REDEEMING TIME

THE WORKING CLASS IN AMERICAN HISTORY

Editorial Advisors
James R. Barrett, Julie Greene, William P. Jones, Alice Kessler-Harris, and Nelson Lichtenstein

Redeeming Time

Protestantism and Chicago's Eight-Hour Movement, 1866–1912

WILLIAM A. MIROLA

UNIVERSITY OF ILLINOIS PRESS
URBANA, CHICAGO, AND SPRINGFIELD

Manufactured in the United States of America
C 5 4 3 2 1
∞ This book is printed on acid-free paper.

Library of Congress Cataloging-in-Publication Data
Mirola, William A. (William Andrew)
Redeeming time : Protestantism and Chicago's eight-hour movement, 1866–1912 / William A. Mirola.
pages cm — (Working class in American history)
Includes bibliographical references and index.
ISBN 978-0-252-03883-9 (hardback) —
ISBN 978-0-252-09679-2 (e-book)
1. Eight-hour movement—Illinois—Chicago—History. 2. Hours of labor—Illinois—Chicago—History. 3. Labor movement—Illinois—Chicago—History. 4. Labor movement—Religious aspects—Christianity. 5. Protestant work ethic—Illinois—Chicago—History. 6. Protestantism—Illinois—Chicago. I. Title.
HD5126.C45M57 2015
331.25'7097731109034—dc23 2014019855

CONTENTS

PREFACE

In the wake of almost two decades of offshoring, economic contractions following 9/11 and the global economic recession, and antiunion political campaigns waged in many states across the country, the American labor movement has been losing rather than gaining ground. According to the Bureau of Labor Statistics, in 2012 union membership figures dropped to 14.4 million, a meager 11.3 percent of all wage and salary workers in the labor force. This figure represents a high of 36 percent of public-sector workers but only 6.6 percent of workers in the private sector. Beginning in 1995, under the leadership of John Sweeney, the American Federation of Labor–Congress of Industrial Organizations (AFL-CIO) focused its attention on ways to stem this slow bleeding of members and union power. Many union leaders committed energy, personnel, and money to revitalize a lethargic labor movement by organizing more workers and winning contracts, especially among service-sector employees. An equally significant part of the labor movement's revitalizing strategy since then has been a focused effort to build bridges with religious groups of all faiths to strengthen its own moral legitimacy in local communities and to help reduce the heightened alienation many Americans profess toward organized labor.

Although people both inside and outside of the labor movement may wonder about the strategic relevance of attempting to build alliances with religious organizations, such alliances have been significant at many key moments in American labor history. Congregations and clergy across the denominational spectrum brought much-needed spiritual and material resources to the embattled labor movement. The religious community, in the past as well as now, was seen as a collective entity that could help restore a moral framework for union activities generally. Since most religious groups maintain commitments to furthering social justice causes and fighting for the downtrodden in society, enlisting those commitments for economic justice struggles remains a logical strategic move on labor's part. In addition to building on shared beliefs in social justice, sympathetic people of faith have been important to workers engaged in strikes or lockouts. By offering food, clothing, financial assistance, and other resources to needy workers, the religious community provided instrumental as well as moral support to labor many times in the past. They continue to do so today.

Fortuitously, in 1996, a national organization, the National Interfaith Committee for Worker Justice (NICWJ), emerged on the heels of John Sweeney's election as AFL-CIO president. Established in Chicago by activist Kim Bobo and others, the National Interfaith Committee has been at the forefront of efforts on the part of concerned members of the religious community to engage with the labor movement. Since its founding, the NICWJ has become an umbrella organization with many chapters in cities across the country. Through its chapters, the NICWJ supported national campaigns to improve conditions for poultry workers and farmworkers, among others. Promoting living-wage campaigns has also been a central battleground for NICWJ-affiliated organizations. More recently, the NICWJ has been organizing in opposition to antiunion and right-to-work legislation in states such as Wisconsin and Indiana. On an educational front, the NICWJ continues to encourage congregations to participate in their "Labor-in-the-Pulpit" program in which representatives of organized labor are invited to speak at church services or in synagogues the weekend of Labor Day.

What is interesting about both the labor movement's campaign to attract the interest of the religious community and religious activists' desire to assist the labor movement is that both groups seem to see what they are doing as something new and charting new waters. While both groups point to their respective histories to support their efforts, in doing so they highlight the success stories of these alliances. Few among them know enough about the specific histories of church-labor relations in concrete struggles to understand the complexities of how and why they have emerged in the past but then seemed to fade again. Little critical analysis has been done on these past relationships to make sense of both the possibilities that exist for alliance success as well as the constraints that limit them today.

Both labor and religious activists bring a stirring idealism to contemporary labor conflicts. But questions remain: Is this simply wishful thinking on the part of each group about what religious support might mean for labor's struggles generally? Or does this idealism spring from witnessing the experience of real-life religious leaders and laypeople in communities playing pivotal roles in the successful outcomes of local labor conflicts? Perhaps it is both. In any case, the relationship between religion and the labor movement is complex. Since the 1990s, in strikes and lockouts across the country, individual clergy and other people of faith have stood with workers in their time of need, and these alliances have been central to the success of numerous campaigns. To be sure, these alliances helped develop mutual admiration between labor and supporters from within the religious community. However, frustration has also accompanied hope in these alliances. In talking to striking workers, one hears expectations that clergy will be conduits for labor education in their congregations and denominations. Some union members assume support for the physical or emotional well-being of individual striking or locked-out workers means religious activists will support the principle of unionism, strike tactics, and the working-class language of combat. Workers are frustrated to find that the willingness of clergy to sign petitions protesting employers' actions is not synonymous with a willingness to join other instrumental tactics in a union's strategy.

Religious activists too are offended when union members discuss their contributions as if they were pawns on a giant chessboard where labor strategists plot moves against their corporate counterparts. Others are uncomfortable with aspects of picket-line dynamics such as the use of profanity, racial or homophobic epithets, and the tenor of violence when striking workers confront the scabs or hired security guards driving past them to get to work. Union activists ask themselves why religious supporters don't act like striking workers, and religious supporters ask themselves why workers don't act more like middle-class churchgoers.

Hope and possibility. Frustration and constraint. Both sets of concepts paradoxically characterize church-labor coalitions. What is often underemphasized is that both possibilities and constraints governing these alliances are products of history. Industrial development created cultures that embraced capitalism and cultures that resisted it. Conflicts between these two cultures also set in motion new ways to think about economic life in communities and new ways of fighting changes that seem to threaten a community's well-being. For activists on both sides of contemporary church-labor alliances, how they understand the conflicts in which they become involved and how each sees their relationship to the other and to employers are shaped by the historical legacy of past conflicts and alliances.

It is ironic that today, people of faith remain hesitant to fight in and over the arena of capitalist economics and industrial conditions. Many Americans, especially white middle- and upper-class individuals, whether they claim to be religious or not, consider economics to be outside the purview of faith. But such sentiments were not always assumed to be true. The questions of how goods and services are produced, who produces them, under what conditions, and who reaps the rewards of production have historically been addressed as moral questions. The Hebrew scriptures and the Qur'an both highlight divine expectations that human economic arrangements were to be just and non-exploitative. Living out the requirements of faith in economic terms meant that wages were to be paid fairly and on time, working conditions were to be humane and as safe as possible, and the rich were required to care for the needs of the poor. In precapitalist economies, the needs of the community took precedence over the wants of the individual, and these moral codes restrained those with more wealth from organizing the economy to benefit themselves at the expense of others. Moreover, economic arrangements were as much subject to religious oversight as any other aspect of community life.

Beginning in the eighteenth century, however, industrial capitalism changed all these moral rules. The economy was left to the invisible hand of the free market, and no one, least of all clergy, had a say in its operation. If wages were low, it was because the skill level of the work or the productivity of the individual worker was low. If hours were long and work was unsafe, such realities were inevitable, as employers were under pressure to keep costs down and individual workers were free to accept this kind of work or not. If a few men got rich at the expense of the masses of their employees, it was market forces and the lack of motivation of the poor that kept this group on top of the economic heap. Capitalism created its own morality and logic rooted in the process of profit accumulation in which the community logic of mutuality and religious morality was assumed to have no place.

But the logic and morality of the capitalist market were never as simple as this, nor was the market adopted without contest. As the new industrial economy expanded, employers increasingly ran afoul of an older preindustrial morality. Those who were the first to join the industrial proletariat were immediately aware of capitalism's new reality: long hours for low wages, unemployment, and the deskilling of work through technological innovation. Immigrants, swelling the ranks of America's urban labor force, took what work they could find. This brave new industrial world was polarized, as Jane Addams (1960, 83) observed in her autobiographical work, *Twenty Years at Hull House*, with "over-accumulation at one end of society and destitution at the other." As tension and frustration exploded in the factories and on the streets of America's cities, the public feeling increasingly reflected the sense that something had to be done. Who better than congregations and clergy to step in to address these centrifugal industrial forces and help those most hurt by them?

The story of Protestantism and the eight-hour movement in Chicago recounted here represents only debates and struggles over one specific industrial condition, the hours of labor. The struggle for the eight-hour day was a central narrative to industrial capitalism and its impact on community life. Redeeming time by limiting the hours Americans spent at work was the foundational progressive reform on which others were built, including mandatory education for children, heightened civic engagement for adults, and a stronger moral community overall. But as we will see, the ideas of industrial "redemption" and "time" meant different things at different stages of the eight-hour movement to workers, employers, and clergy.

It is important to note that Chicago Protestants, rather than the city's entire religious community, take center stage alongside workers and employers in this struggle because of the religious and cultural hegemony they still possessed in this period. Roman Catholics, of course, were resident in Chicago in superior numbers. Catholic priests were on the front lines of the impact of industrialization on the poor immigrants in their parishes and neighborhoods. But well into the first decade of the twentieth century, Catholics also were a culturally embattled minority religious group. Anti-immigrant and anti-Catholic feeling ran parallel in the minds of many native-born Protestant Americans in the nineteenth century. The native-born feared the newcomers would erode the bases of America's growing prominence: democracy in the political realm, laissez-faire capitalism in the economic realm, and Protestantism in the religious realm. Although the Roman Catholic Church engaged in political battles over parochial education in the nineteenth century and Pope Leo XIII issued his famous encyclical *Rerum Novarum* in support of moderate labor reform in 1891, at the local and national levels the Catholic hierarchy was neither publicly visible nor active in the debates over the legitimacy of eight-hour reform until well into the twentieth century (K. Fones-Wolf 1989; Hobgood 1991). Catholic workers, rather than developing a critical language rooted in church teaching, embraced the general religious language used by the labor movement that remained Protestant in approach, though theologically general enough to prevent internal sectarian divides (Halker 1991).

As religious leaders in the city, Protestant clergy were called upon publicly to act on behalf of Chicago workers, even those who were not themselves Protestant. Clergy were presumed to be in a privileged position to do so, especially since the overwhelming majority of the city's economic and social elite sat in their pews Sunday after Sunday. For their part, Protestant clergy saw themselves as losing their moral influence in Chicago, as industrial relations grew increasingly antagonistic and polarized. An intervention had to be made in the feud between capital and labor, and clergy saw themselves to be the ones best to make it.

But if workers hoped clergy would intervene and clergy slowly accepted it as their duty to do so, employers recognized neither worker hopes nor clergy duty. The market was already governed by a morality in which all actions were weighed against their impact on the ability of employers to increase their profits. Any attempt to limit profit accumulation through either religious or political interventions in the market's dynamics was seen as fighting against the natural laws of political economy at best and as anti-American at worst. Neither workers nor clergy exercised the legitimate authority of employers to alter industrial conditions. Their duty then was to stay out of the economic realm, leaving its dynamics to those who knew it best: employers alone.

The story of the eight-hour movement is a central narrative in America's industrial development. It is in the context of this late-nineteenth- and early-twentieth-century reform movement that the reader can identify the origins of several features of the contemporary economic landscape. First, the reader can trace to this period the origins of American church involvement, or lack thereof, in economic questions. Second, readers will observe that labor's pragmatic unionism, focusing on concrete goals as opposed to broader and more radical ideologies, as the principal strategy of American unions for achieving industrial reforms also has its roots in this period. Third, it is in this period when the American economic consciousness becomes dominated by the market's untouchable morality of profit accumulation. Let the reader note, however, that these three issues are all closely related. When church and state both proved ineffectual for achieving labor's reform goals, the American Federation of Labor turned to the language of collaborating with employers to boost profits and productivity as the ideological justification for reforms such as the eight-hour day.

What follows, then, is an examination of the development of what might be termed a doctrine of "separation of church and economy," rooted in the conflicts over what an industrial community is and how it should be ordered. This "separation" was not inevitable. It was constructed through the debates and often violent struggles among specific groups of people at the local level that grew to have a national impact and continues to be played out today. Clergy, their congregations, workers, and employers, through their actions and inactions, laid the groundwork for all future American industrial relations that would be negotiated with reference only to the logic of the market and collective bargaining but not to religious values. Consequently, clergy, as the arbiters of community morality, lost their legitimacy to speak and act as such whenever the social problems they sought to address involved the routine operations of capitalism.

Today, corporations continue to fight union expansion, repeal labor reforms in place since the 1930s, and employ strikebreakers, police, and the National Guard in ways that parallel Chicago in the nineteenth century. In another remarkable parallel, the labor movement once again seeks support from American clergy, Protestant, Catholic, Jewish, and Muslim, as the basis for building community support for workers' rights and economic justice. Denominational bodies and interfaith groups support workers during strikes and to fight for improved conditions and living wages. In the end, however, the struggle to redeem time, whether in the nineteenth century or today, is a struggle over the construction of new moralities of work and leisure in the face of changing economic conditions. In the same ways Chicago's eight-hour movement profoundly altered community life for workers, employers, and clergy in the last century, so too will the contemporary struggles to create new moralities to govern work and leisure alter global community life in the next hundred years.

This project began as a doctoral dissertation in the Department of Sociology at Indiana University (IU), Bloomington. From the very beginning, I received strong support for bringing to light the intersection of religion, social class, and movements for industrial change. I would like to acknowledge the many individuals who contributed their intellectual and moral support to this work early on. Larry Griffin, Michael Wallace, James Wood, Randy Hodson, Suzanne Staggenborg, and Robert Orsi all provided extensive comments on this project and gave me the confidence to tell this fascinating story from America's labor history as a sociologist rather than as a historian. Other equally important intellectual contributions have come from many colleagues over the years. I want to offer hearty thanks to Anne Figert, Chris Botsko, Mitch Berbrier, Aileen Schulte, Regina Werum, Sabine Reible, Sean Creighton, and the past members of IU Sociology's Political Economy Workshop for lengthy discussions that helped me build a theoretical framework for this project.

More recent insights have come from my friends and colleagues who participated with me in the Pew Charitable Trust's Young Scholars in American Religion Program through the Center for the Study of Religion and American Culture from 1997 to 1999, especially Wade Clark Roof, Patricia Chang, Lori Beaman, Mike Emerson, Rich Wood, Sue Monahan, Wendy Young, Eric Gormly, Conrad Kanagy, and Bill MacDonald. Rhys Williams gave me guidance in organizing and effectively communicating the theoretical points that underpin my historical analysis, as did anonymous reviewers at *Social Problems* and *Social Science History*, where earlier parts of this study were published. I am intellectually indebted to Bruce Laurie, Bruce C. Nelson, Ken Fones-Wolf, Eric Hirsch, Rick Fantasia, and Richard Schneirov, all of whose work helped inform my thinking on the role of faith in working-class movements. My colleagues in the history program at Marian University, Raymond Haberski and Mary Ellen Lennon, encouraged me to see this manuscript through its revision and have provided crucial feedback on my writing to bridge the disciplinary differences between historical and sociological writing styles. I have also found the insights and recommendations of reviewers from the University of Illinois Press, editors Richard Martin and Laurie Matheson, and reviewer James Barrett to be invaluable to improving both the organization and the content of this study. This project would not be what it is without them. The Reverend Darren Cushman-Wood, the first old-school labor pastor I ever met, provided insights into contemporary church-labor relations and fueled my thinking about the possibilities and frustrations that inevitably attend them. Of course, though all of the aforementioned played significant parts in the completion of this research, the final responsibility for all the shortcomings of this work are mine.

Grants from a variety of foundations and institutes afforded me the financial support to travel to archives for extensive data collection and for minimizing my teaching responsibilities in order to complete the project in a timely fashion. In particular, I wish to thank the Center on Philanthropy at Indiana University–Purdue University, Indianapolis; the Louisville Center for the Study of Protestantism and American Culture; and the Marian University Professional Development Committee, all of which funded my work on this project over the years.

Practical assistance came from many sources, but I particularly want to thank the library staff at the Chicago Historical Museum for their good humor, despite my constant interruptions, and for their endless searches, suggestions, and general companionship during those long hours in the reference room. Thanks also go to the staff members at the Newberry Library, the State Historical Society of Wisconsin, Seabury-Western Episcopal Seminary, and Garrett-Evangelical Theological Seminary. The Indiana University and Marian University library staffs both endured complex requests for interlibrary loan sources.

Finally, I wish to thank my family and friends for their love and support over the years it has taken to get this manuscript to press, especially my partner, Dr. James LeGrand. I am indebted to Lori Beaman for the push to "just do it" during the low points of the writing process and for the reminders of the need for aesthetic diversions and champagne along one's intellectual journey. Finally, I am grateful to Dr. Eric R. Wright, a former colleague at Indiana University and longtime friend, who provided constant advice and encouragement since I started this project twenty years ago.

REDEEMING TIME

INTRODUCTION

Protestantism and Labor Reform Movements

> The millions who toil beneath the shadow of "the stacks" stand as one in desiring the sincere cooperation of those who pray beneath the "steeples," to the end that the world may be made better and mankind nobler. Will they cooperate?
>
> —William C. Pomeroy, *Stacks and Steeples: A Reply to an Address by Rev. William A. Burch* (1894)

> Whatever may be true about the established church, in which the clergy are dependent upon a privileged class for their living, it is certainly not true that ministers in this country generally "assume the role of protecting property and privilege" to the neglect of the rights of the poor. Whether they are always as outspoken as they ought to be, against oppressive monopolies when the monopolist occupies the front pew, is another question.
>
> —*Northwestern Christian Advocate,* February 3, 1893, 24

It was a cold February day in 1894 when English reformer William T. Stead, author of the controversial social analysis *If Christ Came to Chicago,* presided at a two-and-a-half-hour meeting of workers, social reformers, and the interested public at Bricklayers' Hall in Chicago. The hall was filled with people who had come to hear William C. Pomeroy, general organizer for the American Federation of Labor, and Rev. William A. Burch, pastor of Hamlin Avenue Methodist Church, debate the possibility of ministers and wage earners joining forces in support of industrial reform. Burch and Pomeroy both bemoaned the lack of cooperation between Protestant leaders and the labor movement. Yet while Burch hoped for more mutual understanding between the two, he minimized the industrial conditions and actions of employers that continued to fuel class hatred in the aftermath of the Haymarket affair, the Homestead steel strike, and the Pullman strike. As many clergy had done before him, Burch placed blame on labor agitators and misguided leaders for keeping workers apart from the church. Pomeroy in turn criticized

Chicago's Protestant clergy for their ignorance of industrial conditions and their cowardice in refusing to condemn the actions of wealthy members of their congregations (Stead 1894; Pomeroy 1894). In 1894 the divides between "steeples and stacks" as well as the ongoing hostility between capital and labor seemed as unbridgeable as ever.

Steeples and stacks and capital and labor are two familiar binaries in the broad narrative of American religious and labor histories in the years following the Civil War. The labor question intruded into the lives of late-nineteenth-century Americans, whether they toiled in factories, sat in the privileged front pews of churches, or preached in the pulpits of those churches. It was a question that covered many different facets of the industrial experience of the working classes, from the right to organize unions to the question of wages and working conditions. But more than any of these, the central issue that generated a movement within the labor movement was overwork and the hours of labor.

Shortening the workday and reducing the workweek were umbrella issues for the American labor movement.[1] Reducing the hours of labor linked a host of other industrial reforms and spawned a class-based consciousness among American workers that no other issue had done previously or since. The eight-hour day was salient to native-born and immigrant workers, to labor radicals and conservatives, to the skilled and unskilled, and to men and women, and Chicago's workers were at the center of it all. Overwork and long hours were the basis for some of the most contentious conflicts between employers and their workers in Chicago, and they forced Protestant clergy, willing or no, to engage the labor question.

Though Boston and New York City witnessed extensive mobilization around the eight-hour day, immediately following the Civil War Chicago gained a reputation as the focal point, as the *Chicago Tribune* (*CT*) put it, for "the whole civilized world" to reduce the length of the workday and workweek (July 5, 1879, 2). Between 1867 and 1912, workers achieved an eight-hour day through strikes in various industries, including stonecutting, carpentry, typographical work, and a host of others. Women and child workers also won shorter workdays through precedent-setting legislation in Illinois in 1893 and 1909. To Chicago's wage earners, the eight-hour day was more than simply an economic issue; it was a moral issue, rooted in working-class religious culture, encompassing beliefs about work, industrial justice, leisure, education, civic duty, and health. It was a means to "redeem time" for workers.

But facing staunch resistance from employers, eight-hour reformers realized that to achieve shorter hours workers had to garner support from and build coalitions with other powerful individuals and organizations in the city. Although the exponential growth of Roman Catholics and Jewish immigrants was shifting the religious balance of power in Chicago, Protestant clergy were a logical choice. Protestant leaders saw themselves and were generally perceived as the moral arbiters of the community. Protestants dominated the city's economic and political life as well as its privileged religious culture in the late nineteenth century.

Nevertheless, given the overwhelming numbers of Chicago workers who were from Catholic backgrounds, it may seem ironic that Protestant clergy became the object of labor coalition building. In the urban centers of the United States, the Roman Catholic Church, especially through the work of women religious and other religious orders, attended to the needs of immigrant workers for health care, education, and other social services that helped newly arriving immigrants to find shelter, food, and work and to settle into local neighborhoods and parishes that were segregated by ethnicity (McDonough 1992; McGreevy 2003). Henry Browne (1949), in his classic work on the Catholic Church and the Knights of Labor, argues that specific engagement with labor reform did not enter into the church's educational and service-oriented programs until well after *Rerum Novarum* was issued in 1891. There are some references to Catholic priests becoming involved in labor conflicts in the 1870s and 1880s, but they are relatively few (Fink 1985; Craig 1992; McCartin and McCartin 2007; Hobgood 1991). Some priests in the twentieth century were more directly involved with the labor movement. Catholic priests serving parishes around the Chicago stockyards, for example, supported the 1904 strike of packinghouse workers (Barrett 1987, 174). In the early 1900s, Catholics followed the lead of many Protestant churches in observing Labor Sundays in parishes where priests addressed labor issues (Karson 1958). But in the twentieth century, the Catholic Church's main focus was in opposing the growth of socialism and, through both official and grassroots pressure, shaping the ideology and strategy of unions affiliated with the American Federation of Labor (Karson 1958).

However, beyond these examples, the evidence that Catholic clergy were actively engaged with the public work of industrial reform in the nineteenth century remains quite limited. Across the course of this study, there are almost no occasions when Catholic clergy were noted as being present in the public events and conflicts around Chicago's eight-hour movement. This is not to suggest that Catholicism did not shape the lives or thinking of immigrant workers, but within the labor movement it did so in a less visible way. Halker (1991, 142) notes that Catholic workers, when joining forces with other workers, typically adopted a nonsectarian religious language that argued that "society did not measure up to the standards of Christianity, that workers enjoyed God's favor and that the [labor] movement embodied Christian principles." It is likely that Catholic workers made the same distinction between their Christian faith and the actions of the church as an institution and its clergy that other workers and labor leaders did (Craig 1991; Gutman 1966; Burns 2008). This is an area that deserves a great deal more scholarly attention.

Consequently, it was the language of Protestantism that permeated the religious and civic culture of cities such as Chicago, and, prior to 1900, it was largely Protestant traditions and leaders that provided the moral agenda for the labor movement and for the related multitude of reform movements spawned in the Progressive Era (K. Fones-Wolf 1989; Gutman 1966; May 1963). Handy (1991, 99) notes that even into the first decade of the twentieth century, fewer than 15 percent of social reformers were from religious traditions outside of Protestantism. Uriah Stephens, founder of the Knights of Labor; anarchist leaders Albert Parsons and Samuel Fielden; novelist Upton Sinclair; labor leaders Ira Steward, Henry George, and Wendell Phillips; and Settlement House founders Jane Addams, Florence Kelly, and Graham Taylor, among many others, were all from Protestant backgrounds and were major Gilded Age reformers who aided in constructing a new morality of leisure that would redeem time for workingmen and -women.

From labor's strategic viewpoint, it made sense to create alliances with clergy. Clergy, after all, claimed to uphold Christ's humanitarian mandates to feed the hungry, clothe the naked, and protect the widows and orphans, all of which were desperately needed by workers facing the harsh conditions of work within unregulated industrial capitalism. Clergy also regularly expressed concern for the moral climate of the city and the desire to transform Chicago into a "city on the hill," characterized by high moral standards, temperance, and dignity, embodied by strong adherence to Protestant beliefs and practice (Foster 2002). These were moral goals that workers frequently expressed as parallels to their own desires. Another element made clergy ideal candidates for joining the fight for shorter hours in the 1860s: the clergy's own recent history as movement activists. Protestant clergy had taken public stands to end slavery in the abolitionist movement (Oshatz 2010). They continued as leaders in the temperance movement, and, significantly for shorter-hours reformers, they were organizing to shut down businesses on Sundays to combat what they saw as a significant challenge to the moral and religious life of Chicago: a seven-day workweek in industrial production

(Mirola 1999). Clergy seemed, at least initially, ideal allies for eight-hour advocates.

Yet building coalitions between steeple and stacks to redeem time through eight-hour workdays was never as easy as it seemed. Eight-hour religious rhetoric needed to correspond to the religious ideas of clergy for effective alliance building to occur, and bridging this rhetorical gap was no small challenge. The very idea that time needed to be redeemed was a hotly contested claim that went right to the core of the debate over what values would dominate in the new industrial order. Redemption, a familiar religious theme, invokes the idea of salvation or at least some form of a spiritual transformation. Workers believed that shorter working hours would transform their lives spiritually by providing more time for religious observance, education, and civic engagement. But the very idea that time needed redemption was completely foreign to employers. For them, time was, and is, money. The hours of labor were decided on the basis of production costs and returns on investment, not the personal or spiritual needs of workers. Time was central to profit accumulation and, consequently, had no need for redemption. It only needed to be made as efficient and productive as possible. For clergy, redeeming time also meant different things. Many Protestant clergy believed time needed redemption because too many workingmen and -women spent their limited leisure in saloons and theaters, while too few were in churches on Sunday mornings. In the 1860s and 1870s, the last thing most Protestant clergy would have wanted was for workers to have more time for drinking and other sinful activities. Morally lax workers themselves needed to be redeemed, and then the length of the workday would be irrelevant. Though Protestant ideas about time and work changed across the 1890s and 1900s to embrace the implications of redeeming time articulated by labor, some clergy remained suspicious of any reduction of working hours, while others reiterated employers' views that the hours of labor were an economic question, not a religious one. Clearly, these competing ideas set up workers, employers, and clergy for rhetorical as well as political conflict.

The work of religious coalition building for the eight-hour movement also was complicated by sets of conflicting expectations about how clergy could help the labor movement in practical terms. Workers presumed that Christian employers would be more amenable to such reform if their own ministers were making the appeals. If employers refused to cooperate and listen to the clergy, workers expected ministers to condemn these propertied and privileged employers even if they sat in their pews. In the mid–nineteenth century, however, most clergy were trying to determine exactly how to define what constituted moral behavior in the new industrial economy, just as they had to rethink their views on slavery as a social sin before the Civil War (Oshatz 2007). Much to the surprise of workers, there was no immediate recognition by clergy that eight-hour reform would make either Chicago better or its working-class citizens nobler. Nor were clergy quick to condemn employers in their congregations. Most clergy's views of labor were shaped by fear. When clergy did side with labor, they more often expressed support for the general principle of workers' right to organize, itself a radical claim at the time, *not* the relative justice of any specific demand for industrial reform.[2]

Consequently, contested meanings, mutual suspicion, conflicts regarding strategies and tactics, and, above all, difficulties in translating rhetorical support into practical action plagued Chicago's eight-hour movement and its relations with local clergy. These dynamics were exacerbated by employers who resisted any attempts to impose reform, religiously justified or not. Christian employers were reticent to shorten hours in any way, and Protestant clergy did little more than offer verbal support for labor. Half a century of making religious appeals for the eight-hour day with little to no practical action only confirmed in labor reformers' minds the inability of clergy as well as their religious arguments, on their own, to alter industrial policy or politics.

This study offers a critical look at religious rhetoric and coalition-building strategies of Chicago's eight-hour movement to move us beyond a simplistic and idealistic look at the role of religion in the American labor movement. Religious rhetoric and the actions of Protestant clergy both played important roles in the fight for the eight-hour workday. In constructing eight-hour religious rhetoric, reformers employed a multifaceted logic, rooted in familiar Protestant religious narratives and values, to highlight the problems of overwork as oppressive, immoral, and anti-Christian and legitimized the eight-hour system as the Christian, moral alternative. However, this was in no way a smooth, linear process. At the center of this strategic process were debates between groups of workers themselves and between workers, employers, and clergy over the *legitimate* religious implications of eight-hour reform and the future of industrial capitalism. Behind every religious appeal was a contest over whose religious meanings would ultimately define industrial conditions and conflicts in Chicago.

Between 1866 and 1912, the movement to redeem time through the adoption of a universal eight-hour workday for American workers was one of the last battles fought in the war between the conquering factory system with its new free-market ethos and the remnants of an older, premodern craft-based production and value system. In this struggle, employers, workers, and clergy fought over whose vision of work and leisure time would claim moral legitimacy. And as the results of this contest in Chicago show, religion conformed itself to the ascendant ideology of private property and the free market, rather than the reverse. There was nothing inevitable to this outcome, as some scholars have suggested (Burns 2013). It happened step by step, through the unfolding debates and practical actions of workers, employers, and clergy responding to events in Chicago over time.

Protestantism and American Labor History

Thousands of pages have been written about the American labor movement and on the nineteenth-century debates and conflicts among workers, employers, and clergy, over how best to restabilize the social order in an era characterized as a world turned upside down (Hill 1984; Hobsbawm 1983). Industrial capitalism transformed whole communities and the lives of people in them in late-eighteenth- and nineteenth-century America. It transformed the nature and condition of life and work for the working classes. Old methods of production were replaced by new technologies. With the advent of the factory system, work increasingly moved from homes in small communities to the cities, turning farmers and craftsmen into an industrial proletariat characterized by a growing animosity directed toward the upper classes (Green 2006). Industrialization transformed the lives of employers, who could be swimming in wealth one minute and paupers the next, as extreme economic cycles turned from boom to bust and back again every few years. Industrial conditions also transformed Protestant clergy. Urban ministers, on the one hand, felt their moral authority diminishing to irrelevance in a world dominated by moneymaking, individual fulfillment and pleasure, and the increasingly volatile struggles between capital and labor. On the other hand, these clergy wanted to ensure that Protestant morality remained the guiding principle in the new industrial order in the wake of the expanding numbers of Roman Catholics and Jews (Foster 2002; Rossinow 2005; Cantwell 2012).

Out of the transformations of life for individuals within each of these three groups—workers, employers, and clergy—came a profound transformation of the social relationships between them and how each thought about the other. Religious faith provided one shared lens for thinking and, more important, for talking about these social upheavals for all three groups in many urban communities. As the two quotes that begin this chapter suggest, the labor question was not simply an economic question concerning only the relationship between capital and labor. As a religious question, it addressed the morality of the new industrial order along with the role of clergy and their relationships to both employers and their workers. The labor question, especially as it addressed the hours of labor, pressed the issue of whether the new culture of the market could be guided by religious principles and the question of who would have the right to define the morality of industrial conditions.

Despite the assertion that religion "still languishes in the shadows of late-nineteenth-century history," examining Protestantism's role in the emergence of industrial capitalism is not new intellectual territory for historians and social scientists, though scholars' approaches to it have changed dramatically (Carter 2010, 322). Prior to the 1960s, scholars informed by early Marxist and Weberian approaches to religion did not concern themselves with extensive explorations of religious faith in the labor movement. For those from a Marxist bent, religion was best understood as a tool of elite control because it diverted the attention of discontented workers away from their own oppression and alienation resulting from capitalism and their own power to abolish them through revolutionary action (Marx 1986; Beckford 1989; McLellan 1987). For those influenced by German theorist Max Weber, Protestantism was less important as a means for controlling workers than as a means for capitalists to legitimate their own social positions and ultimately the entire structure of industrial society. Theological beliefs drawn from Calvinism provided a religious understanding that associated wealth with divine approval and poverty with sin (Weber 1958).

Unfortunately, while such analytic approaches seem simplistic formulations today, they influenced the theoretical assumptions underlying much past work on religion in the American labor movement. Many scholars limited their study to studying labor's political battles or the impact of class, ethnicity, or immigration status on the actions of workers (Foner 1982; Davis 1986; Montgomery 1987). As a result, labor history was dominated by class analysis whose aim has been to explain the forces encouraging or inhibiting the formation of a Marxian class consciousness within the labor movement and the degree to which organized labor was able to work toward the creation of a new economic order (Berlanstein 1993). Within the confines of traditional Marxist thought, there was not much place for accounting for religion except as an obstacle to labor mobilization. It was taken for granted that religious leaders, especially Protestants, typically encouraged working people to be content with their place and opposed attempts by labor to alter industrial conditions. The assumption that faith in general was a barrier to the development of workers' class consciousness therefore rendered accounting for the religious dimensions of the labor question in the nineteenth century unnecessary (E. Fones-Wolf and K. Fones-Wolf 2010).

A reappraisal of religion's role in shaping industrial capitalism began in the 1960s. The publication of Herbert Gutman's (1966) essay on Protestantism and the American labor movement and E. P. Thompson's *The Making of the English Working Class* (1966) set in motion a new labor historiography with its renewed attention to examining working-class lives and culture even if they themselves did not always provide the best intellectual examples of doing so (Berlanstein 1993; Salvatore 1998).[3] In the social sciences, the cultural turn of the late 1980s, accompanied by renewed interest in social movement activism, brought attention to examining the ways religion shapes individuals' sense of identity and gives meaning and direction to their actions (C. Smith 1996a). Today, increasing numbers of scholars cite the importance of faith along with class, race, ethnicity, and gender as a potent force in working-class life and industrial struggles of the past and present (McCartin and McCartin 2007; Bruno 2008).[4]

Much of the historical work in this area, though episodic in its appearance in published form, documents the religious beliefs of different groups within the American working class and the ways religion shaped the labor movement in the nineteenth century (Laurie 1980; Callahan 2009; Carter 2010; K. Fones-Wolf 1989; McTighe 1994; Murphy 1992).[5] As Gutman originally described, American workers in the years after the Civil War were a "transitional generation" (1966, 95). Native-born white workers, coming from Presbyterian, Baptist, Methodist, Congregationalist as well as many other evangelical and Holiness traditions, experienced the upheavals of industrial change through the lens of antebellum evangelical Protestant beliefs that emphasized individual perfectionism, the possibility for a new heaven on earth, and that God would judge those who perpetuate injustice (Cantwell 2012; Carter 2010; E. Hirsch 1990; Bruno 2008). Immigrant workers carried their religious values and experiences from the Old World, where established religious traditions worked hand in hand with the state and local aristocracy. Whether they were Protestants, Catholics, or Jews, some immigrants' faith imported suspicion of clergy and institutional religion. For others, churches and synagogues provided ties to home and tradition. For both native-born and immigrant, religion could provide identity, meaning, and direction for their actions (Gutman 1966; Halker 1991; Craig 1992; Burns 2008, 2013; Carter 2013; Nelson 1991; Pride 1987; Barrett 1987).

This scholarship provides the foundation for this study in identifying the many ways religious elements permeated reform demands of the labor movement throughout the nineteenth century. Themes highlighting the humanity of the historical Jesus and his focus on creating a society based on solidarity and equality rather than one built on class divisions were common in the rhetoric of workers demanding industrial reforms (Burns 2013; Sinclair 1952). Many historians have underscored how labor's religious rhetoric was often used to articulate a vision of a moral economy taken from preindustrial experiences in small towns and organized around faith. In this moral economy, the community shared the productive wealth created by labor, in contrast to the spreading capitalist economy where accumulation of profit by any means necessary was the only moral law (Cantwell 2012; Thompson 1966; K. Fones-Wolf 1989; Grob 1961). Workers in conservative craft unions, the Knights of Labor, and even those affiliated with socialist and anarchist organizations took up and amplified different aspects of these religious themes in response to concrete events in unfolding industrial conflict (Burns 2013; G. Smith 2000; K. Fones-Wolf 1989; B. Nelson 1991). More important, these beliefs motivated them into practical action to change their worlds. It is important to note, however, that in using religious ideas drawn from past experience, workers carried no illusions about returning to some mythic preindustrial past. They saw the possibilities for social change and a humane economy emerging out of their industrial present, rooted in their understanding of authentic faith. The chief weakness of this work, however, continues to be the manner in which working-class religiosity is disconnected from the religiosity of employers and clergy in their local communities as well as examined independently of workers' concrete industrial struggles with them.

Religious historians, for their part, have written extensively on the impact of industrialization on the thinking of clergy, especially on the beliefs of Protestant reformers and the rise of social Christianity, more commonly known as the Social Gospel.[6] This scholarship also is foundational for the analysis that follows, because Protestant clergy spoke out regarding the eight-hour movement. But the literature here offers a conflicted and unresolved view of the role of Protestantism as a force shaping labor reform. If labor historians have assumed that Protestant clergy did little to support labor in the nineteenth century, reading the literature on the Social Gospel movement creates the impression that clergy were on the front lines of the labor movement. As definitive independent characterizations, both of these conclusions are limited, because in both bodies of literature scholars examine clergy separately from local industrial dynamics, addressing clergy thinking and action in general or national terms rather than situating their rhetoric and actions in the context of what was going on in their communities. As my analysis shows, clergy responded to what was happening immediately around them and, as community leaders, were drawn into local industrial conflicts. Their responses to these conflicts, whether opposition to or support for labor, emerged from their relationships with both business elites and wage earners in their own communities.

So how did clergy engage the industrial changes in the late nineteenth century? In analyzing the rhetoric used by clergy in addressing labor reform, scholars have emphasized how the language of the Protestant work ethic was used as a theological basis for their sustained religious opposition to any industrial reform. The work ethic, with its implicit view toward the natural depravity of humans, was used against workers by contending that any increase in leisure through a decrease in work could only result in an increase in vice and profligate living habits (Labor Research Association 1942; Levitan and Belous 1977). Workers, especially those in skilled trades who often were native-born Protestants, occasionally adopted this language, and even some radical labor leaders such as Eugene Debs espoused this idealized work ethic, disparaging idleness among the unskilled (Rodgers 1978; Burns 2013). Historians have also highlighted that Protestant clergy adopted evangelicalism and revivalism to remedy the social ills through the regeneration of individual souls. In contrast to the present day, Protestants from all denominations placed heavy importance on soul-saving and missionary work, at home and abroad. Holding revivals was a common expression of this commitment to redeeming souls, and by extension revivals, it was hoped, would strengthen a community's Protestant foundations at the same time. Studies of the great revivals, such as those led by Dwight L. Moody, in the late nineteenth century note revivals went hand in hand with periods of political and social unrest (Sizer 1992; Kinsley 1946). Revivalism, like the work ethic, was linked to defending existing social relations between capital and labor. "Moody's sermons reinforced existing Protestant attitudes about political economy. They condemned any lazy man who refused available work regardless of wages offered and asserted the credibility of the Protestant work ethic" (Robertson 1989, 156). For clergy, in contrast to the experiences of workers, the dominant Protestant culture of the late nineteenth century laid the foundation for clergy's opposition to labor reform, especially in Chicago.

Yet this is not the whole story. Despite extensive clergy opposition to the labor movement, social historians point out that religious leaders also often found themselves at odds with the new industrial order and its disruption of community life and traditional religious values (Hackett 1991; C. Johnson

1989).[7] The theological impulses of the Protestant work ethic and revivalism also provided clergy with a stepping-stone to address the labor movement more favorably. While preachers like Moody swayed many in the middle class, the experiences of mission and rescue workers among the poor gave them an almost unparalleled knowledge of poverty and the economic causes of many of the socially disruptive behaviors they considered to be sin. Working-class men and women turned to saloons for an escape from work. Such knowledge led many Protestants to support reforms called for by organized labor because they encountered the problems firsthand. As a result, the work of revivalists as early as the 1870s was geared both toward correcting public opinion in its "Christian" attitudes toward the poor and needy and over time toward correcting the economic mechanisms that resulted in poverty and need (Magnuson 1977). Committed to the virtues of hard work, an evangelical faith, sobriety, and a belief in creating social institutions that reflected Christian values in the here and now, Protestant clergy and increasing numbers of those in their pews openly sympathized with the plight of labor and attempted to mobilize the church to come to the aid of the workers through a wide range of religious, economic, and political programs geared toward local circumstances (G. Smith 2000).

This transformation of Protestant thinking grew out of the notion that individual moral regeneration was pointless without an associated regeneration of the industrial environment within which the individual lived and worked (Baltzell 1964; Oshatz 2010). The Social Gospel redefined the language of Protestantism and its public approach to industrial reform in ways that paralleled the religious rhetoric in the labor movement yet appealed uniquely to ministers and laity in congregations (G. Smith 2000). Social Gospel theology and calls for industrial reforms were circulated in newspapers, some as early as the 1870s, as well as in novels, poems, tracts, and many other formats. Although some scholars have suggested that the contributors to these papers were too simplistic or idealistic in their analyses and proposed solutions to industrial conflict, a socially motivated Christianity was not merely reactionary or utopian. It was an active attempt by clergy and laity to analyze and reshape the industrial order along Protestant interests and appealed to a broad Protestant audience (Hudson 1984; Hopkins 1940; Aiken and McDonnell 1970; G. Smith 2000).

What is significant about these conflicting historical narratives documenting the role of religious leaders in American labor history is that they point back to a common basis for clergy action. Protestant clergy, even though they often were removed from the day-to-day relations of industrial production, had a vested interest in ensuring that the relationship between workers and employers did not disrupt the stability of their communities (Form and Miller 1960; J. Miller 1993). Clergy entered industrial struggles when they perceived the stability of local communities to be threatened, regardless of whether the threat came as a result of the actions of workers or employers. Essential to getting clergy to enter industrial struggles was their redefinition of what actually threatened social stability in the urban industrial centers of the late nineteenth century. As clergy spoke less about the disruptive moral laxity of the poor and more about the industrial conditions shaping working-class lives, Protestants changed their political actions.

For all the work that has examined religion in working-class culture or the relationships between religious leaders and the labor movement since the 1960s, few social historians have examined in much detail how the faith of nineteenth-century employers impacted their thinking and actions when faced with the labor question. Many studies simply ignore the possibility that there was any intersection of faith and work for industrialists. Other studies suggest some industrialists took a position akin to the divine right of kings when considering the religious dimensions of wealth and poverty. Hopkins notes, for instance, that "John D. Rockefeller asserted that God gave him his fortune and another spokesman for big business defended dictatorial and monopolistic policies on the grounds that the wealth of the nation had been given into the keeping of its Christian businessmen" (1940, 97). Industrialists undoubtedly adopted this morally grandiose attitude. In his study of the Chicago Sunday Evening Club, founded by Protestant businessmen, bankers, and lawyers in 1908, Heidebrecht describes these men as economic leaders who were also prominent churchmen, "driven by a loyalty to the church and desire to follow in Christianity's philanthropic and ethical spirit" (1989, 28). Yet Heidebrecht also underscores that theirs was a "businessman's religion" (1989, 4): practical, efficient, one that reflected individual initiative and personal responsibility, all characteristics they perceived themselves as exhibiting in their lives and work.

Gary Smith's (2010) study of social Christianity provides one of the most focused discussions of how faith shaped the thinking and the actions of employers. In two separate chapters, Smith unpacks the ways in which five businessmen, in different parts of the country and in different industries, merged their faith and business practice. What unites their stories is their commitment to applying the Golden Rule to their various businesses and treating their employees and customers fairly but all the while defending the capitalist system. Some even went so far as to support living wages and reasonable working conditions for their employees as a reflection of "some kind of forward step toward making men rather than merely making money" (G. Smith 2010, 262). Employers may have used a religious lens to think about their actions as businessmen, but here too is a conflicted picture of religion's role in the labor question.

Clearly, these examples suggest that Protestantism in intertwined with the American labor movement in complex ways. Yet when scholars have recognized the importance of this relationship, they have approached it by treating the experiences of workers, employers, and clergy as separate from each other rather than seeing them as a unified story. Changing industrial conditions in local communities impacted the religious thinking of resident workers, their employers, and Protestant clergy *collectively*, yet rarely are these issues framed in a way to show this. Even in excellent community-based studies of the labor movement, religion enters the narratives as a side note, if it is mentioned at all. There are relatively few studies that explicitly examine the religious dimensions of industrial conflict through the relationships between workers, employers, and clergy together.[8] Religious thinking and its expression in the language people use are never static. Thinking and language change as the local relationships between people change and as the world around them changes (Orsi 2003). How different groups spoke about the religious significance of the labor question evolved in response to the outcomes of concrete industrial conflicts, as workers and employers organized to enforce or resist specific industrial reforms. As this study will show, it was also shaped by which group was speaking. Different groups of workers employed different religious messages in calling for reform. Employers made less explicit use of religion to craft arguments to counter labor demands. Clergy entered these conflicts in several different roles, as partisans, as arbiters, and as moral adjudicators, but in each case they remained clergy, and their positions as such shaped what they said regarding the labor question and how they said it. Ultimately, the debates and conflicts *between* these groups over time shaped their religious understanding of the labor question generally and the eight-hour day in particular.

Religion, Labor Movement Strategy, and the Eight-Hour Day

It took Christian Smith's *Disruptive Religion* (1996) to prompt renewed interest in the role of religion in social movement analysis. As Smith observed in his critical introduction, prior generations of scholars assumed that only material, economic, and political forces mattered in understanding the rise of a social movement. And as is the case in the field of labor history, while new social movement case studies underscore the diverse resources that religious groups bring to social movements, few of them explicitly address the development of religious rhetoric, or religious *framing*, by activists, their supporters, and opponents (Isaac 2008).

Framing originally comes from the work of Erving Goffman (1972, 1981) and, across the past two decades, has become one of the three major currents of analysis used in studies of social movements. In general terms, framing involves the creation of a movement language that allows for a meaningful interpretation of events and circumstances (Snow and Benford 2005, 209; Westby 2005). Framing is a strategic process in that movements select from among many available cultural and ideological sources to build a language that can effectively diagnose the underlying causes of its grievances, identify heroes and villains in social struggles, and offer legitimate solutions for confronting and changing the social structures contributing to unjust social arrangements (Zald 1996). Because strategic frames are reflected in movement rhetoric, analyzing their construction and transformation requires a close examination of available texts, speeches, pamphlets, and other written, spoken, and pictorial or artistic expressions of movement leaders and rank-and-file activists as well as those groups with whom a movement is engaged, either as opponents or as engaged outsiders (Zald 1996; Johnston 2005; Isaac 2008).

As a movement constructs its rhetoric for mobilizing collective action and achieving goals, there are always struggles over what to say and how to say it effectively (Snow and Benford 1992; Snow et al. 1986; Haydu 1999). Faith traditions frequently provide a basis for the *religious framing* work of a social movement and those groups from outside related to it. Religious language, however, must make sense to, or resonate with, the people that the movement is trying to mobilize (Snow et al. 1986; Snow and Benford 1992). When religion occupies a prominent place in the culture of a community, it can provide an important basis for mobilizing people to act (C. Smith 1996a). But religious meanings are never self-evident, and consequently employing religious language by a social movement can generate debates over legitimate religious meanings between factions within a movement, between leaders and rank-and-file participants, or between a movement, the elite it is challenging, and other social groups (Williams and Blackburn 1996; Ellingson 1995; Steinberg 1999).

Even when everyone shares the same religious understanding of the issues, religious rhetoric must be perceived to be instrumentally credible, that is, it must be perceived as contributing to the movement's growth and success in tangible ways (Snow and Benford 1992; Snow et al. 1986). In other words, there must be a perceived payoff for using a particular linguistic form. Valocchi's (1996) work on how integration became the dominant ideology of the American civil rights movement is suggestive of how instrumental credibility operates. Although there were many civil rights ideologies within the movement, the rhetoric of integration fitted within the logic of American politics and was a politically moderate way to frame the goals of the movement. Political moderation secured the sympathy and resources of the political elite and those African American individuals and groups who controlled needed financial resources and were suspicious of more militant movement organizations such as the Student Nonviolent Coordinating Committee and the Congress of Racial Equality (Haines 1984). Movements select among ideological components in ways that ensure that the resonance of cultural forms at the micro level is transformed into resource flows or political victories (and hence instrumental credibility) at the macro level. Religious rhetoric will remain a strategic part of a movement's framing provided it generates more resources for a movement, more coalitions, more money, more access to elites, or, at a minimum, it does not hurt the resources a movement already has (Johnston 2005, 253). This is not to suggest that if religious frames do not do these things that movement participants, as individuals, will discard their religious identities and values, only that religious rhetoric will become a less and less visible part of a movement's strategic resources.

Although many studies assert the importance of religion to social movements, there are relatively few studies that examine the processes of strategic religious framing and rhetorical disputes resulting from the interplay of interactions between a movement, elites, and key outsiders over time, and almost no others that do this in the context of labor activism. As these processes and disputes occurred in the late-nineteenth-century labor movement, religious rhetoric and strategic framing were shaped by the relationships between the labor movement's unique class-based religious culture, articulated in the speeches, newspapers, pamphlets, and verbal observations of its labor leaders and rank-and-file workingmen and -women; the broader religious culture of the time, articulated most visibly in sermons, the religious press, pamphlets, and speeches by local clergy; and the seemingly nonreligious culture of industrial capitalism. Herein lay the challenges that Chicago's eight-hour movement faced: how to create intra- and interclass consensus around the eight-hour day as a religious and moral reform in ways that created effective alliances to counter resistant employers and achieve shorter hours for workers.

My analysis of the eight-hour movement focuses on the changing religious debates among workers, employers, and Protestant clergy over instituting the eight-hour workday in Chicago, as expressed in the press, meeting deliberations, pamphlets, speeches, and sermons. It moves beyond previous work on religion and labor in two key ways. First, while many studies find the need to begin with a justification for even considering the religious aspects of labor history, I take the religious cultures of workers, employers, and clergy as the starting point for my historical analysis. All three groups were immersed in a vibrant, Protestant-dominated, religious culture. Religion was potentially useful for interpreting and arguing about industrial conditions in the late nineteenth century for all three sets of actors, albeit at different times and in different ways. Based on that assumption, I describe the changing ways religious rhetoric entered the public debates over eight-hour reform between workers, employers, and clergy. But religious rhetoric gradually faded from use in the eight-hour movement. Why? Gutman (1966), in his original essay, points out that religious rhetoric dissipated from labor speeches and writings after 1900, but few scholars discuss how or why this happened. By focusing on the specific conflicts within the eight-hour movement, I answer this question by examining the factors contributing to a shift away from the use of religious rhetoric to mobilize workers, challenge employers, and build coalitions with clergy as strategies in the labor movement's efforts to reduce the hours of labor.

Second, although some scholars are uncomfortable with any attempt to view religion as an instrumental tool to achieve the goals of the labor movement, I am examining religion and religious rhetoric from precisely that approach. I would never countenance the reduction of religious beliefs to economic or political interests, but I do recognize that faith can reflect them in its own unique fashion. Yet religious faith brings its own unique identity interests that are distinct from interests rooted in class, race, gender, or any other social base. Mobilizing religion in the eight-hour movement emerged from the individual faith commitments of labor leaders and rank-and-file workers along with other sympathizers, but mobilizing religion was also a strategy for winning a shorter workday. Mobilizing workers to act, shaming employers to concede to worker demands, and enticing clergy to support shorter-hours reform were hoped-for instrumental outcomes desired by the eight-hour movement as the result of employing religious rhetoric. This approach allows for a more objective look at religious resources, in the same ways that one might examine and evaluate any other set of material or cultural resources being employed by a movement. Perhaps it is the evaluative component of the analysis of religion that disturbs so many people, both in the academy and outside of it. It is difficult to think about situations where religion "works" to promote desired social changes and where it "fails." In a sentimental way, many of us who study religion want to assume religion makes positive contributions to movements simply because it is religion! But for movements challenging the elite, there is little room for sentimentality. Do religious resources get movements closer to their social change goals, or do they not? This question was posed frequently by labor activists in the nineteenth century, though the answer changed over time and local context.

Looking Forward

This book addresses the historical process of religious strategic framing around the eight-hour workday, and as such it is a study in historical sociology rather than pure labor history. While the narrative that follows taps many of the historical topics addressed in this chapter—immigration, temperance, the settlement house movement, the Social Gospel, and so on—it is not a study of any one of them. I do not intend to explain the emergence of the Social Gospel per se, or provide a study of how shorter hours came to be adopted in practical terms by Chicago employers. Many events from the broader narrative of Chicago's labor history, such as the Pullman strike of 1894, receive only passing mention. What follows is a focused analysis of exploring the intersection between Chicago's eight-hour movement and Protestant religious culture over a fifty-year time span, from 1866 to 1912. In considering the eight-hour movement from the vantage point of workers, this process involves examining how working-class religious culture and ideas were woven into strategic eight-hour rhetoric by labor leaders and rank-and-file workers. It also documents how this religious rhetoric was rewoven in response to the outcome of particular campaigns to enforce the eight-hour system. For Protestant clergy, religious values regarding work and leisure were transformed across the late nineteenth century as a result of the labor movement's struggle to achieve shorter hours. In addition to transforming how clergy *spoke,* the ongoing conflicts between Chicago workers and employers and the public debates with the labor movement transformed what they were willing to *do,* through alliances with the labor movement, to see the eight-hour day enacted as industrial policy.

Examining religious rhetoric within the eight-hour movement highlights both the potential as well as the limitations of religious culture and religious leaders to act as forces in industrial reform. Throughout history, clergy and people of faith have helped many social movements be successful. But as late-nineteenth-century workers discovered in the eight-hour movement, speaking a shared language of faith does not guarantee success, either in winning strikes, achieving legislative outcomes, or building alliances with religious leaders.

The remaining chapters cover the near half century of rhetorical struggle and religious framing disputes over the implementation of the eight-hour workday in Chicago. Though debates over the eight-hour system took place on multiple playing fields, involving different sets of contenders, this project pays special attention to conflicts on the religious playing field. On religious grounds, workers, Protestant clergy, and sometimes employers engaged in a contest over the religious meaning of work and leisure in industrial capitalism as it unfolded in Chicago. Chapter 1, "A City of Industrial and Religious Extremes," details the case of Chicago and nineteenth-century Protestantism, the development of factions within the eight-hour movement, and the relationship between labor reformers, employers, and Protestant clergy in the city.

In chapter 2, I examine the first eight-hour-day campaign of 1866–67 in Chicago, which resulted in the first eight-hour law in the United States. This chapter situates this opening campaign within the larger movement for shorter hours for labor across the nineteenth century and discusses its implications for subsequent eight-hour protest in Chicago. Through the historical narrative, I explore how workers and clergy initially contested the religious meaning of the eight-hour system and the legitimacy of legislating limitations on overwork. The chapter also discusses employers' responses, both rhetorically and politically, to the new eight-hour law.

Chapters 3 and 4 highlight the period from economic crisis of 1873 through the eight-hour campaign of 1886 and the aftermath of the Haymarket affair. This was the most intense period of class hostility and industrial conflict and debate over the eight-hour system among workers, employers, and clergy. The analysis follows how the three main factions within the Chicago labor movement (craft unionists, the Knights of Labor, and the revolutionary Central Labor Union [CLU]) employed religious language in the lead-up to the events of 1886 and immediately after it. I argue that the reticence of employers to reduce overwork and the visceral class hatred emerging between employers and workers both began to shift clergy attitudes to be more sympathetic of worker demands in this period.

Chapter 5 follows several key eight-hour campaign successes and losses in the 1890s and their impact on the religious framing among workers and clergy. It was in 1893 that Illinois enacted the "Sweatshop Act" that limited the workdays of women and children to eight hours. The 1890s is significant as the period in which eight-hour support among Protestant clergy was strengthened as the result of a new social consciousness regarding labor reform.

Chapter 6 ends the narrative of the relationship between Protestant clergy and the eight-hour movement in Chicago by focusing on three key events: the ongoing fight for shorter hours for women, the conflict between typographical workers and the Methodist Church over shorter hours at a Methodist publishing house, and the construction of the Social Creed of the Churches. The chapter shows the decline in religious framing in the eight-hour movement in favor of political and economic arguments at a time when Protestant denominations were establishing committees and commissions to engage the labor movement and its reform goals. Finally, the conclusion of this volume discusses the theoretical implications of Protestant engagement with the eight-hour movement for developing a broader understanding of the possibilities and constraints surrounding religion as a basis for activism around economic and industrial issues.

CHAPTER 1

A City of Industrial and Religious Extremes

Whether it is the nineteenth century or the twenty-first century, Chicago remains a city on the move and one that is difficult to describe definitively as a result (D. Miller 1996; Pacyga 2009). Yet from its beginning, Chicago, more than other urban centers in the late nineteenth century, was recognized as a city of extremes (D. Miller 1996). But it was its industrial development and its religious life that set Chicago apart most from its urban peers. The city embodied the economic transition from a preindustrial order, supported by merchants, farmers, artisans, and small producers, to the new capitalist order dominated by capitalists who held control of the new large-scale industrial factories. In economic terms, the concentration of capital in the city, the use of steam power to increase productive efficiency, the scale of manufacturing firms, and the size of its labor force all grew rapidly in scope and scale (Jentz and Schneirov 2012). Aided by the railways and demands for goods of all kinds as a result of the Civil War and Southern Reconstruction, Chicago's transformation into a manufacturing giant and hub for transcontinental mobility and commerce was firmly fixed by the 1860s (D. Miller 1996; Pacyga 2009).

But the disruptive social consequences of speedy industrial expansion were also beginning to make themselves felt. Within a decade of its founding, not only was Chicago becoming known as a center for trade, but it was also establishing class divides that would make it infamous as a center of industrial conflict. Donald Miller (1996, 135) reports data from the 1848–49 U.S. Census that showed that the top 10 percent owned 94 percent of the city's growing wealth (the top 25 percent owned all of it), while the bottom 74 percent were classed as "destitute." The divide between the haves and have-nots was expanding as a direct result of and in proportion to the city's economic growth.

Table 1. Chicago's Native-Born and Foreign-Born Populations, 1870–1910

	1870	1880	1890	1900	1910
Native-born	154,420	298,326	244,327	383,268	491,365
	(51.6%)	(59.3%)	(22.2%)	(22.6%)	(22.5%)
Foreign-born[a]	144,557	204,859	855,523	1,315,307	1,693,918
	(48.4%)	(40.7%)	(77.8%)	(77.4%)	(77.5%)
Total	298,977	503,185	1,099,850	1,698,575	2,185,283

Sources: U.S. Census Bureau 1870, 1880, 1890, 1900, 1910; City of Chicago 1970.
[a] Figures derived from the addition of foreign-born and native-born children of (one or both) foreign-born parents census categories.

But while the reality of Chicago's economic opportunities was available for a relatively small number, the dream that it was available to all would not be deterred. More and more people from a diverse range of economic and ethnic backgrounds arrived in the city daily. The dramatic nature of the transformation of the population can be exemplified in one report that during one twenty-four-hour period in 1857, thirty-four hundred immigrants arrived in the city by rail (Pierce 1940, 2:6). Initially fed by an influx of native-born workers from New England and those from Britain, Chicago's labor force was quickly supplemented by a steady stream of workers arriving from Ireland, Germany, and Scandinavia. By 1860 more than 80 percent of all of its workers were foreign-born (Jentz and Schneirov 2012, 18). U.S. Census data in table 1 show that Chicago tripled its population between 1860 and 1870. Between 1870 and 1880, a decade dominated by the Great Fire, a prolonged economic depression, and the great railroad strike of 1877, Chicago grew by another two hundred thousand people. The city's population doubled again by 1890, 77 percent of whom were foreign-born, and it increased again by another seven hundred thousand at the start of the twentieth century. And though immigrants increasingly fed the ranks of Chicago's working classes, early on they also fed the ranks of employers. Jentz and Schneirov (2012, 40) point out that Chicago's economic growth was so great during the 1860s that it presented opportunities for immigrants to become manufacturers themselves and that foreign-born men, primarily of British and German decent, owned 64 percent of Chicago manufacturing establishments by 1870.

But whether destined to be workers or employers, the city's immigrants were drawn by the prospect of making money. Monetary gain was so much a part of Chicago's history that it provoked reformer William T. Stead to observe: "This vast heterogeneous community, which has been collected together from all quarters of the known world, knows only one common bond. They are staying to make money. The quest for the almighty dollar is their Holy Grail" (1894, 123). And Rev. Stead was on target: making money was the order of the day, every day, in Chicago. Although New York City dominated the industrial and commercial life of the nation, Chicago was not far behind, ranking sixth nationally in 1880 in the number of manufacturing establishments but third in numbers of employees, wages, invested capital, and profits (Pierce 1940, 3:533). By 1900 it was the nation's second-largest industrial center. Dominant among its industries were meatpacking, printing, lumber and furniture construction, garment making, wagon manufacturing, and the railroads. Furthermore, some of the most renowned nineteenth-century industrialists, merchants, and businessmen claimed Chicago as home. Among these were some of the most prominent and familiar industrialists such as George Pullman, Cyrus H. McCormick, Marshall Field, Potter Palmer, Philip D. Armour, Gustavus F. Swift, and Arthur A. and Charles P. Libby. But there were many more whose names figure in the history of the eight-hour movement, such as banker Lyman Gage, wholesale dry goods purveyor John V. Farwell Jr., and building-trade employers H. G. Loomis and E. B. Phillips.

As the century progressed, the concentration of the economic and social power and wealth of these men and their families created for them a world within a world in Chicago. Especially in the years following the Great Fire of 1871, the wealthy were insulated from the negative effects of the industrial expansion they helped bring about, and they rebuilt their homes in more exclusive areas south and north, while the west side became increasingly the domain of the working classes (Pacyga 2009; Cantwell 2012). The upper classes exerted their influence over society less through direct control of politics and more through creating exclusive social spaces and institutions through which they maintained their economic and cultural control (Jaher 1982; Khan 2011). Prosperous employers lived in the segregated neighborhoods near the lakeshore, building mansion next to mansion as a conspicuous display of their upper-class status. Beyond living in isolation, their wealth also allowed them to socialize in isolation. Belonging to the same exclusive clubs, the Board of Trade, and churches, attending only social functions given by others in one's class, sending children to the same elite preparatory schools and colleges, and encouraging intermarriage to build family alliances were all crucial ways for the elite to create a class identity that was visible along Michigan Avenue, Prairie Avenue, and State and Rush Streets.

The social isolation of Chicago's elite had a contradictory element to it as well. While the upper classes preferred to socialize with others like themselves, they reveled in the public displays of wealth and conspicuous consumption that achieved this period's naming as the "Gilded Age" by Mark Twain and others. The extravagant displays of the wealthy were simultaneously something to be marveled at as well as deplored. The *Chicago Tribune* gave front-page coverage to sumptuous balls and parties given by the city's well-to-do. Then, as now, the lives of the upper classes were something akin to a fairy tale that many Chicagoans of lesser means followed devotedly. The upper classes were the celebrities of their day. However, not every aspect of elite lifestyles went without criticism. For example, when Marshall Field spent seventy-five thousand dollars on a seventeenth birthday party for his son in 1886, the public, religious, and labor presses united in their belief that this was a needless waste of money when so many in the city were without basic necessities. However, when millionaires such as John D. Rockefeller helped fund the construction of the University of Chicago and its seminaries, fewer voices were raised in protest.

But wealth from expanding industrial interests did more than create a material paradise for elites in Chicago; it also shaped how upper-class individuals, especially those who were employers, viewed the world of work and the workers themselves. Insofar as work itself was concerned, the preindustrial communitarian morality that privileged the rights of the community as a community to benefit from productive enterprises had been replaced by the culture of the free market and moral values that made private property preeminent (Tilly 1978; Cantwell 2012). Market forces inevitably worked for the good of the community, so it was argued, as long as individual employers were free from regulations or other constraints on their single-minded pursuit of profit. Employers had the absolute right to order productive processes, including the wages and hours of their employees free from any outside interference. Such interference was to be opposed as impractical, dangerous, and un-American, whether it came from workers themselves, consumers or others in the broader community, religious leaders, or politicians (Haydu 1999; Isaac 2008). If social disparities of wealth resulted from industrialization, it was not the fault of employers; rather, it was due to the moral inferiority of workers, prone to laziness and intemperance, or their unwillingness to work hard and improve their condition in life. Workers and consumers alike either had the right to accept the employment or goods they were presented with or were free to go elsewhere. This new morality of work, rooted in the market economy, was the bedrock logic on which upper-class employers stood when confronted by efforts to reform industrial conditions. Jentz and Schneirov argue that, in their exclusive community institutions, upper-class employers became "politically self-conscious" (2012, 59), transforming and dominating political life by acting collectively as an elite interest group, challenging any law or ordinance that hurt their economic interests.

As the nineteenth century progressed, employers faced ever more challenges to their economic, political, and social power in the city. Chicago not only became famous for its explosive industrial growth and upper-class extravagance, but also became notorious for the horrendous conditions that accompanied its economic development and the intensity of labor reform movements to change or end them. Extreme economic hardship for workers was the price of unregulated industrial expansion. Long hours, low wages, life-threatening working conditions, and the constant of unemployment were taken-for-granted realities under the new industrial economy. A lack of state regulation, due in part to organized resistance from employer blocs, meant that the ebbs and flows of capitalist expansion were attended by frequent depressions that cycled through at least once a decade. Some were more severe than others for the city's economic elite, but all devastated workers. Typically, in the manufacturing establishments that didn't shutter their doors, employers slashed wages and, where possible, mechanized production to further cut costs (Jentz and Schneirov 2012, 156). When the economic recoveries finally arrived, bringing economic rewards to the industrial barons such as John D. Rockefeller, J. P. Morgan, and Andrew Carnegie, they brought little more than the possibility of jobs to desperate workers (Foner 1982; Duis 1998). Thousands of workers, including ever-greater numbers of transient workers, more familiar as tramps, competed for jobs following depressions, driving down wages and increasing hours, as employers could set the terms for hiring. For other residents, including Protestant clergy, it became more and more difficult either to remain ignorant of the life conditions the city's immigrant workers faced or to remain unencumbered by the intensifying conflicts between capital and labor.

When wages were increased, they rarely kept pace with costs of living for workers. Although for some workers wages were reported to have increased from between 15 to 100 percent, clothing costs went up at least 100 percent, fuel costs from 85 to 122 percent, rent 66 percent, and the prices of certain foodstuffs 133 percent. In 1883 workers' annual wages were reported to be some $200 below the estimated cost of living (Foner 1982, 498; Duis 1998). When Pullman workers struck against extraordinary wage cuts in 1894, the contradictions between wages and the cost of living for most workers were played out in the extreme (Carwardine 1894, 69). As Carwardine, himself a Methodist minister in Pullman, reported:

> Wages are paid at the bank. When they go to the bank to receive their two-week pay the half months rent is taken out, and the paycheck cashed. After deducting rent the men invariably had only from one to six dollars or so to live on for two weeks. One man has a pay check in his possession of two cents after paying the rent. Another I saw the other day, for seven cents. The man had worked as a skilled mechanic at ten hours a day for twelve days, and earned $9.07. He keeps a widowed mother, and pays the rent, the house being in his name. His half-month's rent amounted to $9.00. The seven cents was his, but he never claimed it.

Though they initially received relatively good wages for skilled work, workers faced similar scenarios in the meatpacking industry, whose wages and steady employment were continually dropped in the face of mechanization, seasonal layoffs, and an influx of unskilled laborers, including many women (Barrett 1987; Pride 1987). Barrett's (1987, 91) study of working-class life of packinghouse workers includes a 1911 report that the gap between the average weekly wage for male heads of households and the minimum cost of weekly expenses was $5.73 ($9.67 in earnings compared to $15.40 in costs) and that 30 percent of families reported facing such a gap.

The length of the workday was an equally stressful part of life among Chicago workers. Prior to 1881, bakers worked an average of one hundred hours per seven-day workweek, which figures to more than fourteen hours' work per day. Gasworks employees worked eighty-four hours per week, blast-furnace workers averaged seventy-two hours, while streetcar conductors put in seventy hours each week. The majority of other workers, male and female, were held to sixty-hour workweeks, with the exception of women employed in sweatshops that could be forced to put in sixteen-hour days over seven-day weeks (Illinois Bureau of Labor Statistics 1892, 393). Many others, especially immigrants from central Europe, faced irregular working hours in the length of both the workday and the workweek in the meatpacking plants (Barrett 1987). By 1900 the majority of workers (approximately 65 percent of 76,513 employees in 767 establishments surveyed by the Illinois Bureau of Labor Statistics) still worked between ten and thirteen hours daily (Illinois Bureau of Labor Statistics 1902, 270).

But low wages and long workdays were only two of the more readily documented difficulties workers faced. If one was native-born and spoke English, one had a clear advantage in carrying out the routine details of urban life, such basic things as asking for directions, haggling with merchants, and reading rental contracts and the like. Upton Sinclair describes the life of a fictional family of Lithuanian immigrants working in the stockyards, for whom, as newcomers and non-English speakers, even the most mundane activities posed threats.

> There were many such dangers, in which the odds were all against them. Their children were not as well as they had been at home; but how could they know that there was no sewer to their house, and that the drainage of fifteen years was in a cesspool under it? How could they know that the pale-blue milk that they bought around the corner was watered, and doctored with formaldehyde besides? When the children were not well at home, Teta Elzbieta would gather herbs and cure them; now she was obliged to go to the drugstore and buy extracts—and how was she to know that they were all adulterated? How could they find out that their tea and coffee, their sugar and flour, had all been doctored; that their canned peas had been colored with copper salts, and their fruit jams with aniline dyes? And even if they had known it, what good would it have done them, since there was no place within miles of them where any other sort was to be had? (1905, 79)

Eventually, these issues came to the attention of the middle-class public who also were sold these same dangerous, low-quality goods, prompting the formation of consumer leagues that fought for purity standards in food-production industries. Yet prior to the enforcement of such standards, alteration and doctoring of already low-quality food with chemicals and other additives became a further mechanism, beside low wages and long hours, for manufacturers to maintain high profit margins even in relatively bad economic times.

Chicago workers did not simply face these deplorable industrial conditions without question. The level of dissatisfaction among workers and mounting anger at their own economic insecurity are represented in the number of strikes across industries and in the caustic verbal attacks that permeated the labor press, pamphlets, music, and the public speeches of labor leaders (Jentz and Schneirov 2012; K. Fones-Wolf 1989; Halker 1992; Weir 1996). Worker frustration was fueled by the recognition that long-held views of America as a democratic republic built on a foundation of small producers, farmers, and independent craftsmen were being undermined by the new capitalist order controlled by powerful manufacturers (Cantwell 2012; Sutton 1998). Low wages, long hours, and increasingly militant labor demonstrations followed by brutal repression became the consequences of this transformation of industrial life. The Illinois Bureau of Labor Statistics (1888), which began collecting information on industrial conditions in the state only in 1881, reported a total of 2,767 strikes for the years 1881–87. Of this number, strikes to reduce the hours of labor, or occasionally against any increase in hours, accounted for 970, or one-third of the total reported.[1] But unlike employers and the upper classes who had a class consciousness and solidarity rooted in their trade associations, neighborhoods, club memberships, and churches, Chicago's working classes were fragmented by ethnicity and race, gender, religion, language, and skill. These demographic divisions shaped how particular groups of workers fought back against overwork, low pay, and dangerous conditions but often stood in the way of united action to challenge employers (Pride 1987; E. Hirsch 1990; Weir 1996; Tax 1980; Payne 1988; Schneirov 1997).

Three organizational factions dominated the labor movement in late-nineteenth-century Chicago, distinguished by ethnicity and religious commitments: conservative Protestant craft unionists, Protestant and Catholic Knights of Labor, and anticlerical anarchist and socialist revolutionaries. These factions, however, were more porous and fluid than fixed in their divisions. Radicals were members of craft unions and the Knights of Labor, especially at times of radical repression (B. Nelson 1988; Schneirov and Suhrbur 1988). The Knights were unique in their attempt to build a universally inclusive labor organization in which women, African Americans, conservatives, and radicals were welcome, though this was a challenging goal to achieve (Weir 1996; Pride 1987). Craft unions felt the internal pressures from a membership that cut across gender, ethnicity, and ideology, especially after 1870, as German and Irish workers were increasingly fragmented from native-born "Yankee" and British workers (E. Hirsch 1990). All local urban labor-reform movements faced the challenge of creating unity and solidarity while remaining divided by these factions.

According to U.S. Census records, by 1890 U.S.-born residents and those with British nativity made up approximately a quarter of Chicago's working classes, down from 41 percent in 1870 (E. Hirsch 1990, 92; Jentz and Schneirov 2012, 146). These workers typically identified as Protestant and were employed in skilled crafts, as carpenters, printers, ironworkers, and tailors, among others. Being native-born, skilled, and Protestant shaped both the unique challenges they were facing as a class and their definitions of the problems of industrial production and how to reform them. Skilled workers faced particular problems at work. With industrialization came mechanization and a technological revolution that threatened to deskill employment (Gordon, Edwards, and Reich 1982). Being transformed from a skilled into a semiskilled workforce meant a lowering of status and a declining standard of living. But during times of depression and high unemployment, these workers had few options other than to take whatever work was offered (Duis 1998).

Republicanism was a dominant ideological force shaping workers' views of industrial capitalism, many of whom were new to the city from rural communities (Cantwell 2012). America, according to republican thinking, was unique as a Christian republic whereby social and political life was built on the hard work and cooperation of a population whose livelihoods were based on being independent farmers and craftsmen and small-scale producers. Within this ideological understanding of community, property ownership was reasonably balanced, and workers and employers alike contributed to the overall stability of their communities by subsuming individual wealth accumulation to the well-being of the community. British immigrants, bringing with them Chartist beliefs in the need for mutual association among workers to protect their economic and social status, found immediate resonance with this ideology (E. Hirsch 1990).

But alongside republican ideals, nativism, anti-Catholicism, and anti-radicalism were equally common in the views of Anglo-American workers, whether native-born or immigrant. Non-Protestant immigrant workers shared the blame for deteriorating conditions because they were willing to accept whatever work was offered to them, making them a useful group to employ as strikebreakers when skilled workers fought to maintain their economic ground. A strong work ethic, rooted in evangelical Protestantism and support for temperance, was also a part of the worldview of these workers, separating them further from German and Irish immigrants. Encouraged to do so by employers and trade union leaders in the Chicago Trades and Labor Assembly (CTLA), these workers remained committed to beliefs that anyone who was motivated, God-fearing, sober, and committed to the divinely ordained American way of life could climb the social hierarchy of their communities (K. Fones-Wolf 1989; Cantwell 2012).

For much of the other three-quarters of the city's non-Protestant working classes, the Catholic Church was a community institution on which Catholic immigrants depended for material as well as spiritual resources (Higgins and Bole 1993; McGreevy 2003; McDonough 1992; Pride 2012). It is estimated that more than half the members of the national Knights of Labor were Catholic, including the order's leader, Terrance W. Powderly (Browne 1949). In Illinois approximately a third of the 37,974 members of the Knights of Labor were southern German and Irish Catholics (Weir 1996, 93). In the early years of the twentieth century, Irish and German Catholics were estimated to be a majority of the members of the American Federation of Labor and its leadership (Karson 1958, 221).

But in the nineteenth century, Catholicism was a religion under siege. Internally, it was divided along ethnic lines. Externally, Catholicism was characterized by Protestant elites as un-American, was associated with alcohol use, and was seen as contributing to other urban ills (Wuthnow 1988). Catholic leaders felt the competition from the dominant Protestant culture as well as from secular labor organizations that enticed workers with an alternative "religion" built on human solidarity, industrial reform, and justice (Weir 1996). In response, Catholic clergy often took a clear position against any Catholic joining labor organizations such as the Knights of Labor, both for fear of spiritual corruption as well as fears of radicalism in labor organizations (E. Hirsch 1990; Browne 1949; Weir 1996). But even this opposition may have been more tempered than historians have suggested. Higgins and Bole (1993) argue that American bishops understood that the secrecy and oath taking that were a part of nineteenth-century labor's fraternal culture were about protection, not religion, and that Catholic workers were not in danger from joining such organizations. As a result, it was the bishops who drafted an independent statement of support and then proceeded to send James Cardinal Gibbons to Rome for its ratification. Browne summarizes the fear of the American bishops at any outright rejection of unions in a quote from Chicago bishop Thomas Foley, who in 1869 commented that if the church condemned labor organizations, "we might as well close our churches" (1949, 7).

The religious commitments of Catholic workers created a challenge to labor organizations. On the one hand, remaining faithful to the church was important for workers. Terrance Powderly, leader of the Knights of Labor, maintained his orthodoxy by claiming that "six months have never rolled over my head in which I did not perform my duty as a Catholic in approaching the sacraments" (Browne 1949, 191). On the other hand, ending industrial exploitation was also a priority. To juggle these two pressures, labor leaders eventually negotiated a détente with the Roman Catholic hierarchy, who would allow workers to join trade unions so long as they remained reformist rather than revolutionary (Howe 1985; E. Hirsch 1990). For their part, however, it should be noted that Catholic workers didn't wait for this compromise. When Catholic leaders opposed them, workers responded by either ignoring the church's position or leaving it entirely (Weir 1996; Browne 1949).

What linked Protestant and Catholic workers were shared commitments to the reforming industrial conditions through political parties and the ballot. Labor republicanism and belief in the democratic foundation of American life underscored these strategies as the best means to reform industrial conditions. These organizations were committed to the idea that if labor-friendly men could be elected to public office by the working-class majority, then employers could no longer do as they pleased with the full support of government. Strikes as a direct means to challenge employers were not initially perceived as good or even universally effective tactics. The Knights of Labor especially were emphatic about using strikes only as a last resort. For craft unions, the strike had one valid place in labor strategy: as a means to enforce industrial reforms achieved legislatively.

Many eastern and southern European immigrants brought anticlerical and free-thinking traditions with them, later ensconced in various socialist and anarchist labor organizations, and created a religious divide in Chicago between believers and nonbelievers (B. Nelson 1988, 1991). This divide made joining forces around reform efforts easier for "believers" within the Chicago Trades and Labor Assembly and the Knights of Labor while making it more difficult to build them with labor's radical, irreligious wing. Yet even these divides were not insurmountable. Albert Parsons, one of the Haymarket anarchists, was a member of the Knights of Labor, as were many other anarchists in Chicago, while anarchists and socialists made inroads in directing the actions and strategies of craft unions in the Trades and Labor Assembly.

Working-class radicals were distinguished from other workers by more than their antipathy toward organized religion. In confronting the new capitalist order, total abolition of the wage system, not piecemeal reform, became the rallying cry of socialists and anarchists. The Socialist Labor Party (SLP), the Central Labor Union, and local union assemblies dominated by German and Bohemian workers attempted to organize workers around a new vision of the world that could be realized only through the revolutionary destruction of capitalism. But even among radicals, there was no uniform program for social change. The SLP, under the leadership of Thomas J. Morgan, favored the use of the ballot box and the formation of a political party of workers, while using strikes and boycotts to force employers and politicians to capitulate on industrial reform. Anarchists in the CLU distrusted any attempts at reforming the system from within but occasionally compromised on this issue to minimize factionalism during campaigns (B. Nelson 1988; E. Hirsch 1990).

The extremes of wealth and poverty in Chicago set the stage for contentious social unrest and class conflict (Pacyga 2009; Jentz and Schneirov 2012). The less willing upper-class employers were to listen to workers' challenges and alter the conditions of production, the more militant workers became. Workers were less willing to be patient and to rely on legislation to achieve their desired reforms. German, Irish, and Bohemian workers formed independent militias, such as the German Lehr und Wehr Verein and the Bohemian Sharpshooters, as a form of class-based "self-defense" and went so far as to engage in artillery practice in Chicago's parks in preparation for the day they feared the business elites would send troops into their neighborhoods to purge worker dissent (B. Nelson 1988, 151; Pacyga 2009). On Thanksgiving Day 1884, hungry women and children marched along the streets of Chicago's wealthy neighborhoods, demanding food. In response to worker organization and at the behest of employers, National Guard troops and police regularly descended on protesting and striking workers to restore order in the city's railroads, the stockyards, in the Haymarket Square, in Pullman, in bread riots, or whenever elites perceived their control to be threatened. As the Gilded Age unfolded, it seemed clear to more and more residents in the city that another war loomed between capital and labor. Eventually, these conflicts spread into all other parts of community life, providing unasked-for but increasingly firsthand knowledge of industrial conditions to those whose lives had previously been sheltered from them, especially the city's Protestants.

Life in Religious Chicago

Chicago was nationally recognized in the post–Civil War era as a religious center for both Protestants and Catholics. In 1870 there were approximately 125 Protestant churches (87 of which were Baptist, Congregational, Episcopal, Methodist, and Presbyterian), compared to 25 Catholic churches and 5 synagogues (Pierce 1940, 2:511). In 1878 the 5 core Protestant denominations added 10 more churches to their number, and by 1910 that number more than doubled, aided in part by the influx of Protestant immigrants from Scandinavia (*Churches of Chicago* 1878; Chicago Baptist Association 1910; General Congregational Association 1910; Diocese of Chicago 1910; Methodist Episcopal Church 1910; Stevenson 1907). Presbyterians especially reveled in calling Chicago a "Presbyterian City." Andrew Stevenson (1907, 124), in documenting the growth of the Presbyterian Church, USA, since the 1870s, calculated that Presbyterians had grown from 7,235 in 1876 to 26,071 in 95 congregations by 1906. Similar patterns of growth were evident in other denominations as well, allowing the *Chicago Tribune* to boast that "Chicago exceeds all other cities in America in the number of Sunday Schools and churches" (December 12, 1897, 41).

Congregational membership figures expanded with the population. Table 2 shows the increase in membership for the five major Protestant denominations relative to the general population in Chicago. In general, all five

Table 2. Protestant Affiliations in Chicago, 1870–1910

Denomination	1870	1880	1890	1900	1910
Baptist[a]	3,528	4,630[a]	13,506	15,331	17,552[a]
Congregational[b]	2,963	5,244	11,393	19,228[b]	21,697
Episcopal[c]	6,032	5,861	12,452[c]	21,621	28,616
Methodist[d]	5,011	7,779	13,586	24,551	32,210
Presbyterian[e]	3,237	6,816	10,772	15,291	31,376[e]
Total Population	298,977	503,185	1,099,850	1,698,575	2,185,283

[a] Chicago Baptist Association, *Proceedings*. Figures noted are for 1882 and 1906.
[b] General Congregational Association of Illinois, *Minutes*. Figure noted is for 1903.
[c] Diocese of Illinois, *Journal of the Proceedings of Annual Convention*. Figure noted is for 1889.
[d] Rock River Conference of the Methodist Episcopal Church, *Register*.
[e] Presbytery of Chicago, *Handbooks*. Figure noted is for 1913.

churches increased their memberships between 1870 and 1910. The relative numbers of Protestants in the population remained constant, if small, for each denomination, ranging from 0.8 percent for Episcopalians up to 1.4 percent for Methodists and Presbyterians. For instance, in 1890, the total number of these five groups of Protestants in the city was 61,709, or 5.6 percent of the total population. In contrast, the Catholic Archdiocese claimed 262,047 communicants, or 23.8 percent of the city's population. Such comparisons provide a basis for Protestant perceptions that their religious and cultural power was diminishing and intensifying congregational programs for widespread evangelism among non-Protestant newcomers. In *Our Country*, Josiah Strong (1885, 185) contributes to these perceptions by noting that in 1870, there was 1 Protestant church for every 2,433 residents, but by 1890 there was 1 church for every 3,601 Chicagoans.

But while Catholics surpassed Protestants numerically, Chicago remained dominated by Protestant leaders and traditions. As noted earlier, the influence of Protestant culture and social views held a wider currency in Chicago, and Catholics themselves were divided by ethnicity and language (Barrett 1987). Protestant influence was supported by a strong local religious press that promoted Protestant attitudes on a wide variety of social issues, including immigration, commerce, temperance, the "Negro question," the "Chinese question," and, of course, the "labor question." By late 1867, the Congregational *Advance* (November 21, 1867, 2) reported that twenty different religious periodicals were printed in Chicago, not to mention those from the East that circulated in the city as well. Each of the five major Protestant denominations had its own newspapers (usually one regional or citywide paper and several local congregational periodicals). Daily newspapers, thanks to the editorship of Protestant businessmen such as Joseph Medill, furthered Protestant worldviews, through extensive coverage of religious happenings and by including sermon excerpts from the city's leading Protestant pulpits. This permeation of public discourse by Protestant voices reinforced and supplemented Protestant ministers' personal access to economic and political elites, many of whom were members of their own congregations (Jaher 1982).

Denominational affiliation and social class went hand in hand in nineteenth-century Chicago, and many Protestant churches existed as religious reflections of wealth and influence. Employers and other professional businessmen clustered in Episcopalian, Presbyterian, Congregationalist, Methodist, and some ("Northern") Baptist churches. Upper-class churches were found nestled among the mansions along Michigan, State, Rush, Wabash, and Washington Streets on the city's north side and along the exclusive neighborhoods of Prairie and Calumet Avenues on the south side. Jaher (1982, 528) observes that St. James Episcopal Church, the First and Second Presbyterian Churches, and the First Congregational Church were among the most fashionable churches for upper-class Chicagoans.

At the end of the Civil War, only two churches out of twenty-nine of these five denominations were located among Chicago's immigrant and poor neighborhoods: St. Ansgarius (Swedish Episcopal) and one Scottish Presbyterian parish. Both Baptists and Methodists, being centered among the middle class, boasted more churches among the German, Danish, Swedish, and Negro communities (Pierce 1940). Toward the end of the nineteenth century, more Protestant churches had sprung up in working-class areas (Carter 2010). In some cases, churches such as the Western Avenue Methodist Episcopal Church began as a congregation of small business owners, shop clerks, and skilled workers but quickly became dominated by industrial workers as the demographics of the west side neighborhood changed (Cantwell 2012). The class divide in Chicago's religious landscape is important for understanding the attitudes of Protestant employers, specific groups of Protestant clergy, and workers toward industrial reform and the eight-hour movement. Although there are many similarities between Protestant denominations in terms of their class makeup and social attitudes, there are also differences rooted in their demographic composition and theological traditions.

Of the five main Protestant denominations in Chicago, the Episcopalians were the smallest, in numbers of both members and churches. In 1865 there were eleven Episcopalian congregations and one mission in the city. In 1878 there were twenty-eight, which included ten German congregations and two Norwegian ones (*Churches of Chicago* 1878, 10, 13). By the turn of the century, diocesan records report there were ninety-one churches and fifty-four missions in the city (Diocese of Chicago 1901). As "aristocrats" of American Protestantism, the membership lists of Protestant Episcopal churches were dominated by the wealthy (May 1963; Baltzell 1964; Weir 1996). St. James Church, for example, was situated at the heart of the most fashionable neighborhood in the city, on Wabash and Huron Streets. Like many similar churches in the late 1800s, the pews at St. James's were filled by a wealthy upper class (Jaher 1982). Among its parishioners were millionaire Potter Palmer; Samuel Nickerson, a founder of First National Bank; multimillionaire James Dole; banker George Sturges; and many top executives of Chicago railroads and grain companies (Schultz 1986).

Presbyterians attended one of eighteen congregations or six missions in 1878 and one of ninety-five by the middle of the first decade of the twentieth century (*Churches of Chicago* 1878; Stevenson 1907). The class divide seen in Episcopalian congregations was also evidenced in Presbyterian ones. Stevenson (1907) recorded that 540 leading industrialists, bankers, and other economic elites called the Presbytery of Chicago their church home. Included in their number were Cyrus H. McCormick, head of International Harvester; *Chicago Tribune* editor Robert Patterson; wholesale dry goods magnet John V. Farwell; and meatpacker Louis Swift. In addition to these men, Stevenson lists 61 manufacturers and wholesale merchants; 30 bankers; 19 railroad officials; 40 lawyers, judges, and other government officials; 10 meatpacking magnates; 14 lumber magnates; 10 retail merchants; 12 newspapermen; 6 architects; 10 LaSalle Street financiers; 16 publishers; and 28 capitalists. Further, to reinforce Jaher's (1982, 518) point regarding the prominent role the elites play within congregations, Stevenson's list documents that 200 of these men were officers (elders, trustees, and deacons) in their respective congregations. There were several Presbyterian congregations that were home to working-class people, including Englewood Presbyterian, close to the stockyards, and Pullman Presbyterian, in the town of Pullman (Carter 2010).

Chicago Congregationalists had their roots in the Third Presbyterian Church, from which they were ousted in 1851 in that denomination's debates over slavery (Pierce 1940, 2:365). In 1870 there were eleven Congregationalist churches and two missions in the city, although by 1878 there were fifteen churches. As the twentieth century opened, that number increased to seventy-three congregations (General Congregational Association 1900, 4–6). Among the prominent members of these churches were meatpacker Philip Armour; steel and railway magnates; Eugene J. Buffington, president of the Illinois Steel and Indiana Steel Companies; and William Gardner, president of the Chicago Northwestern Railway Company and the St. Paul and Omaha Railway Company (Pride 1987; Heidebrecht 1989). Few wage earners attended any of the city's Congregational churches.

The significance of having these individuals and their families together in the pews of these churches is twofold. First, the sheer numbers of these elites on church rosters meant that these churches themselves became an institutional means to reinforce elite network ties and the exclusivity of their religious cultural capital (Baltzell 1964; T. Nelson 2009). Being a member of elite Presbyterian congregations, for instance, not only meant you would socialize week by week with other elite Presbyterians, but also meant these individuals would find they had more in common with Episcopalians and Congregationalists. This is not to assert that there were no middle-class or working-class individuals in these denominations. Rather, the congregations themselves were segregated geographically, and, over time, they became more and more homogenous along class lines (Cantwell 2012). Second, by building such an exclusive cultural space in their churches, wealthy Protestants could ensure that any individuals from outside elite circles would feel alienated if they attended their services and so would not try to bridge the class divide, as so many voices in the labor press pointed out. Middle-class individuals were kept out of congregations such as St. James's or Fourth Presbyterian's, as were the city's poor, not only because of their class status per se but also because of an elite class culture that made them feel like strangers (Schultz 1986; T. Nelson 2009). This social distance between rich and poor Chicagoans was reinforced by residential segregation, making it unlikely that anyone other than those within a church's neighborhood would attend.

Such demographic characteristics may lead readers to suspect Episcopalians, Presbyterians, and Congregationalists and their clergy were more likely to oppose workers and labor reform. In reality, there was a great deal of variation in how these Protestants viewed the labor question. Episcopalians, as clergy and people of faith, were more inclined to support labor, at least verbally (G. Smith 2000). Of all the mainline Protestant churches, it was the Episcopal Church that first organized a church-sanctioned alliance in support of working-class interests, the Church Association for the Advancement of the Interests of Labor, in 1887, one year after the Haymarket affair, which remained active until 1926 (Hopkins 1940). CAAIL's self-identified tools for action included prayer, sermons, pamphlets, lectures, and the ballot box. New York bishops Henry C. Potter, F. D. Huntington, and James Huntington, the latter of whom was a member of the Knights of Labor, arbitrated strikes and orchestrated the distribution of food and other necessities to families of workers on strike. The Protestant Episcopal Church was the first denomination to recognize and celebrate Labor Sunday in 1890. Episcopalians as a denomination were very receptive to the Social Gospel movement, even in its more radical variation of Christian socialism (G. Smith 2000).

During the first decade of the twentieth century, these three denominations instituted formal offices to collect information regarding the state of industrial relations across the nation. In 1901 the General Convention of the Episcopal Church established the Joint Commission on Relations between Capital and Labor, which included the bishop of Chicago, the Right Reverend Charles Palmerston Anderson (Hood 1990). Together, CAAIL and the Joint Commission brought the structural and ideological power of the Protestant Episcopal Church to bear on industrial problems. In 1903 the Presbyterian Church established the first "Workingmen's Department," formed to present the church's positions to labor, and in 1904 the Department of Church and Labor, to formally examine labor reform issues (Nash 1970). Slower than its denominational siblings, the Congregational Church did not install its labor department head until 1909, when the Reverend Henry A. Atkinson of Atlanta, Georgia, was chosen to act as the secretary of labor and social service of the Congregational Brotherhood.

Locally, individual priests and pastors made efforts to reach out to Chicago's working classes. The Reverend Louis S. Osborne, rector of Trinity Church, for example, was among those Episcopal clergy who worked on a parish level, long before the establishment of any official church department, to bring the interests of the church and working people into closer alignment. Trinity Church sponsored a "Workingman's Club," which held an annual service at the church and made a library, a reading room, and game rooms available to neighborhood workingmen (*CT,* June 1, 1885; *Knights of Labor,* November 3, 1888). In addition to both CAAIL and the Joint Commission, the Episcopal Diocese of Chicago created its own Committee on Social Service, headed by the Reverend P. C. Wolcott. The committee's 1909 report urged "the study of existing social and economic problems in light of the Gospel of Jesus Christ." It also encouraged all Christians to "join in every movement for the advancement of the interests of labor, in particular, such movements as seek to obtain fairer wages and shorter hours" (*Living Church,* June 26, 1909, 302). But for all of these developments, it is important to assess how much these programmatic developments really impacted the labor movement. Robert Weir (1996, 83–84), in his work on the Knights of Labor, offers his realistic assessment tinged with a bit of sarcasm, that Episcopalians were the best Gilded Age Protestantism had to offer labor. Most Protestants in fact demonstrated at best a tepid engagement with the labor question, and, for all their best intentions, elite Protestants seldom seemed able to question the fundamental assumptions underlying the capitalist industrial order.

Methodist and Baptist congregations, in contrast, reflected more class diversity in their pews and in their approach to the labor movement. Lenhart's (1981) analysis of Chicago Methodists found a majority (65 percent) were from middle- and upper-class backgrounds, but the remaining third (35 percent) were working-class, predominantly native-born skilled factory operatives (see also Cantwell 2012). Although Baptists drew from a rural population and history, Chicago Baptist churches had more industrialists in their pews than did the Methodists. The First Baptist Church, for example, included Charles Walker, one of the founders and the first president of the Chicago Board of Trade, and Robert Harris and F. E. Hinkley, both presidents of railroads, in its pews (Stackhouse 1933). Other elites representing such diverse manufacturing interests as iron, jewelry, general merchandise, tailoring, banks, mills, book publishing, and architecture were also among local Baptists.

Methodists were a stronghold for Chicago's middle class and bastions of revivalism and were key supporters of Dwight L. Moody's citywide efforts to spread Protestant piety and combat the spread of Catholicism, alcohol, and Sabbath desecration through mass evangelism (Jentz and Schneirov 2012; D. Miller 1996). Conversion as a means to win new church members was not lost on church leaders or on the church press. As the largest denomination in the city, they focused on their own material and numerical growth. Their theological emphases on hard work and frugality, accumulation, and charity complemented their material interests nicely (Lenhart 1981; May 1963). Cantwell (2012, 94) also describes how, for many nineteenth-century Methodists, there was an obligation to take care of the spiritual and material needs of everyone rooted in the preindustrial experiences of their life in rural communities. This ideal of community life in which those with greater resources had responsibilities to care for those with less became a basis for Methodists' critique of the emerging industrial order.

Baptists were similar to Methodists in both material and theological emphases. Local Baptists helped to lead Chicago's temperance and Sunday-closing movements. Baptists, like other Protestant denominations, were dependent on industrialists and entrepreneurs for their own financial survival, for the expansion of their mission societies, for the revivals themselves, and for the support of local charitable and philanthropic enterprises. The Chicago Baptist Association, for example, praised John D. Rockefeller, himself a Baptist, for being a multimillion-dollar donor to the association and to its seminary at the University of Chicago (*Standard,* December 31, 1910, 4). Marshall Field, George Armour, Cyrus McCormick, and John V. Farwell all contributed financially to the success of local revival efforts (Jentz and Schneirov 2012, 191). In turn, church leaders backed manufacturers in their battles with workers as the perceived enemies of property, freedom, and sobriety to the point that, after the 1877 railroad strikes, local Baptists supported the purchase of a Gatling gun by the Citizen's Association for the purpose of "mowing down a thousand men (strikers, no doubt) in a few seconds" (Stackhouse 1933, 83).

Like their Protestant counterparts, most Methodists and the Baptists did not form relationships with the labor movement until the twentieth century, despite being two denominations that had significant numbers of wage earners as members of their churches. In December 1907, twenty years after Episcopalians founded CAAIL, Methodist pastors and laypeople formed an unofficial society to address industrial reform, called the Methodist Federation for Social Service. The federation saw its own raison d'être as "a response to a demand manifesting itself throughout the denomination indicating a rising interest in the larger fulfillment of the second great commandment of Jesus Christ, and a recognition of the responsibility of the Church to meet the social problems of the day with a Christian answer" (*Northwestern Christian Advocate* [*NWCA*], April 1, 1908, 13). The Methodist Federation began with the task of educating Methodists through leaflets, monographs, and books, promoting a Christian perspective on industrial problems. Most important, the federation expressly stated that such intellectual study was required to be practical and would result in action geared toward remedying the problems it confronted. People in the pews were receptive to this new attention to the labor question and wanted to hear more. While the Methodist Federation tried to remedy many different kinds of social problems, raising wages and the improving the conditions of labor ranked high on its list.

Like its denominational brethren, the Baptist Church maintained a small but influential prolabor minority that included well-known advocate of social Christianity Walter Rauschenbusch, and on the whole the Baptist *Standard* was reasonably friendly to working people's interests (Hopkins 1940). The Northern Baptist Convention organized the Social Service Commission in 1909 "to study what was being done by Baptists churches in the field of social service," with a hope of stimulating more congregations to be socially involved (*Standard,* February 20, 1909, 8). The Reverend George T. Webb circulated a survey to Chicago's Baptist congregations that gives a clear sense of what service meant. Webb inquired about classes in "applied Christianity," kindergartens, charitable work, gymnasiums, citizenship movements, temperance, work with immigrants, work with trade unions, employment bureaus, and many other programs. The growth of these programs signaled the arrival of the "new consciousness" that aimed to apply Christian teaching to social conditions (*Standard,* January 7, 1911, 5).

But unlike other Protestant groups, this consciousness was perhaps less new in practice. Baptists had been friendlier in some ways toward labor reform efforts in both their actions and also the ways they spoke about them (Hopkins 1940). What was central to the Baptist approach to industrial conditions was a belief that an individual's moral state was directly related to the social conditions that surrounded him or her (White and Hopkins 1976; Oshatz 2010; Bowman 2007). It was this tenet that provided a basis for the Baptist presence in both the temperance and the Sabbatarian movements. Efforts to close saloons or eliminate Sunday work were part of a larger moral project to eliminate vice at a social level, which in turn would contribute to the strengthening of church efforts to raise the moral state of individuals. Labor reform was framed in much the same way. When the Illinois Baptist Association, for instance, took the lead in supporting workingwomen in their efforts to achieve a ten-hour workday in 1909, this obvious partisan move by Baptists was not taken simply out of a belief in the inherent goodness of shorter hours. Rather, it was taken because long hours were detrimental to the moral condition of women as a group, who in turn were believed to be responsible for the moral character of their individual families (*Chicago Daily Socialist,* October 22, 1909, 2). Shortening their workday meant redeeming time for women workers everywhere and creating a new set of social conditions that would support their redemption as individuals.

Of course, any of these clergy who supported industrial reform had detractors. Employers regarded them with suspicion and generally classed them in the same group as socialists or anarchists, or they simply dismissed them and their opinions (Weir 1996; Mirola 1999). Radicals within the labor movement, and even some moderates, continued to deride them as tools of employers who were unwilling to expound a full and practical critique of capitalism. Burns, in his analysis of the thinking of radical Christian leaders in this period, cites George Herron's critique of Walter Rauschenbush and other Social Gospel advocates as "spoiling everything they have touched" and working only in the interest of the church, "in order that the Church may save itself by bridling and saddling the working class" (2012, 79). Employers and workers both were also unwilling to accept a model of social relations in which clergy would lead both classes to industrial peace (G. Smith 2000; Weir 1996). Nevertheless, these clergy continued to work for industrial reform and were able to continue their efforts because they operated within their own denominational contexts. Their positions as leaders of local congregations certainly made them vulnerable to pressures from their congregants to temper their support for labor, but their positions also freed them to address industrial reform as nonpartisan community leaders.

Protestant clergy found themselves enmeshed in intensifying industrial conflicts that demanded their attention and input. Employers had their own economic resources and political connections to mobilize against labor and enjoyed religious defense of their interests by fiat. Earlier in the century, employers expected the implicit support of their religious leaders in upholding business interests, and so long as clergy used their moral authority to bolster this economic system, they were believed to be doing their jobs. Later in the century, employers had made a clear divide with their faith. Faith was personal and was the focus of Sunday devotion. But on Monday morning, it was capitalist values that became the driving forces shaping employers' behaviors and decision making. Labor, however, lacking access to other resources, depended on the support of churches and others to stand with them to enact and enforce labor reform. Because Protestant church leaders were initially slow to champion labor causes, workers organized without them and either used their own interpretations of biblical injunctions against wealth and oppression to legitimize the moral rightness of their cause, in many cases turning the Bible against the clergy, or rejected institutional religion totally. The Railroad Conductors' Brotherhood, in its April 1978 *Monthly Magazine,* best describes the complex life of Protestant Chicago as the eight-hour movement took shape:

> We are living in a charitable, Christian country, where a hundred thousand preachers are paid annually to preach for the benefit of sinners, and the expenses of a hundred thousand churches have to be paid; where Baptists rival Congregationalists by having a larger dome on their church, and the Congregationalists the Methodists by having a more eloquent preacher, and the Methodists the Episcopalians by having a more elaborate chandelier; and the preachers keep up antagonism by overthrowing their old doctrines, and want extra money for trying to build up new, not thinking that they are professed followers of the Messiah, who taught charity, humility, peace and good will toward all. Now, if half, or even one-third of the money appropriated to the Church and quarrelling preachers was given to the starving masses of our great metropolis of the West, we should lessen our prison tax and houses of correction. (167)

Convincing Protestants to build alliances with a movement whose aim was to improve the city's moral condition by reforming the conditions of labor was as much a part of the mobilization task set before eight-hour reformers as was the task of mobilizing workers themselves.

Beneath the manifest economic and political conflicts that characterized Chicago's eight-hour movement was a debate between workers, employers, and clergy over the religious and moral significance of redeeming time through shorter hours for labor. In the development of their respective rhetoric in this debate, eight-hour advocates and employers fought over whether the hours of labor carried any religious significance whatsoever. Clergy responded to the struggles for reform from their positions as embedded community leaders. Protestant values about work, leisure, and community relations shaped how clergy approached local eight-hour conflicts and provided the basis for initially opposing shorter hours but also for their later support for the movement. But it was the local events that took place around the eight-hour movement between 1866 and 1912 that shaped how employers, workers, and clergy came to understand the eight-hour day, framed its legitimacy, and addressed each other's actions.

CHAPTER 2

Opening Eight-Hour Protests and the 1867 Eight-Hour Law

The great debate over the length of the workday began long before the Gilded Age and carried on concurrently in early-nineteenth-century Europe as well as in the United States (Robertson 1893; Rae 1894). As industrialization, the wage system, and class polarization expanded in advance of and following the Civil War, the new industrial working classes faced profound contradictions between their lived experiences with the factory system and their republican ideals regarding how the economy and community life ought to operate (Montgomery 1981; Weir 1996). A generation of native-born workers and immigrants from Britain, Ireland, and Germany all found themselves caught between their commitments to and experiences within preindustrial economies based on independent producers operating within reasonably balanced markets and close-knit communities and the chaos of the new urban, industrial order (Sutton 1998; Cantwell 2012). The older world was quickly disappearing, and workers organized around reforms that initially were meant to help preserve it; chief among these reforms was a shortening of the hours of labor through the eight-hour day. As Jentz and Schneirov argue, "The eight-hour movement prompted the first public recognition of how capitalism was affecting American life" (2012, 81).

America's westward expansion was driving the rapid industrialization of eastern cities, and workers faced twelve- and thirteen-hour days, with longer days being required in summer and shorter days in winter. With the advent of gas lighting, employers required longer hours because they were not dependent on the sun. The introduction of twenty-four-hour industry, a boon for new manufacturers, was a distinct break with older traditions and customs regulating the natural order of work in preindustrial, agrarian communities. Some workers went so far as to condemn the use of artificial light as unscriptural, for violating the divine order of creation, based on evening and morning constituting a day in the biblical account of creation (Roediger and Foner 1989, 52). Gas lighting allowed employers to abolish the evening with constant light and work. To contemporary readers, this may seem to be an odd argument. However, it illustrates the important point that work was never reducible to the economics of production and making a living for past generations of workers. Work was tied to the life of communities and always was regulated by community religious and moral beliefs and codes of conduct. As Roediger and Foner (1989, 17) note, "Fairs, days off, long meals, and social drinking during the day gave place to a rhythm of work . . . set by machinery and by the demands of masters pressured by merchant capitalists." Religious observances were also disrupted in the new order, with seven-day workweeks challenging the demands of personal and collective devotions for Christians and Jews (Pollard 2009; Hunnicutt 1988). Religious ideals and language provided workers with a significant ideological foundation from which they would challenge overwork and long hours (Lazerow 1986, 1987; Murphy 1992; Sutton 1998; Burns 2013).

The 1820s through the 1850s saw the maturation of early American trade unionism in its fight for a ten-hour day (Roediger and Foner 1989; Foner 1982). Industrial New England, with its textile mills, factories, and shipyards, occupied center stage for the ten-hour movement. Workers, both men and women, in this era employed a two-pronged strategy in fighting for ten hours (Murphy 1992). First, labor reformers used strikes both defensively, when employers tried to lengthen the workday, and offensively, to encourage uncooperative employers to go along with a "voluntary" adoption of shorter hours. Second, reformers pressured local, state, and federal politicians to legislate shorter hours in a variety of bills (Stone 1852). Both strategies succeeded. In the 1840s, strikes forced employers to grant shorter hours across various industries, and in the 1850s seven states passed ten-hour laws and more than fourteen others entered into debates on the subject.

In the context of both strikes and politics, religious rhetoric emerged as significant means for framing arguments for the ten-hour day, as it later would be for the eight-hour day. The antebellum religious arguments rested on several key points. First, God ordained that everyone fulfill a variety of religious and social duties. Male workers demanded shorter hours as a means to gain the necessary leisure to conduct themselves as true men, who were obligated to both provide for their families and be engaged citizens in the public sphere (Weir 1996; Sutton 1998; Cantwell 2012). Working-class women argued in a similar vein that their need to fulfill their religious obligations and the sacred duties of motherhood was central to their demand for shorter workdays (Lazerow 1987; Murphy 1992; Payne 1988). Second, as noted in Sutton's work on evangelical artisans in antebellum Baltimore, evangelical Methodists and Baptists active as trade union leaders argued for the ten-hour system to counter the growth of greedy manufacturers and financiers by employing biblical mandates to support "a communitarian preference for social justice within a producerist context" (1998, 250). Third, reformers asserted that all of the social evils decried among the working classes such as drinking, gambling, laziness, and so forth had as their root cause violations of God's law through overwork and the enforced idleness from too few people working for too many hours while others remained unemployed (Foner 1982; Roediger and Foner 1989; Hunnicutt 1988, Oshatz 2010).

In addition to crafting these religious arguments, reformers also carefully considered the potential audience for them. As Foner (1982, 118) observes, the success of ten-hour strikes was dependent on public support. Religious rhetoric was used in the strategic hope of persuading Christian politicians, employers, and the public at large to accept the moral justice of the ten-hour demand. Ten-hour reformers also used these arguments to make direct appeal for support from clergy (Lazerow 1987). Clergy understood themselves and were understood by others to be the moral arbiters of their communities and as such were invited to stand with workers for what to them was a divinely ordained industrial reform (May 1963; Sutton 1998). Ministers from the working-class churches typically did not need much convincing and joined publicly in support of shorter hours (Sutton 1998). To entice other ministers, reformers argued that the "true" religion that Christ taught required people not simply to participate in prescribed religious forms and ceremonies, but to improve the lives of the needy in concrete ways (Lazerow 1986, 1987). In advocating the ten-hour system, clergy evidenced, in the minds of workers, a living out of authentic Christian values.

Progressive ministers testified to the beneficial impact of shorter workdays, and their statements were circulated far and wide. In a report to the Massachusetts Legislature from the Committee on the Hours of Labor, James Stone included the observations of numerous civic leaders from across England who testified before Parliament in support of a ten-hour bill in 1847. Stone recounts the testimonies of Protestant as well as Catholic clergy in detail. Rev. Sharples of Blackburn reported that "immediately from the passing of the Ten Hours Bill, reading rooms and schools for mutual instruction sprung up on all sides." Another minister, "in a dense population," testified that "the majority of the regular attenders consist of persons engaged in factories. Their conduct and spiritual condition are the most satisfactory of any persons attending church. Deeply would they grieve, and deeply should I grieve, if the legislature sanctioned a system, which must entirely deprive them of these benefits, and would very deeply injure their moral and religious character" (1852, 13). Despite strong anti-Catholic feeling in England at this time, even Catholic priests from Bolton and Stockport were cited, stating, "The number of factory workers attending schools has more than doubled. There is not the slightest doubt that the social, moral, and physical condition of the factory workers has been improved." These clergy clearly reinforced the point that ten-hour reformers wanted to make: that fewer hours for work meant more time for self-improvement, not idleness and dissipation. With clergy testimony from England being used as testimony and precedent for reform in Massachusetts, it is clear that the moral authority of clergy carried over time and place, from England to New England and from New England to Chicago. Labor reformers knew this and attempted to employ the moral authority of the clergy for their own political ends.

From Ten to Eight Hours

With this historical precedent, protest for eight hours grew and expanded westward to Chicago. The Civil War expanded trade unionism in urban centers of the East Coast as well as in the Midwest, as rising costs of living outpaced wages. The first eight-hour movement began shortly before the end of the Civil War, spearheaded by Boston mechanic Ira Steward and George McNeill and was soon taken up by native-born and British craft workers joined by German and Irish workers in Chicago (Montgomery 1981; Jentz and Schneirov 2012; Green 2006). Nascent unions such as the International Typographical Union (ITU, founded in 1852), the Brotherhood of Locomotive Engineers (1863), and others, including iron molders (1857), machinists and blacksmiths (1859), and masons and bricklayers (1859), provided the leadership for eight-hour agitation in the city. In 1864 the Chicago Trades Assembly (CTA) was established and organized twenty-four trade unions with more than eighty-five hundred members (Pierce 1940, 2:168). The *Workingman's Advocate* (*WA*), edited by Scottish printer Andrew C. Cameron, was the voice of the CTA and, until 1879, the main labor newspaper in the Midwest, and its clarion call was for a new law reducing the hours of labor.

Chicago workers had become increasingly alienated from President Lincoln's war policies, especially the 1863 Draft Law that stipulated all male citizens between the ages of twenty and thirty-five and all unmarried men between thirty-five and forty-five were subject to military duty. A mass meeting was organized by the CTA calling for a third labor party, setting both Republicans and Democrats scrambling to appease workers by taking up the eight-hour day as a central campaign issue. In 1865 Cameron formed Chicago's Grand Eight Hour League as a political organization independent of both the Republican and the Democratic Parties, with fourteen branches operating across the city hosting mass meetings, further pushing state and local politicians to support eight-hour reform. In the elections of 1866, all seven candidates who pledged support for eight-hour reform were elected to office (Jentz and Schneirov 2012, 91). The league's class-based political pressure worked to bring an eight-hour ordinance covering municipal workers for a vote before Chicago's Common Council. The council split, however, and Mayor Rice sided with the no votes (Beckner 1929; Pierce 1940, vol. 3). Several months later, however, pressure from labor forced the council to pass the ordinance.

With this success, eight-hour agitation continued both at the city and at the state levels. In the spring of 1866, the *Chicago Tribune* reported more than twenty-six strikes related to shorter hours and wages in the East among railroad workers, car drivers, shipbuilders, caulkers, joiners, and carpenters (January 20, 1866, 2; April 15, 1866, 2; April 20, 1866, 2; May 8, 1866, 2; *WA*, May 12, 1866). The editors of the Republican *Tribune* noted that every branch of trade unionism had embraced the eight-hour system, but, in their opinion, demanding shorter hours was unreasonable and "only Capital will triumph" (May 8, 1866, 2). The editors were correct. Not one of these strikes successfully shortened hours (*CT*, May 17, 1866, 2).

Initial eight-hour agitation quickly produced new arguments for shorter hours that capitalized on the themes of freedom and equality that had been crafted by the abolitionist movement to end slavery but also on themes familiar to those steeped in a heavily Protestant religious culture. From its inception, the *Workingman's Advocate* framed eight hours in religious terms that would resonate with the evangelical Protestant morality of native-born and British workers. Despite the fact that this group was increasingly a minority among Chicago's working class, their religious values as applied to the eight-hour system appealed to German Lutherans and Irish Catholics who were experiencing the increasingly chaotic and oppressive effects of the manufacturing economy (Jentz and Schneirov 2012, 87). As the prior generation argued about the ten-hour system, the institution of an eight-hour workday was a key component of sustaining republican institutions and creating a divinely ordered society of free men. In recounting a speech before the New

York Legislature by the Honorable George A. Brandreth, the *Workingman's Advocate* embraced Brandreth's religious framing of the eight-hour question:

> Traditions informs us that Solomon, when he was building a temple to the Most High promulgated a decree for the men employed upon the great work, "eight hours shall be dedicated to labor, eight to rest, recreation, refreshment, and the worship of Jehovah, and eight to sleep." Thus the stones and timbers of that edifice consecrated to the Supreme Being was kept unpolluted by the sweat of slaves, or of laborers exhausted by overwork and painful toil. It appears then that the weekly day of rest and the eight-hour system are alike derived from that once illustrious chosen people. Taking our warrant from the divine authority, we have established the Sabbath by statute and penalty; and why not in like manner now make an enactment for the eight-hour rule? (April 21, 1866, 1)

The eight-hour day not only came from "a divine source," but was "sustained by the Gospel of Christ," with the Bible as "the rock of truth" on which all labor reform was grounded (*WA*, April 21, 1866, 1; November 16, 1867, 2). Workers imbued a spiritual depth to industrial reform. "We are not in the dark, in these upheavals of society," stated one anonymous workingman. "God is in them saying, 'Let there be light'" (A Workingman 1866, 7). Religious metaphors and injunctions were interwoven with the economics of shorter hours and the political debates on how best to achieve it.

Reformers also drew on themes from two other key Protestant movements of the time: Sabbatarianism and temperance. Violations of the Sabbath and alcohol consumption were tied up in a collection of social threats to middle- and upper-class moral sensibilities that included fears of Catholicism, immigrants, unemployment, gambling, and other vices, all of which seemed to be encroaching simultaneously on the cultural hegemony so long enjoyed by Chicago's Protestant establishment. Sunday work was a direct violation of the Protestant Sabbath and the divine injunctions and social customs that allowed only religious observance and works of charity on Sundays. Alcohol consumption violated Protestant sensibilities rooted in evangelical theology and biblical injunctions that prohibited drunkenness. It also reflected their fears of a changing religious landscape, as immigrant Roman Catholics, Lutherans, and freethinkers flooded the city without any religious injunctions guarding them from drink. But for eight-hour reformers, these Protestant movements provided a new dimension to labor's religious rhetoric. Shorter hours would lead to the moral improvement of workers. Andrew Cameron, himself an evangelical Methodist, argued the saloons were escapes from overwork and poverty.

> How has intemperance been combated? A few sermons which are not listened to; a few municipal ordinances which are not paid attention to. Instead of preaching and punishing, a cure should be applied, and for that the cause of the evil should be known—The evil excessive hours of labor! Think of the twelve hours that these men spend in the workshops . . . so exhausting, so monotonous, follow him in the snow and frost when he quits his shop. . . . Enter with him into the frightful dog-hole where his meal is scarcely ever ready, for his wife is at work like himself . . . where he cannot breathe, because the air fit for breathing is dearer still than wine. . . . Do you know many men, even among those who are most eloquent on drunkenness, who would resist the attraction of the pleasant tap room, well-lighted, well warmed, with its glittering pots, its dusty bottles, its gay companions, and all the semblance of happiness, which hides him from the want of real happiness? (*WA*, April 28, 1866, 1)

Intemperance did not result from sin or any inherent moral laxity of workers but was due to the industrial conditions workers endured. Reformers were also quick to point out the hypocrisy of temperance leaders who condemned saloons and drinking from the comfort of middle- and upper-class communities where the conditions of life provided alternatives to saloons in the form of rest, leisure, and plenty. Eight-hour reformers appealed to Protestant clergy to support the movement as a more practical way to achieve their own desired ends of a Christian community.

On June 4, 1866, Chicago journeymen stonecutters along with those in Marquette, Illinois, struck for a nine-hour day. Three days earlier, the stonecutters had proposed a nine-hour day, which employers refused, and employers offered workers a reduction of one hour on Saturdays, which the stonecutters rejected (*CT*, June 25, 1866, 4). The standing committee of the union, Thomas Marshall, A. McBeath, and J. Smith, in a letter to the *Tribune*, stated that the stonecutters were striking for nine hours' pay for nine hours' work at the old rate of wages that was paid them by the day, not by the hour (June 26, 1866, 2). But this demand violated the logic of the new industrial order that newspaper editors were expert in articulating.

> We are in favor of the fullest human liberty in obtaining all that the labor of a workingman is fairly worth. But coercion and extortion are as odious when attempted by those who have labor to sell as by those who have bread, meat, coal, or tenements. The attempt to shorten days works without lessening wages is like a combination of bakers to lessen the size of a loaf while maintaining its price, or of grocers to declare twelve ounces instead of sixteen to be a pound of sugar, or of coal men to sell 1,800 pounds of coal and style it a ton. Values cannot be so changed. (June 19, 1866, 2)

Employers in the building trades corroborated the *Tribune*'s claims. On June 21, employers and architects met to formulate a united course of action to resist the striking stonecutters. H. G. Loomis, E. B. Phillips, W. W. Boynington, F. A. Sproehnle, and L. H. Boldenweck described the stonecutters' strike as uncalled for, unjustifiable, and causeless. As a consequence, they would use all legitimate means in their power to resist the demand for shorter hours and not employ any stonecutter who would not return to work under the ten-hour system. Further, these men agreed to not work with any company who employed union stonecutters. But despite this show of unity, employers were divided in their approach to organizing among their workers. While the representatives of twelve companies signed statements refusing to work with those who hired union men, many others did not. They did, however, unanimously adopt a resolution stating: "We recognize the right of the journeymen stonecutters to associate themselves together in any way that they may consider beneficial to them, but we do not recognize the right of any body of men to dictate to us as to the manner in which we conduct our business" (*CT,* June 22, 1866, 4). In response, 150 striking stonecutters held their own meeting several days later to reply to their bosses. The workers appealed to Chicago's business community and the public to support them and "repudiate the unholy alliance entered into by some of the employing capitalists to crush our labor organizations, which are founded on the principles of equal justice, alike to employer and employee" (*CT,* June 25, 1866, 4).

The press ridiculed workers for waging a "bootless war against the laws of political economy that would only end in humiliation, failure, and loss" (*CT,* June 23, 1866, 2). From the perspective of the *Tribune*, "If a resolution would change the value of a day's work the stonecutters are at fault in not resolving that their employers should pay them full wages for one hour's work instead of nine. That would afford them eight hours more for recreation and study. Their resolutions would as speedily effect one purpose as the other" (June 27, 1866, 2). The city's newspapers expressed sentiments that ignored the industrial realities under which workingmen and -women labored. In adopting the idea of free labor, their claim was made that workers had full choice over what number of hours and what rate of wages they would tolerate on the job. Should an individual worker find their conditions of labor acceptable regardless of hours or wages, no one had the right to interfere with them. That employers act in an organized fashion to create similar conditions in all industries including what were acceptable levels of production, leaving workers no choice but to accept these conditions, did not even enter the editors' or the public's thinking. The *Tribune* also used familiar abolitionist themes of coercion, slavery, and even the whip and the lash in its antiunion framing of the eight-hour strike, observing:

> In every strike there are a large number who, contrary to their own judgment, find their right to control their labor destroyed, and themselves made the slaves of a tyrannical mass of men who rule them as despotically as the late southern slaveholder ruled his negro. Indeed, these labor associations enslave labor as manifestly as does African slavery, the chief difference being that the latter enslaves labor for the benefit of the master, while the former fetters it for the pretended benefit of the workman. But the question underlying the whole system of labor associations is, whether labor needs to be enslaved at all. (June 27, 1866, 2)

In the face of opposition, the journeymen stonecutters demonstrated the power of their union when facing organized employers. Despite their stated resistance, employers conceded, and eight months later, to the satisfaction of both parties, the journeymen stonecutters worked on the eight-hour system, initially for $3.50 per day and then for $4 per day (*CT,* May 1, 1867, 4).

Although the stonecutters won an eight-hour day by means of a strike, the leaders of the eight-hour movement remained committed to using political means to achieve it (*WA,* August 18, 1866, 2). But the political process to enact shorter hours posed its own problems. Andrew Cameron ran for a seat in the Illinois Legislature as a Democrat, hoping for strong support at the polls from workers, especially among the Irish, with the goal to make the eight-hour day a legislative reality once he was elected. In shifting from a traditional Republican position, Cameron's choice to run with the Democrats was strategic, as he hoped to force both parties to embrace labor reform in the struggle for workers' votes (Montgomery 1981). But the editors of the *Tribune* saw the difficulty in fighting for economic and industrial change through political means at once. "That the Republican Party will carry the State in the coming election is perfectly certain. How the eight-hour movement can derive any advantage from sending Democrats to a legislature where the Republicans have a majority is difficult to see. In the nature of things, Mr. Cameron's influence as an eight-hour advocate would be impaired or destroyed by his political affiliations. On the other hand, if elected, he will be bound to support political measures distasteful to a majority of the workingmen" (November 1, 1866, 2). So long as labor sympathizers in political office were in the minority, there would be no way to enact labor reforms that workers elected them to carry out. They would be forced either to stand their ground and be doomed to irrelevancy or to compromise and lose the support of their electoral base. Neither option offered much hope.

One example of the partial victories so often afforded by the political process is illustrated in the *Tribune*'s report on the state Republican Party convention in receiving resolutions from delegates who were eight-hour supporters. A delegate from Kane County, Illinois, offered a resolution that favored "eight hours being made a legal day's work for the mechanics and laborers in cities, factories, and all public works." A delegate from LaSalle amended this resolution in a way that shifted the resolution's intent from support for a concrete legislative action to a principled support for the spirit of the eight-hour movement: "Resolved, That we are in favor of that kind of legislation which shall tend to alleviate the hardships, shorten the hours of labor and improve the conditions of the laboring classes" (August 14, 1866, 2). The convention moved that the latter resolution be adopted, and it passed unanimously. What did the eight-hour movement gain from this move? It gained a general support for the spirit of the movement without any practical requirement for elected officials to translate it into concrete action. For their part, Republican officials could claim that they had dealt with and supported reducing the hours of labor without actually enacting reform.

In January and February 1867, Illinois was poised to be the first state to enact an eight-hour law, and it received close attention by other state legislatures, especially those of New York, Pennsylvania, and Massachusetts, which were also close to taking such a step. The Honorable H. M. Shepard, with the support of Representatives Lester Bond and Joseph Reynolds, both strong advocates for the eight-hour movement, offered resolutions in the Illinois Legislature expressing support for the movement, which were adopted (*CT*, February 2, 1867, 1; February 19, 1867, 1). A version of the eight-hour bill passed the Illinois House of Representatives by a vote of fifty to eleven.

As soon as the eight-hour bill was passed, local employer associations passed resolutions rejecting the new law. Illinois employers argued they would be at a competitive disadvantage with neighboring states that did not have eight-hour laws. The costs of production would increase as well, they claimed, forcing many businesses out and increasing unemployment. Consumer price increases were also predicted to follow from the eight-hour law. Neither could Chicago workers themselves, they argued on meteorological grounds, benefit from such a law.

> In our cold climate, out-door labor can only be successfully prosecuted a little more than half the year. Take masonry for instance. New bricks are

> seldom made and delivered before the first of June; after the fifteenth of November, the weather is unfit to lay them. Ought then this short season of less than six months to be still further abridged by cutting off one-fifth of the balance? . . . Is it not unwise to say that a mason shall not work more than eight hours a day, when for five months in the year it is almost impossible and quite impractical and unprofitable for him to work at all? What sympathy does he deserve who pleads poverty in winter and yet refuses to earn only four-fifths of what he might readily earn in summer? Were the whole year like June and September some argument might be possibly urged in behalf of such a law. (*CT,* March 17, 1867, 2)

But while they tried to present a unified front, employers were not of one mind about the eight-hour movement (see Montgomery 1981). At a meeting at the Masonic Temple, seventy employing mechanics and master builders engaged in heated debate over resolutions to challenge the forthcoming state law and over the move from paying workers by the day to paying them by the hour (Pierce 1940, vol. 2). At least two employers openly opposed the group's resolutions to resist the eight-hour day. Mr. Knight believed their resolutions were attempts to dodge the law without actually coming out and saying that is what they intended to do. Seth Paine, a master mechanic from New England, also opposed the resolutions and spoke of the rights of workers to have rest and chances to develop their intellects. Paine recalled fourteen hours constituting an acceptable day's work, but clearly that was no long the case. Paine argued that "the tendency of the age is to lift up man. It has been begun with the slave on the plantation. These resolutions ignore the humanity of men and treat him as a horse or an ox" (*CT,* March 17, 1867, 2). Paine's logic showed there was some hope that the strategic rhetoric used by eight-hour reformers might resonate with some employers, but the voices of Paine and Knight were clearly the minority. The employing mechanics' resolution opposing eight hours passed, and the results of their deliberations were circulated to other employer associations.

A test of employer resolve followed quickly on the heels of this meeting. In April 1867, the Illinois eight-hour bill became law and would go into effect on May 1. In content the law simply stated that eight hours would be a legal day's work, when no contracts existed to the contrary, and the bill did not include any mechanism for enforcement (*CT,* April 30, 1867, 2). Yet the law was a cause for great celebration, as the Grand Eight Hour League and its affiliated trade unions planned for a parade and mass demonstration on May Day to enforce the eight-hour day, with thousands of Chicago workers participating in a general walkout (*CT,* April 18, 1867, 3).

Contested Interpretations of the 1867 Law

The new law and planned demonstration generated intense public debate about the eight-hour question. The entire city seemed occupied with the eight-hour movement, from "the divine in his pulpit to the boy baby who prattles to mamma at bedtime" (*CT,* May 8, 1867, 4). Eight-hour advocates and their allies continued to use religious language and values to frame both the eight-hour day and its impact on Chicago. In a response to questions about the impact of the eight-hour system on his life, one worker interviewed by the *Tribune* reported seeing a direct benefit of eight hours to his religious life. "I think I would be a more constant churchgoer. I should not feel compelled to make the Sabbath a day for bodily rest and a good sermon would make double the impression upon a man free from weariness. The Sunday's sermon now comes at the end of six day's work" (March 26, 1867, 2). However, eight-hour advocates, such as "Mechanic" in his letter to the *Tribune,* wanted intellectual and moral independence, not just a chance to blindly follow clergy.

> The priest says to the working man: "O, thou man of toil, wouldst thou know the way to Heaven, and avoid the hell, pay me a portion of your wages, so that I can preach to you, and you can believe and be saved" . . . but all this must change. A revolution is at hand, and although peaceful, quiet, legal, orderly, yet a revolution nevertheless. . . . [T]he first gun has fired, the keynote has sounded. The Eight Hour System has passed into law. . . . [U]nder its influence we laboring men will have rest, leisure, and opportunity to study the laws of nature and the word of God for ourselves, and thus avoid paying the priest. (April 20, 1867, 2)

Protestant reformers within the CTA reminded workers that the successful transformation of Chicago through the eight-hour law required their own willingness to be transformed as individuals, another familiar evangelical theme. "Mechanic" argued that workers must deserve these better conditions. "Nor can any laboring man hope to have his condition bettered whilst he is *himself* unworthy; nor can he expect that friends will have the heart to help him whilst he prostitutes all the faculties of his manhood at the gaming dens, grog shops, cribs, and other hot beds of hell. The worst opponents of success are the worst class of working men themselves" (*CT,* April 5, 1867, 2). Beneath this statement is a sentiment similar to that of most Protestants in the city, namely, that poor, foreign-born, Catholic workers were overrunning the city and themselves contributed to its low moral culture. Even eight-hour reformers shared these discriminatory attitudes and made them fear they would not win public support as a result of the behavior of the more "undeserving" elements in the working class. Protestant leaders in the CTA had to exercise caution with such language, however, so as to not alienate German and Irish workers from the movement.

Employers argued against any regulation of hours in terms of competition with manufacturers either in other states or in other countries. "How delighted England will be to see this suicidal policy inaugurated here," said one employer in a letter to the *Tribune* (May 1, 1867, 2). So, faced with a new law that would damage production and profit, employers carried through on their promise to resist the eight-hour system. Joseph Medill, the owner and editor of the *Tribune,* along with the editors of the other newspapers in the city, opposed the eight-hour day on purely economic grounds. Ideologically, the law of supply and demand was the moral of the day, and the *Tribune* consistently reinforced the acceptance of that law as embodying the "immutable and unshakable" principles of political economy (December 16, 1866, 2; March 26, 1867, 2; April 4, 1867, 2; April 9, 1867, 2; May 12, 1867, 2). Consequently, Medill and the *Tribune*'s journalists characterized the eight-hour movement alternately as "causeless and indefensible struggles," as "consummate folly and stupidity," "ill-devised," "suicidal," "disastrous," and "humbug and tomfoolery" (June 23, 1866, 2; May 23, 1867, 2; June 2, 1867, 4; June 16, 1867, 4; August 23, 1867, 4).

In no way did the movement's appeals on religious grounds move Christian employers to support the law or newspaper editors to accept labor's religious redefinition of the injustice of long hours. In fact, just the reverse was true. In publishing a portion of the 1866 report from the Massachusetts Commission on the Hours of Labor that favored the adoption of the eight-hour system in that state, the *Tribune* ridiculed eight-hour reformer Edward H. Rogers's minority report that supported the law for burying "his points in a mass of quotations of both prose and poetry, having little reference to the subject, and certain to weary and repel the reader" (March 26, 1867, 2). This unwillingness to concede even the slightest bit of justice to the eight-hour cause pushed unions such as the Chicago Typographical Union to link the *Tribune* and the *Times* as clear enemies of labor (Pierce 1940, vol. 2).

In rare instances, the newspapers drew frames against the eight-hour system from the temperance crusade. The propensity of working-class immigrants to frequent saloons was an additional reason for the *Tribune* to oppose the eight-hour law, though even here they still argued on economic rather than spiritual grounds.

> The expenditures of the past year in this city for liquors, tobacco, cigars, theatricals, billiards, and gambling, amounted to eight millions of dollars. . . . One-third of the wages of thousands of employees is absorbed by indulging their appetites and tastes for those luxuries and practices. . . . [O]f course they cannot continue in the enjoyment of these things to the same degree if their earnings are reduced to the extent of the proposed abbreviation of their labor. . . . [T]he question between them and their employers to settle is: Shall the latter gratuitously donate the money to pay for liquors, cigars, amusements, and keno or shall the former be obliged to do without them, or work enough extra time over eight hours to pay for those things? (March 22, 1867, 2)

Of course, the use of intemperance by the newspapers as an argument against shortening the workday occasionally included a more sophisticated analysis that indicated a lack of alternatives to saloon going. Also from the 1866 Massachusetts report on the eight-hour system, the *Tribune* included an argument similar to the one advanced by Jules Simon in the *Workingman's Advocate:*

> Would the workingman spend his additional leisure in a wise and useful manner, so that it would really contribute to his elevation and improvement, or in such a way as to injure himself and his family? . . . [N]either libraries, reading rooms, or places of social resort are provided by the State, or by the Church, or by society, as a general fact; and therefore operatives, unless they have homes of their own are turned into the street to find a place of resort and social enjoyment wherever they can; and as there is but one place where they are always welcome, and that is the lager beer saloon or some similar beneficent institution(!) . . . Such being the unquestionable condition of things, it cannot be wondered that many are led to the belief that the less leisure the working people . . . have the better. (March 26, 1867, 2)

But unlike Simon's temperance-based support for shorter hours, the *Tribune* did not call for this "unquestionable condition of things" to be rectified so that alternatives to saloons would be available to workers. The *Tribune* accepted the world as it was.

Protestant clergy too accepted this world and opposed this first eight-hour campaign and maintained their distance from the movement. Protestant beliefs in the inherent virtue of hard (and continuous) work were dominant and viewed as common sense (Hunnicutt 1988; Rodgers 1978). A few ministers expressed tepid sympathy that eight hours might improve the spiritual condition of workers. Sabbatarian clergy, probably the most open to considering the moral benefits of shorter hours, tried to abolish Sunday work the year before, both by direct appeals to employers and by a new state law. Both strategies met the same end: absolute resistance or complete disregard from employers (Mirola 1999). Religious claims from either labor or clergy were no longer legitimate within a capitalist moral order that made the rights of employers to order business as they saw fit paramount, free from any alternative claims by faith, employees, or the state. Most clergy accepted the logic of employers and newspaper editors that the economic laws of trade were unalterable.

May 1 and the General Strike

As the deadline for inaugurating the eight-hour system loomed, employers went on the offensive. In seventy industries, employers had preemptively shifted from paying wages by the day to by the hour, exempting them from the law and allowing them to continue to operate under the ten-hour system (Montgomery 1981). Employers in the plumbing trade hinted they might need to give in for a short time if their employees struck. Employers of house builders, ship carpenters, and iron molders all reported that the eight-hour law would impact them the most and expected trouble from their workers. All of these employers refused to pay ten hours' wages for eight hours' work, and they all refused to tolerate shorter hours in their shops. Other employers, such as those employing carpenters, reported no fear of a strike because their workers were desperate for work due to high levels of unemployment resulting from bad weather the previous winter (*CT,* April 18, 1867, 3). Still others demanded their employees to commit to work ten-hour days or be fired prior to May 1. Such was the case at the machine shop of Fuller and Ford, where all eight-hour men, a quarter of their employees, were fired (Pierce 1940, 2:177). P. W. Gates, president of the Chicago Eagle Works, issued an advance ultimatum to his workers, requiring them to agree in writing to work ten hours or the shop would be closed and the men fired.

These reports notwithstanding, a few employers dissented. The "boss painters," after lengthy deliberations, decided to obey the law as stated and work under the eight-hour system but at eight hours of pay, leaving it to the painters themselves to work more if they chose. The journeyman painters rejected this offer and proposed an eight-hour day at the rate of nine hours' wages (*CT,* April 30, 1867, 2; April 30, 1867, 4). This proposal in the end split the solidarity of the boss painters. As of May 1, eight shops employing the painters would give nine hours' pay for eight hours' work, and three shops would pay eight hours' wages for eight hours' work (*CT,* May 1, 1867, 4).

As he had done during the stonecutters' eight-hour strike, Seth Paine wrote a lengthy letter to the *Tribune,* again challenging the newspaper's opposition to shorter hours. Paine reminded the *Tribune*'s editor and readers that they were incorrect to assume that individual workers had the right to choose the conditions of their labor not because they could not attempt to do so but because employers would not permit it. Paine stood almost alone as an employer in arguing that workers needed more time for spiritual and mental improvement and that workers who were more rested would be more, not less, productive. In comparing workers to southern slaves, Paine asserted that under the ten-hour system, workers "do not work as they might for the self same reason that the slave on the plantation does not. Neither the mechanic nor slave sees his interest in doing it." Paine also appealed to employers' economic interests, arguing that the eight-hour system would be financially desirable. Well-rested workers were more productive, not less, improving profits for manufacturers. Finally, Paine speculated about the eight-hour system's impact on the civic life of Chicago. Cooperation on eight-hour reform, he asserted, would "beget oneness in social life, gradually reduces the distance between rich and poor, lessens the gulf that separates employer and employee, brings master and servant on a common platform, and ultimately in universal brotherhood, bringing about the age of harmony, and making possible the approach of heaven and earth." Indicting his own class, however, Paine noted that Chicago employers resisted the idea that the working class could work together with their employers, "so the war goes on" (March 30, 1867, 2).

On May 1, the long-anticipated general strike and mass demonstration arrived. The *Tribune* anticipated that close to fifteen thousand workers would be marching in the streets in the largest parade the city had yet seen. Of these, the editors speculated, only ten thousand would use the general strike as a means to force employers to go along with the new law, the other five thousand workers being already employed under different contractual terms than those stipulated by the terms of the legislation (May 1, 1867, 2). Twenty-four trade unions were represented in the parade, along with an assortment of workers from a variety of railroads, iron and rolling mills, the Laborer's Benevolent Association, the Union Veterans' Society, and five bands providing music. Mayor John B. Rice gave the opening address to the crowd gathered on the lakeshore, but, much to the dismay of employers and the editors of the *Tribune,* in addition to supporting the eight-hour law, Rice asserted that he did not believe the interests of capital and labor were the same; rather, they were antagonistic toward one another, with capital trying to get as much work from employees for the lowest wages, while employees desired to get the highest wages for his or her labor. Yet Rice believed compromise was possible and encouraged workers to face the coming conflict with employers reasonably, calmly, and with conciliation. Governor Richard J. Oglesby sent a letter that was read to the crowd supporting the eight-hour day and the intention of Chicago workers, "in a kind but decided and peaceful manner, to insist upon their rights only" (*CT,* May 2, 1867, 4).

Representatives from the Illinois Legislature and prominent laborer leaders also offered their support. Congressman A. J. Kuykendale took Mayor Rice's comments further in linking the eight-hour struggle back to abolitionism. He asserted, "Capital and labor never have or can unite. Capital will never be content unless it controls labor. . . . [I]f they do not control capital it will own labor as slaves. . . . If all the wealth is produced by labor, it ought to be subservient to labor, otherwise labor is as completely the slave as the African ever was. We must not stop with freeing the African and allow ourselves to be slaves." The Honorable Henry M. Shepard also addressed the crowds with his assurance that, with "this bright sun shining upon us so brilliantly, it is a sign that the Deity smiles approvingly on our cause. . . . And if God and Right are on our side, what man can stand up against us?" (*CT,* May 2, 1867, 4). Among the crowds, this author of the eight-hour bill was a hero, witnessed by the biblical metaphor on one placard carried in the parade that read, "The Shepard that takes care of his flock" (*CT,* May 2, 1867, 3). Richard Trevellick, whose legacy as a successful leader who won shorter hours for shipbuilders and caulkers in New Orleans in the 1850s as well as eight-hour days for workers in Australia and New Zealand, echoed Shepard's religious rhetoric (Roediger and Foner 1989). Trevellick "believed this to be God's work. The day must be divided into sleep, recreation and amusement, with the one-third for labor. This was a divine law" (*CT,* May 2, 1867, 4). That the eight-hour law flowed logically from the realms of religion and morality as much as from the political economy of industrial capitalism was taken for granted by all present.

But in the weeks that followed, the practical task of enforcing the eight-hour law remained for trade unions, and the perils of depending solely on a legislative strategy grew clearer with each passing day (Pierce 1940, vol. 2; Montgomery 1981). The various trade unions sent out groups of men, or "committees," with the task of appealing to their fellow workers to not give in and work ten-hour days. These appeals took various forms, as the *Tribune* was only too happy to report. In addition to making reasoned, calm appeals, others resorted to ever more extreme and physical means of coercion to convince ten-hour men to not break the strike. Riots and rumors of riots unfolded in Bridgeport but also in the western and northern divisions of the city, anywhere shops were operating on the ten-hour system. Following the first reports, the rioters and mob violence decried by the *Tribune* and *Times* editors were acknowledged not to be seven or eight hundred men roaming the streets, threatening violence and murder to any worker caught going back to work, but only small groups of unemployed youths who were often intoxicated, disrupting the peace. Nevertheless, the newspapers perpetuated the idea that the eight-hour movement was connected to threats of mob violence and riots, while simultaneously reporting they were not.

Reports of disorder continued in subsequent days. Crowds of two to three hundred gathered outside rolling mills, planing mills, and lumberyards, drawn out by "profanity, the excitement of liquor, and the willful misrepresentation of injustice of employers" (*CT,* May 4, 1867, 4). These crowds were met by police forces armed with clubs and revolvers that were posted throughout the area, with the Chicago Light Artillery standing in readiness at the Armory. The police arrested men presumed to be the leaders of the riots, and the crowds disbanded. Such actions elicited a flurry of proclamations from the mayor's office as well as from the CTA. Mayor Rice warned that the police were sworn to use whatever force was necessary to maintain order in the city, whether men worked eight or ten hours (*CT,* May 4, 1867, 2). The Central Executive Committee of the CTA issued a statement to workers rejecting any connection to the violence in the streets but to warn them that mob violence is a "suicidal policy that plays into the hands of our enemies" (*CT,* May 6, 1867, 4). Andrew Cameron and two other members of the Executive Committee, George Darling and Josiah Boyce, met with Governor Oglesby to state emphatically that the CTA had nothing to do with the mobs. These disturbances raged on for two days but then gave way to a rainy weekend in the city, which the newspapers believed kept things quiet. Mayor Rice faced criticism from employers and both the secular and the religious presses for seeming to concur with labor reformers' assertions that capitalists and workers had antagonistic interests, as reported in the Methodist *Northwestern Christian Advocate* (May 22, 1867, 164). Rice also alienated workers by telling the Central Executive Committee of the CTA that the time had not yet come for the eight-hour day and advised them to go back to work on the ten-hour plan (*CT,* May 11, 1867, 4).

In the days following the mass demonstration, few shops operated on the eight-hour system. Employers who still contracted labor by the day took different approaches to the question of wages. In most cases, workers who did work eight hours accepted a reduction in wages, sometimes receiving nine hours' wages but more often eight hours' wages. In other places, workers were required to put in ten-hour days but were paid time and a quarter. Few entire industries were on the eight-hour system, though the city's tanners and curriers, stonecutters, plumbers and gas fitters, painters, and carpenters all were reported as operating successfully under the system (*CT,* May 20, 1867, 4). The rest mandated ten-hour days. Where workers refused to work ten hours, as fifty workers at the Brunswick and Bros. billiard establishment did, they were promptly fired. Employers at the Franklin Iron Works posted a sign, "Ten Hours or Death," to make their point (*CT,* May 7, 1867, 4). Even the municipal workers, who initially were granted an eight-hour day by the Common Council in April, petitioned to go back to the ten-hour day. The *Tribune* smugly observed that "workers found what the demagogues had told them about the value of two hours for 'improving their minds' was moonshine. What they needed most was money with which to buy flour and meat, potatoes and groceries, fuel and clothing, and to pay their house rent" (May 16, 1867, 2).

The *Tribune* kept up daily reports on the progress of the strikes, while they lasted. There was a running debate between the eight-hour central committee headed by Andrew Cameron and the editors of the *Tribune* over the actual numbers of workers in the movement and its associated strikes. Some three weeks after the May Day celebration mentioned here, the *Tribune* (May 20, 1867, 4) allowed for five or six thousand workers sharing in the movement ("a minority of workers"). Of these, by the end of June, the paper conceded there were two thousand eight-hour men still out of work, although Cameron maintained that a full five thousand were still in active support of the strike. But one by one, most shops resumed work at a ten-hour workday. In August 1867, Cameron proposed a resolution to the National Labor Union, stating that it was "inexpedient for any state or locality under existing circumstances to attempt to secure the adoption of the eight-hour system, until the same be recognized by national legislation" (*CT,* August 26, 1867, 2). The eight-hour movement needed more time to redeem time.

Contested Framing Following the 1867 Campaign

While the eight-hour movement had argued for shorter hours on economic and political grounds, eight-hour reform was simultaneously a *religious* cause and needed to remain one. If labor's claims are "presented under other auspices, we cease to merit the attention of the public and will be regarded, even by those who befriend us, with suspicion and distrust" (*WA,* May 9,

1868, 2). If workers had more time to devote to their own spiritual growth, they would be less likely to be seduced either by liquor or by infidelity (*WA*, October 21, 1868; May 19, 1870). For conservative Anglo-American Protestant workers, there was no reform "*without* Christianity" (*WA*, November 16, 1867, 2). The economics and politics of the eight-hour system were infused with moral significance to the same extent that evangelical Protestantism possessed economic and political implications. The eight-hour day was to be championed as an expression of genuine Christianity that would generate religious commitment, spiritual development, and temperance in Chicago's working classes (*WA*, November 16, 1867, 2; June 17, 1871). William Taylor from the Illinois Central Railroad shops made his plea for temperance clear: "The workingmen should quit drinking lager beer and liquor, live soberly, and they will succeed" (*CT*, May 11, 1867, 4).

Two other rhetorical themes emerged alongside these religious claims. First, advocates continued to link the eight-hour movement and abolitionism. German railroad worker Mr. Swager from the Illinois Central Shops, speaking to a mass meeting of railroad strikers, reminded his listeners that "they settled the black labor question, and we're just now girding up our loins to fight the white labor question. . . . If it were not for the Trade Unions, the workingmen would all be driven like a flock of sheep into their slave pens." Swager went on, however, to cast both the May 1 demonstration and the continuing struggle to enforce the law in evangelistic terms, all the while asserting the superiority of a labor rally over any led by churches: "This was a good revival. He was glad that the workingmen of this city were able to carry on a revival which was of far more importance than any revival ever carried on by the Methodists, Baptists, or any other sect" (*CT*, May 10, 1867, 4; May 11, 1867, 4). Mr. Hayes, a machinist at the Eagle Works, argued that "on the First of May, 1867, the Declaration of Independence, No. 2, and the liberation of the white man should have taken effect" (*CT*, May 16, 1867, 4). Despite the failure of the law, shortening the workday and freeing workers from industrial slavery went hand in hand for reformers.

As the strike went on and employer resistance increased, a second rhetorical theme wove together the hypocrisy of Christian employers in not acquiescing to what was a divinely ordained reform. Said one striker, "They took away the State Street Market where the laboring classes could buy their food from the farmers. They must have a market house on every square inch. They build churches here a-plenty, but who will think that they care for the souls of the workingman when they work their bodies to death? It is all hypocrisy" (*CT*, May 7, 1867, 4). Eight-hour framing challenged the antidemocratic actions of capitalists in refusing to recognize laws that were inconvenient to their class interests (Montgomery 1981). William Taylor from the CTA asked a rhetorical question: "Can a law be passed that benefits the laboring classes that capitalists must respect?" (*CT*, May 16, 1867, 4). The answer from the perspective of workers was no. Eight-hour frames needed this elaboration, not only to couch shorter hours in religious terms to garner support but also to offer explanations for its seeming failure.

As the legitimizing voice of Chicago employers, local newspapers made claims about the folly not only of the eight-hour movement but also of all challenges to the new industrial order. The *Tribune* downplayed interest in the eight-hour day even among workers, concluding that "barely a tenth [of all Chicago workers] have an interest in behalf of the adoption of the eight-hour restriction of labor" (May 10, 1867, 2). Eight-hour reform, the editor went on to say, "has been cut up into jokes and is used only to spice conversation with" (May 10, 1867, 4). But always the same conclusion was drawn to explain this state of affairs: "A concerted attempt was made to circumvent the laws of political economy and it failed. An attempt to circumvent the law of gravitation would have met with equal success" (May 10, 1867, 2).

A central theme in the press's framing of the eight-hour movement was to discredit the idea of antagonistic class interests as well as the idea that employers had control over wages. "There can be no such thing as an antagonism between capital and labor. . . . We affirm it is impossible for employers as a general rule to obtain an undue proportion of the products of capital and labor. . . . [T]hey have little control of prices, taxes, costs, wages, etc. as well as the owner's personal expense of living and supporting his family. . . . [L]aborers receive all that capitalists can afford to pay them." Again, the laws of economics were invoked to reinforce this idea but also to limit attempts by trade unions to challenge these laws. "Wages must be governed by the natural laws which control in these matters. . . . It is by enabling the workingman to get from his employer the full value of his labor, as regulated by the unobstructed laws of supply and demand, that the unions help him. When they lose sight of this, and attempt to fix arbitrarily the price of wages and, prohibiting the laborer from making his own bargain and then attempt to bargain for higher wages, they go far astray from any good. They become a tyranny and a curse to labor, a mischief and wrong to capital, and a vast injury to society" (*CT*, May 8, 1867, 2).

Local newspapers also called into question the legitimacy of leaders in the CTA and its unions. "The eight-hour law has become a fanaticism with them. Fanatics are always sincere," argued the *Tribune* to reformers' criticism that they were now labor's enemies (May 12, 1867, 2). The editors even offered an analysis of what kinds of men were fueling the movement. "There is no doubt that the trade union strikes have been engineered by a few parties—mostly reckless men with no families to care for—who have mounted a high horse and terrified those with wives and little ones dependent on them, into joining the movement" (May 16, 1867, 4). In the end, the editors claimed workers were pushed further into poverty by the strike and were betrayed by their leaders, but workers saw the error of their ways, that "two hours gained for recreation were not worth the cost," when faced with deprivations that were made more acute, as strikers remained unwilling to work in the ten-hour system (May 11, 1867, 2; June 2, 1867, 4; June 16, 1867, 4). By June the papers could report to their uneasy readerships that "anarchy and mob law have yielded to the inevitable laws of trade" and that "all establishments are back on the ten-hour plan" (*CT*, June 2, 1867, 4).

If Chicago's Protestant congregations were among those discussing the eight-hour movement at length, as the *Tribune* suggested, there is not a tremendous amount of evidence to support this. Clergy, of course, did discuss the movement and often responded to the charges of inaction laid at their door by workers. But this first period of eight-hour protest was met with quiet caution from clergy, as is evidenced by the editor of the Methodist *Northwestern Christian Advocate:*

> With the desire of laboring men to secure more time for recreation, mental improvement, and devotion, we have the warmest sympathy. It is finally decided in this country capital is not to own labor, but that laborers are free. They are more than free. They are sovereigns. It will be dangerous to entrust the functions of sovereignty to men ignorant and stolid. We have sympathy with the desire of the laborer to secure as much time as possible from exhaustive toil, and feel that employers cannot be too careful to concede this right to secure intelligent labor, to secure contented labor. (May 22, 1867, 164)

However, this backhanded support was balanced by two stipulations: that the rights to freedom of contract and community peace and stability were maintained. The Methodist paper reiterated the economic claims of the *Tribune* that it was impossible to concede ten hours' wages for only eight hours' work. Furthermore, labor reformers had no right to prohibit their fellow workers from working under the ten-hour plan if they so wished, relying on the military power of the state to ensure that was the case. But even as they reminded workers of the willingness of the Dearborn Light Artillery to maintain order at any cost, the editors stayed hopeful that "no bloodshed would occur" (May 8, 1867, 149). The clergy and the religious press also built both their modest support and their opposition on a rejection of class antagonisms, trusting that employers and workers would act in the spirit of conciliation (*NWCA*, May 22, 1867, 164). However, such hope was difficult to sustain in a religious culture that associated working-class status and poverty with moral laxity.

The 1867 campaign provoked the Congregationalist paper the *Advance* to compare Chicago's working-class communities to the biblical city of Sodom, whose corruption, attributed to idleness, resulted in its complete destruction by God. The editor concluded:

> It is a very significant that in Scripture Sodom's aggravated iniquity is traced to idleness and "fullness of bread." Her fertile soil and well-watered plain enabled her to live luxuriously, leaving unemployed time on her hands, one of the most corrupting elements of her social life. We might select out of the community today thousands who could not safely be trusted with an hour's leisure beyond what they now enjoy. If it were secured for them, it would only be abused and perverted into a curse. . . . [T]he indiscriminate bestowal of [leisure], as society is now constituted, would prove a great and deplorable evil. . . . But to this end it is essential that Christianity should pervade the masses. They must be taught that dissipation is the reverse of recreation. (October 3, 1867, 2)

The desire for a shorter workday was interpreted as one more expression of the moral laxity of the workers—a condition that made them more susceptible to the appeals of corrupting labor agitators.

> Few indeed are doing as much wrong to the laboring class as those who pretend to redress its wrongs. . . . Instead of bringing labor and capital together, they have set them farther apart. Instead of reconciling the laboring with other classes, they have drawn it off to a greater degree of isolation. . . . They are the inevitable result of making the cause political. Strike that key-note and all sorts of harshness and discords follow through the quivering air. . . . No effort to raise an individual, none to raise a class, none to perfect humanity, but needs a spiritual motive and a spiritual guidance. This movement in behalf of the laboring classes is or ought to be a spiritual, even more than a social, one. . . . Only religion itself, one and undivided, can breast these prejudices; only religion can stay these passions, pacify these strikes, and set the toiling multitudes in the direction of justice and happiness. . . . Such a power—where shall it be found? Where but in the Church of Christ, whose whole work, from its foundation to the present hour, is one long service, social and spiritual. (*Advance*, February 8, 1872, 2)

Only by a clear embrace of Christian teachings could leisure be safely procured for workers.

But the clergy were divided in mind both about workers as a class and about the eight-hour movement as a whole. Rev. Dr. W. W. Everts, speaking to his congregation at First Baptist Church, gave this mixed message:

> Christ came of the common people. He was not from the nobility. His father was a carpenter, and he worked as such. . . . [T]he Church guards the rights of the common people, by upholding the Sabbath which was given as a day of rest, and which the laboring classes cannot give up to toil without becoming the slaves of capital . . . standing as the champion of the rights of the masses. . . . Religious communities should be judged by their regard for the poor. A Church that glories in display and aristocratic connections should be feared. The true Church will call in the poor, not to keep them poor, as the Catholic Church does, but to raise and benefit them. Churches that do not what they can for the poor are weak and of a low grade.

Even as Everts claimed that Christ and Christ's church embraced the poor, he offered this observation about the eight-hour strikes:

> The speaker here alluded to the late differences between workingmen and employers. . . . [H]e would rejoice in their advancement, but he deprecated the actions of trade unions which sought to force conditions which could not yet be obtained. The natural result of Gospel principles would be to elevate and liberate the laboring classes, as it had been in the past; but when he heard, while abroad, of the strikes which were taking place here, he found that they were originated by bad men for selfish purposes; and especially when he heard that the saloon keepers unanimously favored them, he feared that they did so in order to gain more custom from those who would have more time to spend with them. (*CT*, September 16, 1867, 4)

Suspicion and fear of the working class and anyone who supported and encouraged them to organize for change were rooted too deeply in the minds of Protestant clergy to be changed easily.

Despite resistance from employers, the press, and Chicago churches, Andrew Cameron used the *Workingman's Advocate* as the voice of the eight-hour movement to direct its religious appeals to clergy, who were concurrently launching a campaign to instate Sabbath observance in Chicago with a law prohibiting Sunday work (Mirola 1999). By aligning arguments in favor of a shorter workday with those of a shorter workweek, labor leaders strategically attempted to entice clergy into support for the eight-hour movement as a logical extension of Sabbatarianism. Eight-hour reformers argued that if Chicago could enforce Sabbath observance through the law, then the same could be done for an eight-hour day. "No class is as deeply interested in the observance of the Sabbath as a day of rest as our workingmen. Its sanctity is their safeguard, and the recognition of its claims is indispensable to the perpetuation of our republican institutions. 'Six days shalt thou labor and do all the work but the seventh is the Sabbath of the Lord thy God; in it thou shalt not work,' is an injunction so plain and imperative that he who reads may run" (*WA*, November 14, 1868, 2). But despite Cameron's claims that workers wanted to protect Sundays as a day of rest and shorter workdays for spiritual development, clergy remained convinced that more time off would lead to debauchery and intemperance.

Because the eight-hour law of 1867 did not address hourly contracts explicitly, this legal loophole enabled employers to maintain longer workdays by contracting work by the hour, rather than by the day. But regardless of the tactics employers used, any regulation of their control over the operation of their businesses was resisted. Even attempts by President Ulysses S. Grant to enact federal eight-hour laws first covering workers in the navy's shipyards in 1869, and later covering all government workers in 1872, were similarly ignored (Bonnett 1956). Legislative defeat pushed reformers to reframe subversion of the eight-hour law in religious terms, attributing its failure to the moral bankruptcy of employers and to the hypocrisy of clergy. Capitalist greed, from the point of view of workers, perpetuated the injustice of overwork, exacerbated by employers' use of Christianity to justify their power (*WA*, May 9, 1868, 2). The eight-hour law was overturned because so-called Christian capitalists "repudiated all righteous human enactments including God and all His laws" whenever they did not suit them. Clergy, for their part, were accused of being "political clackers," who claimed to follow the teachings of Christ, "while they actually abet the robbery of the widow and orphan. They are guilty of a fraud which even an atheist would scorn to commit" (*WA*, November 16, 1867, 2). Because Protestant ministers did nothing more than support the unscrupulous actions of the wealthy members of their congregations, they stood accused of "wearing the livery of heaven but serving the devil" (*WA*, November 16, 1867, 2).

In the years following the defeats of 1867 campaign, Chicago's eight-hour movement fragmented along ethnic and religious lines. Native-born and British labor leaders, such as Cameron and Trevellick, continued to try to speak for a multiethnic labor movement, but they faced the rising leadership of Irish Catholics and German Lutherans and freethinkers, who had their own ideas of how best to challenge manufacturers (Montgomery 1981; Jentz and Schneirov 2012). Cameron carried on with his strategy of appealing to clergy to do their prophetic duty and support the eight-hour movement through the *Workingman's Advocate.* He argued that clergy ought to support the eight-hour day, because if Christian leaders were involved in the movement, then the goal of eight hours for spiritual development in workers would be ensured (May 19, 1870, 2; June 17, 1871, 4). In addition, Cameron warned that clergy support for the movement would ensure that workers would not be "seduced into infidelity" by radicals as a direct result of continued clergy opposition to reform (March 26, 1870, 4).

Most religious leaders responded by asking Christian employers to be more charitable toward their workers, but they came no closer to supporting the eight-hour movement. The response of the *Workingman's Advocate* to these kinds of appeals by clergy was scathing. Clergy asking wealthy industrialists such as John Jacob Astor to exercise self-denial and distribute his resources in charity was like "Satan rebuking sin" (June 17, 1871, 4). From the perspective of eight-hour reformers, the evils of overwork and clergy inaction were both rooted in the same social problem: the social consequences of unregulated industrial capitalism.

Yet labor reformers also believed that ignorance of industrial conditions stood in the way of clergy taking their proper place on the side of workers. Protestant clergy accepted that the eight-hour cause was more complicated than they originally thought and that the future of industrial society depended on the church intervening in the class struggles of employers and their workers. As a writer for the *Workingman's Advocate* pointed out, "To think that the Church can ignore it, and go on as if nothing were shaking the body politic, and disturbing the souls of people, would be to stultify ourselves" (May 19, 1870, 1).

By 1870 the Trades Assembly disbanded, and workers in specific industries were dependent on the strength of their unions, if they had one. The sentiments of many existing trade unions, especially those dominated by German and eastern European immigrants and of Chicago's wage earners generally, pronounced legislative attempts to secure short hours a farce. Like the ten-hour laws put in place before, the actions of well-intentioned reformers and politicians proved insufficient to enforce a legal reduction in the hours of labor. The working classes were left to rely on their own organized strength in the aftermath of the 1867 campaign, as employers themselves were doing (Green 2006, 24; Bonnett 1956). But a change was in the air. The effort to bring in the eight-hour day in 1867 failed because the movement needed more time to build its organizational base and mobilize workers effectively "to advertise truth as widely as falsehood had been articulated" (*WA*, July 13, 1872, 2).

Eight-hour advocates remained divided over strategy. Anglo-American workers joined with the Lassallean faction of German workers to maintain a focus on the ballot box to win the shorter workday (E. Hirsch 1990). Appealing to themes of social regeneration and moral improvement, hard work, temperance, respect for the Sabbath, abolitionism, and biblical injunctions regarding work, these conservative craft workers challenged the business elite through a religious and political language rooted in evangelical Protestantism fused with radical republicanism. Their firm belief was that the eight-hour day was the first step in the renewal of a people's republic in which wage earners could be independent citizens, working cooperatively within a balanced economic order, not one dominated by a few powerful manufacturers. Radical German, Irish, and Bohemian workers increasingly adopted a more revolutionary approach, rejecting the idea that employers would allow workers to reform any aspect of the industrial system through legal means. For these workers, capital and labor were irreconcilable, and battles over who set the terms of the new economic order would only intensify (Green 2006). The Protestant religious establishment was suspect as well, as much for its attempt to control the behavior of new immigrants whose community institutions of beer gardens and Sunday picnics and parades violated Yankee Puritanism as for its reticence to support industrial reform.

In the defeat of the nation's first eight-hour law, new debates over how to redeem time in Chicago began within the working classes and between them, their employers, and Protestant clergy. Religious language was used by supporters of the eight-hour day in these debates but with little effect. Nevertheless, it was understood by all sides that there was a *moral* basis to the shorter-hours question, but what and whose morality would define it were yet to be determined.

CHAPTER 3

Eight Hours and the Financial Crisis of 1873

As a new decade began, Chicago workers remained angry and frustrated by the lack of enforcement of the Illinois eight-hour law and by the ongoing resistance of employers both to the moral pressure of reformers' arguments and to their attempt to enforce the eight-hour law through strikes. Union efforts at putting the eight-hour system to work were largely unsuccessful, so very few workers except the journeyman stonecutters actually worked shorter hours in their trades. Yet despite what seemed to be the general failure of the 1867 eight-hour campaign and the fragmentation of the movement into conservative and radical factions, Yankee, British, German, and Irish trade unionists kept the goal of redeeming time through the eight-hour system as the centerpiece of labor activism in the new decade. But differences in strategy and tactics on how best to shorten the workday, either through the ballot box, strikes, some combination of the two, or a complete social revolution, kept the eight-hour movement divided (E. Hirsch 1990).

In March 1873, the reorganized Trades Assembly organized a mass meeting to discuss the eight-hour question. Native-born and British skilled craft unionists continued to base the moral logic of the eight-hour system on the biblical foundations that had been used in 1867. Referring to the biblical account that the laborers who built the temple of God for the Israelite King Solomon worked only eight hours a day, Mr. Newland posed the following question at one such meeting: "Why should not all [Christ's] followers become advocates of the movement? The workingmen deserved it, and . . . the day was coming when they would have it" (*CT,* March 15, 1873, 7). At least two speakers, Mr. Newland and Frank Lawler, a ship carpenter, agreed that divisions among workers, not employers, were responsible for the failure of the 1867 movement and that the eight-hour day would become reality only when workers organized as a body to enforce the law.

But there were clear points of disagreement among these skilled trade unionists. At this same meeting, another speaker, Mr. McAvoy, thought the eight-hour day was an unrealistic goal when many workers had not yet achieved a ten-hour day. Mr. Newland countered, however, that "every intelligent workingman—everyone who was trying to educate his family and make them respectable—desired eight hours a day; also that every man who lived from hand to mouth, and visited the saloons, and grasped hands with the bummer politician, wanted ten hours a day." Still others felt that adopting the eight-hour system in Chicago was premature and, reflecting the logic of employers, would only hurt workers if there was not a national eight-hour law, fearing employers could not compete with eastern manufacturers working on the ten-hour system (*CT,* March 15, 1873, 7).

While Chicago workers were too divided and unorganized to do so, the *Tribune* kept the eight-hour question in front of its readers in reporting the deliberations and demonstrations of workers elsewhere in the country. When all the nation's trade unions met as an "Industrial Congress" in Cleveland, Ohio, in July 1873, shorter hours was the central issue in the deliberations reported by the *Tribune.* The report from the Committee on the Hours of Labor produced resolutions that linked the eight-hour system, overtime, and Sunday labor:

> In consideration of the great moral advancement of the producing classes experienced since the general adoption of the ten-hour system, we declare ourselves emphatically in favor of the further reduction of the hours of labor from ten to eight. Every rational mind admits that the astonishing improvements made in machinery, and even the spread and progress of civilization, are to a large extent attributable to a reduction of the daily hours of labor to ten and the additional leisure time for workingmen means an increased opportunity for moral culture and social improvement. We are also opposed to the system of working overtime, it being an injury to the individual as well as to the trade at which he is employed, and we maintain that an employer by inducing or compelling men to work overtime commits an act of inhumanity. We are opposed to the practice of working on Sunday. That day should be a day of rest, and the time of the workingman at his own disposal. (July 19, 1873, 1)

For skilled craft unionists, the eight-hour day was inextricably tied to the social regeneration and moral improvement of wage earners and the overall "progress of civilization." Although this language would resonate with the thinking of many evangelical Protestants, the idea that Sunday was a day for leisure, not for religious observance, would have alienated them again.

In the fall of 1873, Chicago experienced the first financial collapse of the industrial era. The collapse and the depression that followed inaugurated a new phase in the development of the labor movement: the rise to prominence of semiskilled and unskilled immigrants within Chicago's labor movement. As Jentz and Schneirov state, "The 1867 strike had been led by well-organized skilled workers with their own labor movement . . . an extension of the American and European republican revolutionary traditions. . . . [I]n 1873, the crowds of the unskilled took the initiative under new leadership and owed relatively little to antebellum American labor traditions and . . . were closer to a classical wage-earning proletariat than to rebellious journeymen" (2012, 157). Five to seven thousand workers gathered at Turner Hall for a mass meeting organized by German socialists on December 21, 1873 (E. Hirsch 1990). Using quite a different tone from his native-born counterparts in the CTA, A. L. Hernault, a Frenchman, argued to these unemployed workers that "the laws were all made for the aristocrats and none for the laborers, and the rich must be held responsible if the poor starved. . . . What liberty could there be if workingmen were slaves, and the free press forbade them liberty? They were strangled by the free press, the bourgeois, and the priest, who did all in their power to prevent enlightenment among the working classes" (*CT,* December 22, 1873, 1). The next day, ten thousand workers marched on the city council and the Board of Trade, demanding assistance from funds held by the Relief and Aid Society two years after the Great Fire. They also carried banners demanding "BREAD AND WORK" under the eight-hour system (Green 2006). Such a show of unity among Chicago's diverse population of immigrants took the elites by surprise. But employers refused to be cowed by the socialist marches and demands. In their own show of strength, business elites raised seventeen thousand dollars to organize the First Regiment of the Illinois National Guard to prohibit any further disruption from worker demonstrations or strikes (Jentz and Schneirov 2012; Green 2006). The economic gap between the classes grew wider as the result of the depression, but open class hostility grew because business elites refused to make even the smallest concession to worker demands or to accept that employees had any legitimate right to shape the terms of their employment.

Building on the solidarity and strength of the December marches, new socialist labor organizations flourished in Chicago. The city was home to a section of the International Workingmen's Association, originally founded in 1864 by Karl Marx in London, and the Workingmen's Party of Illinois (WPI), founded in 1874 (E. Hirsch 1990; Nelson 1988; Green 1996). Growing numbers of immigrant workers sympathetic to socialist ideas continued to construct a language of protest that emphasized the oppression of workers by employers, the press, and clergy. Playing up the religious hypocrisy of employers, Mr. Arnold, speaking at a mass meeting of workers, noted that "workingmen wanted nothing more but what belonged to them, only reasonable wages, but they objected to the wages of starvation. The men who grow rich on the work of poor laborers called themselves Christians, while in reality they were nothing but Pharisees and hypocrites. The time was not far off when they would rule over these Christian gentlemen who had brought them to the very edge of starvation" (*CT*, January 18, 1874, 16). Carl Klings, a German socialist leader running for office on the Workingmen's Party ticket in 1874, welcomed attacks by powerful business elites that could result only in a better-organized movement.

> That the bourgeois were afraid of the workingmen's associations was best shown by the severe attacks made upon them. They were aware of the fact that the time for action had come, and therefore shook in their boots. By these attacks, their organization had been much benefitted and strengthened. A few years ago they would have been contented with an eight-hour law, as it would have done much toward a peaceable settlement, but the move was defeated, and they therefore not only demanded shorter time but the proceeds of their labor as well. (*CT*, January 19, 1874, 1)

As a group, radical labor leaders were not willing to blame workers for the failure of the initial eight-hour movement in any way and remained committed to using militant action to achieve the eight-hour workday. At a meeting of socialist trade unions in New York, organized by the United Order of Masons, workers debated a general strike to enforce that city's eight-hour law. The newspaper reported that "the proceedings were very violent and disorderly" and that "incendiary speeches were made by prominent Internationalists, denouncing Commodore Vanderbilt. One man wanted him hanged to a lamppost; another said if there was any interference with the 'Eight-Hour' rules, the streets will run with the blood of capitalists" (*CT*, March 27, 1873, 8). Clearly, more radical factions placed the blame for the movement's failure squarely on employers and articulated workers' growing animosity toward employers. In Chicago, however, as Green notes, although the Workingmen's Party lost at the polls and the rule of law seemed to have been restored in the city, "few businessmen felt relaxed" (2006, 52).

The two factions of the Chicago eight-hour movement struggled to regain strength in the 1870s through mass meetings and demonstrations. While both factions supported the goal of reducing the hours of labor, they differed significantly in their view of politics as a means to achieve it (E. Hirsch 1990). With the unity of the 1867 campaign dissolved, each faction held independent meetings and at no point joined together in common cause, illustrating the insurmountable gaps that had developed between Anglo-American and German, Irish, and eastern European workers.

The more conservative, craft unionist faction included stonecutters, tailors, ship carpenters and caulkers, and blacksmiths. Delegates from these unions gathered at the offices of the *Workingman's Advocate,* still under the leadership of Andrew Cameron. The eight-hour day remained the chief goal. These workers argued that the eight-hour law "would be a blessing to the workingman if it were more generally recognized, as it would enable him to devote more attention to the education of himself and his family" (*CT,* April 29, 1874, 3). Holding tightly to antebellum republican ideals, these workers remained committed to the idea that the state could be used to restore the balance of power and the eight-hour day to workers but denounced employers' willingness to subvert the democratic process to secure their own interests. For all of their shared beliefs, even their unity was fragile. Conflicts first emerged over which unions would sponsor and pay for a mass meeting planned in May 1874 (*CT,* May 2, 1874, 5). Others debated who should be invited to speak at the meeting. One delegate recommended a local sympathetic minister, Rev. M. J. Savage from Third Unitarian Church, as someone from the community who would be willing to address a meeting of Chicago workers. But the proposal to invite a clergyman was voted down, as clergy were thought too out of touch to address a union gathering.

When May 18, 1874 arrived, the city's eight-hour advocates hosted two separate mass meetings, reflecting the conservative-radical divide in the movement. The Workingmen's Party of Illinois organized a meeting of five hundred workers at Thielman's Theatre at the corner of Clybourne and Division Streets, while the conservative trade unions held their own meeting at Vorwarts Turner Hall on Twelfth and Halsted Streets. The *Tribune* downplayed the importance of the WPI gathering, given its small numbers, while describing the meeting of the conservative craft unions as one of the largest meetings of workingmen ever held in the city. The newspaper sympathized with craft unionists and emphasized their peaceable and reasonable mood and that there was nothing provocative or incendiary in their speeches.

There were other important differences in how each group approached the eight-hour question. German and English speakers at the WPI meeting asserted that it was a "moral outrage" that "government officials allow the eight-hour law to be violated when there were so many workingmen looking for work, and an equalization of the hours of labor was never more desirable than at present" (*CT,* May 18, 1874, 8). The WPI meeting concluded by passing a resolution that attributed the economic collapse to "reckless production" practices by manufacturers who balanced overproduction with wage and job cuts. The WPI resolution further claimed that "such emergencies will reappear every few years and lead to the entire ruin of the working classes; and . . . can only be prevented by reducing the hours of labor" and called for the enforcement of the eight-hour law "in all branches of business, public and private" (*CT,* May 18, 1874, 8; Jentz and Schneirov 2012, 156).

At Cameron's meeting sponsored by CTA unions, Richard Trevellick kept his appeals tied to the moral-improvement benefits of the eight-hour system, arguing:

> A rational degree of labor improved the physical condition of man . . . but overwork was another affair—it enervated, it depressed, it crushed the working people. Man was not a machine. He required occasional relations. He needed some spare hours to devote to his family; when he did not have this time what was the result? The family was neglected, and if the boys or girls went to the bad, the ministers held up their hands in holy horror and said "What a picture of demoralization." Judging by the circumstances surrounding the overworked people it should hardly be wondered at. (*CT,* May 19, 1874, 4)

Trevellick maintained the charge that overwork drained men and women of the energies necessary to fulfill their domestic, civic, and moral duties, a familiar theme that resonated with these republican trade unionists. But he offered a unique twist on this theme by invoking a caricature of religious leaders harping on the moral laxity of the working classes but lacking the common sense to see how shorter hours would restore their moral integrity. Trevellick, earlier in his speech, also distinguished between good capitalists, those who did right by their employees, and bad capitalists, or "Money-Power," who used their economic power to exploit the law for their own greedy purposes. This distinction further drew from radical republican suspicions of monopolists who were rapidly subverting independent producers and therefore the Republic.

At least as reported by the *Tribune,* neither the WPI nor the CTA speakers used any strong religious argument other than that the eight-hour system was morally desirable and that it was the duty of elected officials to enforce the law. Both craft unionists and WPI members promised to use the ballot box to remove politicians who opposed the eight-hour law, the former backing reform through the existing political parties, while the WPI remained intent on growing a third labor party. Only the WPI saw the eight-hour system as a way to protect workers as a class from the greed of organized employers whose concentrated wealth resulted from unregulated capitalism. Cameron, Trevellick, and their supporters, however, believed overall that workers should embrace capitalism and strive to move up within it, provided there were checks and balances in place to protect them from the power of a growing number of corrupt monopolists.

Employers and the Press

While craft unionists and socialists battled for leadership among Chicago's working classes, the radical charge that employers and the press were actively organized against eight-hour reform could not be ignored. In the 1870s, employer associations became more formalized, and in some cases employers bonded themselves up to one thousand dollars to break up unions in their trades (Bonnett 1956). Newspapers consistently reported that local employers were almost unanimous in their opposition to the eight-hour system, and those who did not join in this opposition faced the censure of other manufacturers. In one instance, the *Tribune,* recounting a New York employer's reticence to give in to demands for shorter hours, stated that "there were so many employers who refused to cooperate with the workingmen that the majority of those who acceded to the demand for eight hours have been compelled to return to the old system or leave the field altogether" (August 12, 1873, 1). As had already been demonstrated during the 1867 campaign, employers simply waited out workers' attempts to enforce the eight-hour system through strikes.

Employers framed their opposition to the eight-hour day exclusively in the logic of the market and supply and demand. The press reinforced employers' logic and downplayed the usefulness of strikes and deprecated the eight-hour movement. The *Tribune,* reflecting on tense class relations in the city, observed that "demagogues will appeal to men whose earnings are thus suddenly reduced and seek to array them in hostility against the employers; but good sense and calm judgment must convince them that, where the reduction is general, embracing every variety of employment in every branch of business, and applicable to all alike, high and low, rich and poor, there must be a general submission to the inevitable and common effort to make the best of it" (October 1, 1873, 4). But as conditions deteriorated and workers did not exhibit "good sense," instead marching on the city council and the Relief and Aid Society, the *Tribune* became more vitriolic in its denunciations of labor. Initially, the press continued to note the impracticality of both the eight-hour system as well as any attempt by government to enforce the "right of employment," as it would take from the working classes "all inducement to take care of themselves and the little ambition they have would be extinguished. They would be reduced to the condition of children. All incentive to foresight and economy, and temperance would be destroyed" (January 2, 1874, 4). Newspaper editors intensified their rhetoric regarding the threat of labor "demagogues" instigating and encouraging violence and the stupidity of workers in allowing themselves to be led astray by them. In the wake of the Tompkins Square Riots in New York City, the *Tribune*'s editors pronounced:

> The workingmen chose to violate the rules deliberately and defiantly. The result was what they might have expected. They came into collision with the police, whose duty it was to enforce the laws. . . . Thirty or forty of them, who were the most prominent in their resistance, were arrested. . . . All this in accordance with the strict observance of justice, and they cannot expect to have sympathy. . . . At the same time, it is to be regretted that the worthless, plotting demagogues, who egged them on to their violence, advised them to procure weapons and resist authorities by force, and roused their passions with inflammatory harangues, cannot be arrested and punished also. . . . [H]ow long will it be before workingmen discover that these demagogues are their worst enemies, and that they have never yet gained anything by following their counsels? (January 20, 1874, 4)

By April the *Tribune*, in observing the increasing frequency of strikes, noted that it was "an evil omen" but reasoned that strikes "produce only evil" and that "the only method of preventing the evil consequences of strikes is to educate the laboring classes to see the remote consequences of even their immediately-successful strikes" (April 2, 1874, 4).

The growing visibility of a more vocal socialist faction of the eight-hour movement also posed a new threat to the establishment.

> These wandering lecturers on the immitigable "hostility of capital to labor," and the "necessity of strikes," and the "assertion of the workingman's power," and such stuff have done much mischief, not by their ability but by the docility of workingmen to their inculcations. They have some superficial knowledge of political economy, some misused statistics, and a stock of stereotyped phrases; and, with an illimitable force of impudence to employ these, they have succeeded in misleading men of more intelligence, but

> more modesty, than themselves. . . . They live on the diseases of industry, and help to make them, that they may live. They are the least, but not the least annoying, of moral insects,—a sort of economical louse, nourished by the workingman's inattention to his own cultivation and condition. They can never see a chance for harmony between employer and his men, except upon the basis of absolute control of one by the other; and, therefore, clamor for strikes. (July 8, 1875, 7)

Two years later, the *Tribune* pronounced its own incendiary warnings to mirror that of the New York "internationalists" quoted above when it issued a warning to radicals: "Every lamp-post in Chicago will be decorated with a Communistic carcass, if necessary to prevent the wholesale incendiarism or punish any attempt at it. It is idle to reason with people who threaten to burn a city. . . . We can only warn them that their threats may have the very opposite effect from what is intended. . . . [T]hey may produce a war of extermination in which the Communistic sentiment, utterly foreign to this country, may be extinguished once and for all" (October 23, 1875, 4). In publishing these ideas, the press played a significant role in shaping elite perspectives that opposed any attempts to change the existing economic order.

But the *Tribune* and the other city newspapers proved to be a double-edged sword to eight-hour opponents, reporting successes of eight-hour protests and recounting the logic of its supporters elsewhere in the country. When the *Tribune* provided a detailed report on the success of the eight-hour system in large textile mills in Massachusetts, it included facts that challenged the logic used by opponents of the eight-hour system. Employers charged that the eight-hour system was economically impractical and unsustainable for large firms, but the fact that large textile mills witnessed no adverse effects countered this logic. In addition, opposition to extending leisure time to workers in fear that they would use the extra time off in morally inappropriate ways, such as by spending more time in the saloons, was specifically rebutted in the Massachusetts report, which documented that the eight-hour system did not result in "moral debauchery, drunkenness, or idleness" (*CT,* May 15, 1873, 2).

Clergy Responses

Protestant leaders watched the intensifying conflicts between capital and labor with growing concern and developed their own approach to these struggles. Clergy only rarely preached on the topic, but a few addressed themselves to the growing class divide in their city. Congregationalist minister Rev.

Henry Ward Beecher, renowned abolitionist and among the most famous American preachers in the nineteenth century, preaching at the Union Park Congregational Church in a sermon titled "Manhood and Money," was one exception. Beecher made direct comparisons between the days of slavery, when one man owned another, and the industrial era, when slavery was masked by the way those who had extensive fortunes increasingly owned industry, government, and even their own employees.

> We have a tyrant that is more tyrannical in possibility in the future than ever slavery was. Slavery is dead, but mammon stands in its place today and there is no Legislature that exists on this continent that could not be crushed or bought by the combinations of such vast treasures as are held in the hands of only three central roads. . . . [O]ur institutions are endangered more today from incorporated capital than from all other influences. . . . It is a monstrous evil. . . . The pulpit speaks of infidelity and unfaith and the growing tendencies of men to wild works of philosophies and opinions. These are great dangers, but the most immediately impending, after all, is the money power. And our liberties, if they are destroyed—that is to say, if the commonwealth, after all, becomes an engine of the few, and exercises the mandate of a power, it will be through the influence of these gigantic corporations holding such money, and, by such money, such control. I look out with a hopeful eye, and I believe that some remedy will be found; but if things go on for another twenty years as they have for the last ten . . . there will be either reformation or revolution, for there are influences at work that will just as surely breed revolution by and by as clouds of summer breed storms. (*CT,* March 1, 1873, 3)

Though Beecher offered no concrete solutions to the growing domination of society by those who controlled "money-power," he had the foresight, in advance of the economic collapse about to occur, to draw links between the resistance of employers to reform and the spread of more revolutionary ideas for achieving industrial change. Beecher was a staunch supporter of abolition and later women's suffrage; however, it is no small irony that in 1873, he condemned the subversion of the Republic by money-power here but four years later would antagonize the American labor movement for condemning strikers in the Great Upheaval of 1877. But for the moment, Protestant ministers, such as the craft unionists in the CTA, viewed industrial expansion in Chicago through an antebellum, republican lens that feared the economic and political domination of a handful of manufacturers. Few ministers paid significant attention to how industrial capitalism was transforming the lives of working people.

Clergy spent more time adapting to the growth of their numbers in Chicago, building new churches, and addressing the increasing religious competition with immigrant Catholicism. Now and again, in sermons and editorials in the religious press, they reflected on why workers were increasingly absent from the city's Protestant churches. The Congregationalist *Advance* suggested that the financial and social costs of pew rents and fashionable clothing were too high for wage earners. "Why doesn't the Congregational Church save the masses? The masses don't want to be saved by the Congregational Church. They cannot afford it. The luxury is too expensive. . . . Roman Catholics and Methodists have always had the poor with them" (March 16, 1873, 533). When ministers did address labor, they typically decried intemperance among the working classes and violations of the Sabbath by working-class immigrants. But the economic crisis of 1873 transformed Protestantism. New theological rhetoric emerged that became the precursor to Social Gospel theology. These ideas found expression in short-lived papers such as *Equity,* published between April 1874 and December 1875, and *Labor Balance,* published between 1877 and 1879 in Boston by the Christian Labor Union.

The Christian Labor Union, founded by a combination of New England Congregationalist and Methodist workers and clergy, was actively engaged with the eight-hour movement in Boston (Craig 1992). The language that these reformers used in support of the eight-hour movement represented a radical departure from most other Protestant clergy who publicly either remained silent on the eight-hour question or adopted the standard frames of employers and the press. The Christian Labor Union employed a unique combination of a republican critique of the new industrial order with a radical reading of the Bible and Protestant theology. Unlike most of their contemporaries, these reformers rejected the simple proposition of both conservative workers such as the Chicago Trades Assembly and the press that workers should use the ballot box to achieve industrial reform. In the first issue of *Equity,* in setting out their ideals, the editors, Methodist ship joiner Edward H. Rogers and the Congregational pastor Rev. Jesse Jones, point out that "to change government is only to change the control of certain surpluses of wealth; but to revolutionize the work system of society is to change the very processes themselves through which wealth is produced, and whereby men get a living." To "revolutionize work" required an organized labor movement to change society matched with the evangelical Protestant ideal of transforming individuals through the power of God.

> The full cure is two-fold—change in persons, and a change in the relations. The persons must be changed, as to find their good in the good of others; rather than in their own gains at the loss of others. Today the hate of each class for the other is growing. . . . [T]he fire of hate must be transformed

> into the life of love. This change can only be wrought by a divine power; and they only can help in that work who carry both classes in their hearts. But society also must be changed. It must be so reformed in structure that the antagonism of positions shall be abolished. . . . We tried to put equal citizens in the place of noble and serf. Does not the very genius of our institutions require that we should also strive to put equal artisans in the place of capitalist and wageman? (April 1874, 1)

Elaborating on their ideas for achieving change four months later, Rogers and Jones were clear about the religious basis for the social transformation of capitalism:

> The only remedy for the immense and multitudinous societal evils which now oppress our land and the world . . . is Jesus Christ. We are well aware how few will sympathize with us and that the naming of this name in such a connection will give offence to almost all people. To many Labor men that name seems far more the symbol and source of ecclesiastical despotism, than the power which will emancipate them from their bondage to capitalists. . . . We would help people to see Jesus as He really was in the wholeness and vastness of His function and work; that so beholding, they may see Labor Reform in its proper place as a part of that work . . . *for the only Labor Reform that will ever succeed is that of which He is the head and life.* (August 1874, 33–34)

Protestants hoped to save society from its many social ills by saving the souls of individuals. But Jones linked the problem that too few working people attended church directly to the problem of overwork. Jones argued:

> Wage laborers in our large centers of population had neither the time nor strength to attend church. . . . [M]en who had been thoroughly tired out by six days of toil were not inclined to burden themselves with church services on Sunday. . . . [E]ight hours work instead of ten was an essential condition of the possibility of saving men. . . . [I]f religious people desired the conversion and elevation of the masses, it was their religious duty to be in favor of reducing the hours of labor to eight, and thus give time to the toilers to attend to their spiritual welfare; and that the whole church ought to be making it one of its objects to obtain so important a result. (June 1874, 21)

For the first time, a Protestant minister emphatically argued that the eight-hour movement was the practical application of evangelical Protestantism and that it was a "religious duty" of Christians to support it.

Because there was no means of achieving eight-hour reform without Christianity, Jones and Edwards redefined the fundamental nature of Christianity as both a religious, or theological, entity and a secular, or practical, social force. "These facts divide Christianity into two immense departments—Religious Christianity, or the work of Jesus concerning God and man; and Secular Christianity, or the work of Jesus concerning man and man. These two thoroughly interpenetrate each other as the blood and nerve system that make lace-work all through the human body; and Christianity can never be thoroughly understood, or correctly taught, much less completely lived, until both these departments are accurately known. . . . JESUS CHRIST IS THE SECULAR, EQUALLY AS THE RELIGIOUS, HEAD AND LEADER OF THE HUMAN RACE." But here too, Jones and Edwards were aware that using Christianity's spiritual and practical elements in support of eight-hour reform was decidedly out of step with how other Protestant leaders understood their mission. But this too was no surprise for them, considering the tepid role that they saw Protestant clergy playing in the abolitionist movement.

> Protestantism not only does not teach, but it strenuously denies that Jesus was a secular leader. Even at the height of the antislavery struggle, the highest ground that was taken by the strongest Bible advocates of emancipation was that slavery was a violation of the law of love, and therefore wrong. Think of it, that the strongest Bible weapon of the Christian antislavery men was an *inference*! And that so far as we know, not one of the whole body of them got hold of and proclaimed the grand fact that Jesus was a *secular* Messiah, and that in announcing his secular Messianic mission, He explicitly declared that He came to free all slaves! We here insist upon this fact, not wholly nor even chiefly because Protestantism is an embodied falsity in this regard, but because that as for this very reason it planted itself right across the way of God's car of Emancipation of Bought Slaves; so now has it planted itself across the way of His car of Emancipation of Wage Slaves . . . and all this because of its fundamentally false position with reference to the work of Jesus Christ: and finally because it is impossible for us to present Jesus in His true light, as the great originator of the Labor Movement . . . without coming at once upon that awful obstacle, the attitude of the Protestant Church. So there was nothing to do but meet it. The work of Jesus as the Leader of all true Labor Reformers will more fully appear as we proceed. (August 1874, 33)

Despite this early sophisticated Protestant support for the eight-hour movement, the ideas of Rogers and Jones and other sympathizers had a limited audience outside of the labor movement. And even this forthright support did little to shift how conservatives and radicals viewed religion and its relationship to eight-hour reform efforts.

Economic Recovery and Eight-Hour Framing

As the 1870s progressed, Chicago's population exploded, increasing from three hundred thousand to a half million, nearly half of whom were immigrant workers, predominantly from Ireland, Germany, and eastern Europe. With this influx of German workers came more radical freethinkers, anarchists, and socialists, and more Irish meant a stronger Catholic population as well as sympathetic Irish nationalists. Immigrant workers, desperate for work, provided a population ripe for conversion by evangelistic leaders in the city's radical labor organizations. Socialists continued to advocate the eight-hour system as the industrial reform that would benefit all workers, skilled and unskilled, employed and unemployed alike (Jentz and Schneirov 2102). Tensions between labor and employers intensified as the end of the depression brought a renewal of employer associations designed to break up union activities in their shops. The formation of the First Regiment of the Illinois National Guard prompted German workers to form their own militia, the Lehr und Wehr Verein, in preparation for a literal class war with employers. Militias were formed by the Irish and by Bohemians with the same purpose. Employers continued to cut wages, driving the anger and desperation of workers to ever more extreme heights (Green 2012). Yet employers ignored this rising tide of frustration, while simultaneously their own fears of these "dangerous" classes led them to act in ways that fueled workers' discontent. Reports of strikes and lockouts peppered the *Tribune,* and the intensifying, virulent conflicts between capital and labor could no longer be ignored by anyone, including Chicago's Protestants.

The Protestant press offered religious solutions to these class divides and the industrial battles they spawned, including the bloody battles that ensued between striking workers, police, and militias during the railroad strike of 1877. Protestant leaders emphasized the need to disseminate the gospel and "correct doctrine" to restore class peace. "Correct doctrine," not surprisingly, told wage earners to remain in their place and condemned any revolt on their part as a reflection of their own low moral character. When wage earners took matters into their own hands and fought for shorter hours or higher wages, ministers reminded them that wealth and poverty were part of the divinely established social order in the Gilded Age and a direct result of one's high or low moral behavior. Rev. H. M. Paynter told his Calvary Tabernacle congregation that "it was not for man to take into his own hands the responsibility of bettering his condition by bloodshed and disorder. The Lord knew all grievances. He even told them, 'Do not strive!' Do not strike.

Don't cry, 'Blood or bread.' He told them to go to their closets and ask for their daily bread" (*CT,* July 30, 1877, 2). Methodist J. S. Smart hypothetically compared workers who made two dollars per day to those making ten dollars, arguing that the former had no right to grumble and complain. "Each but receives the legitimate results of his genius and labor. God hath made them different" (*NWCA,* August 15, 1877, 6).

The fear that too much leisure would exacerbate the moral deterioration of workers and society in general remained the common theme in most Protestant discussions of the eight-hour day. The *Northwestern Christian Advocate* reflected that workers somehow had to work long hours to protect them and society itself from the dangers of leisure. "I believe that for most men more than eight hours work per day is required for the maintenance of physical, mental, and moral health . . . to keep down and utilize the fires of animal nature and passions. I believe that if improvements in machinery should discharge men from the necessity of laboring more than six hours a day, society would rot in measureless and fatal animalism" (July 23, 1877, 2). The long hours of labor resulted in "physical, mental, and moral" well-being for working-class people. In contrast, workers could never be trusted with leisure. Methodist pastor Rev. J. Williamson observed that "at least eighty-five percent of the active sinning is done in human society, not when men are employed, but when they are at leisure." Williamson strongly asserted, "It has been determined by laborious and philosophic experimentation, protracted long enough to effectually settle all intelligent doubt, that the average man must work ten hours a day to earn his bread and shelter. This conclusion I regard as the fiat of God for our century and civilization" (*NWCA,* August 20, 1879, 6). Attorney Walter C. Larned, writing to the Episcopalian *Living Church,* argued that individuals needed more work, not less, to achieve contentment and a high standard of morality:

> More expressly says nobody shall work over six hours a day, in his "Utopia." . . . [T]he natural inference is that it is better to work as little as possible, and . . . that as much leisure time as possible should be allowed to everyone. . . . The amount to be done by each one is measured by what the laziest and most stupid of the community can accomplish. . . . Men will always seek ease and idleness. Only two things can change this law of our nature: one is necessity; the other, the spiritual consciousness that work is noble; that work for others is most noble; that without exercising and taxing his powers, man cannot rise to dignity and true happiness. (March 29, 1879, 391)

Larned's implications here are plain: Chicago's wealthy espoused the appropriate values of discipline in savings and hard work, hence their wealth and power. In contrast, the working classes, the unemployed, and the poor lacked these same values, and the values that they did possess, such as squandering their little income in saloons, keep them impoverished. The praise and the blame for both groups lay in the qualities of the group itself, not in the system of production.

Furthermore, already lax morals of workers made the appeals of eight-hour reformers all the more alluring. Walter C. Larned expressed the view of many Protestants that eight-hour reform was "bait with which to catch all the lazy, and shiftless, and ignorant of any community" (*Living Church,* March 29, 1879, 391). Rev. Dr. W. W. Patton, preaching at the First Congregational Church, condemned both eight-hour reform and the labor organizations that promoted it:

> The fault that has been found, not without reason, with the operation of trades unions and labor leagues, the object of which seemed to be to compel the adoption of the fewest hours of work and the payment of the highest wages, irrespective of the general welfare of the community, or even of other laborers, and to the ruin of employers who were engaged in fulfilling heavy contracts based upon hours and wages as existing at the time. These laboring men, so narrow and selfish in their views and so violent in their proceedings, these tramps, and bummers, and thieves, the very sight of whom is a disgust, are nevertheless our fellowmen and members of the same communities with ourselves. . . . I do not know that they are any more loathsome, physically or morally, than many of those outcast sinners for whose rescue Jesus patiently and lovingly labored. (*Living Church,* July 30, 1877, 2)

As industrial conflicts intensified, some Protestant opinions became more extreme. The Presbyterian *Interior* prescribed its own merciless solutions to labor's militancy. "Strikers must be put down with musketry, not fired to frighten but to kill. The more promptly and vigorously the riots and rebellions are suppressed and a lesson not to be forgotten is taught to the mobs, the better. . . . [T]he general public needs to learn that in letting the communistic tiger loose, and encouraging it, they are letting it loose upon themselves and their own property" (July 16, 1877, 381). For the *Interior* and many business elites, the growing strength of a radical eight-hour movement, carried by unskilled foreign-born workers whose very culture challenged the economic and cultural dominance of native-born Protestant elites, had to be fought with any means available to safeguard Chicago as well as their own power and position in it.

Although all of these polemics must be understood in the context of the elite hysteria and visceral contempt for the labor movement following the strikes and street battles of 1877, they illustrate the basic problems with any labor reform, including the eight-hour day, in the minds of Chicago's Protestants. That thousands of the city's working classes were unemployed resulted from their own low moral standing rather than the activity of employers. More leisure would only make this condition worse. For their part, labor reformers were perceived as demanding and greedy agitators, willing to go to any length to force employers to give them more pay for less work and entice ignorant workers to join them. Some clergy, like Patton, also feared that if workers were granted shorter hours, the economy would be thrown back into depression, disrupting the entire community in the process. Morally and economically, long hours were an inevitable and divinely ordered means to protect the well-being of workers and society as a whole, and employers were justified in resisting any attempts to reduce them.

But in the upheaval of the national railroad strike, while most Protestants' opposition to labor and eight-hour reform was reinforced, it is possible to identify a gradual shift in their thinking as well. While J. S. Smart assumed wage differences were God given and immutable in writing for the *Northwestern Christian Advocate,* he also pointed out that employers were to blame for the extremes to which labor seemed willing to go to change industrial conditions:

> The tendency of capital has always been to increase its volume by oppressing the poor. There have always been men heartless enough to carry this policy to any extreme.... All they want is so to grind them up that gold may flow to their coffers. No matter what name you call it by, it is a real slavery when the poor thus become the hard-driven and ill-fed dependents of the rich. We call it robbing the slave to deprive him of education, of home and domestic comforts, and reward the toil worth hundreds a year to the master, with nothing but a bare subsistence, and so it is. And if by any organization of capital and labor, the same result is reached . . . employer and employee are simply other names for master and slave.

Smart's critique went further and accused employers of violating God's will for human relationships:

> When the [employer] takes advantage of his position to oppress the poor, he becomes a tyrant and betrays the trust God hath reposed in him. With this character we have no sympathy.... The employer has no right to look upon his employee as a mere beast of burden, to be worked and starved to death to make money for him, or as a mere machine, without soul or sense, to be worn out in his service, and then broken up and thrown away.

> He may be poor, may be coarse and lowly, may be ignorant, and even mean and vicious. But he is a man, and Christ died for him. (August 15, 1877, 6)

Sabbath desecration by railroad owners was targeted by Protestant clergy as the principal cause for the violence of that strike. "When thousands of men are systematically deprived of all Sabbath rest and religious privileges, they become a dangerous element to society. . . . The 22d of July, 1877 was but the culmination of thousands of Sabbath desecrations by these railroads. If the railroads would not see such scenes repeated . . . give them their Sabbaths. The godless and Sabbath-desecrating managers should be held responsible for these riots" (*NWCA,* August 29, 1877, 6; Crafts 1885, 234). By shifting blame for industrial conflict from workers to employers, clergy reinforced a moral divide between the interests of sinful employers, on the one hand, and those of God and their employees, on the other.

Likewise, while the Presbyterian *Interior* called for the suppression of workers with the force of arms, the paper also began linking the problem of overwork to employers' insatiable desire to make more money. Mrs. R. W. Frisbee underscored the point that workers had no choice but to work as long as possible. "The trouble is . . . labor and idleness are carried to extremes. The workingman toils from morning until night, until he comes to be a mere human drudge, a machine for making money. He is not to blame for this, but his employer is. If he should object, he is at liberty to leave, for his place could be supplied in an hour. So at the expense of denying himself rest or culture, however much he may desire it, he must succumb to the wishes of his employer or reduce his family to want." Mrs. Frisbee also labeled employer actions criminal by arguing that "murder is a shocking crime and we all turn appalled at its commission, but by what other name can we truthfully call this disregard to the health and strength of another?" Mrs. Frisbee's remedy to the problems of both overwork and unemployment was the eight-hour day, so "those whose hours hang heavily on their hands could only fill them up with the labor that is bowing others down . . . making life a burden too heavy to be borne, and too bitter to last. . . . [The unemployed] would be useful and of consequence; the work would be done, and the work man find time each day for rest and improvement" (October 18, 1877, 1).

The Christian Labor Union's second newspaper, *Labor Balance,* left no doubt that shorter hours led both to the social improvement of workers and to establishing God's kingdom on earth. "When the real religion of Jesus prevails, and his real spirit rules among men, and when all work is done to establish the kingdom of God on earth, then, in no place where men work in large companies, shut in from the sky, will they work more than eight hours a day" (April 1878, 12). Other shifts in Protestant thinking slowly challenged the working-class charges that Christianity remained irrelevant to practical efforts at social transformation.

> They [the working classes] also sometimes feel that while the gospel is rich in promises to the sick and dying, it does not meet the needs of those whose shoulders are bowed with heavy burdens; while it promises a glorious life in the future, it does not fully meet the daily toil of this. And yet it is preeminently to these the Gospel addresses itself. "Come unto me all ye that labor and are heavy laden and I will give you rest," is the call of Christ to the toiling world. . . . He did not become the leader of a class, but he was the savior of men, and responded to the call of suffering from whomsoever it might come. (*Interior*, November 8, 1877, 2)

Clearly, Protestant rhetoric about labor was evolving when workers were reminded that "Christ is the workingman's friend," and his teachings had important political implications for remaking the industrial order. For a small group of Protestants, redeeming the industrial world was as important as redeeming men's and women's souls.

CHAPTER 4

Marching to Haymarket and the 1886 Eight-Hour Campaign

As the 1870s drew to a close, the animosity between Chicago workers and employers continued to grow unabated. Fragmentation continued to plague labor as the eight-hour movement split into three movement factions, spurred on by the immigration waves that flooded the city's working class with more Germans, Irish, Bohemians, and Scandinavians. Approximately thirty thousand native-born mostly Protestant workers were organized into nineteen unions through the Chicago Trades and Labor Assembly. Irish Catholics along with some native-born, Protestant workers joined the Chicago District Assembly of the Knights of Labor. The entrance of Catholic immigrants into the Knights increased their membership from under one thousand in eight local assemblies in 1878 to upwards of twenty-five thousand in eighty-eight locals in 1886 (E. Hirsch 1990). An estimated ten to fifteen thousand radical workers, largely of German and eastern European origin, were organized into twelve unions through the anarchist Central Labor Union, the International Working People's Association (IWPA), and the Socialist Labor Party.

These three factions are simultaneously studies in contrast as well as similarity. The CTLA and Knights were united by a mutual interest in reform and the use of the ballot to achieve specific labor reforms, in contrast to the more revolutionary focus of the CLU. All three factions shared varying degrees of commitment to a republican vision of America grounded in an economy based on independent producers (Fink 1985). Divisions emerged in the CTLA's and Knights' roots in evangelical Protestantism and beliefs that the labor movement could restore the Republic by combating corrupt monopolists, while radicals typically took militant stances against organized religion and refused to join the patriotic displays of the others

(Schneirov 1997; Weir 1996). The Knights of Labor shared more in common with the CLU in their inclusive vision of a movement that included all workers, skilled and unskilled, native-born and foreign-born, men and women, not only those Anglo-American male workers in the skilled crafts. The CLU remained a steady contrast to both the CTLA and the Knights by its disdain for political solutions to industrial conflict and its insistence on the complete overthrow of capitalism through direct action, as much as by its popularity with radicals in Chicago's immigrant communities (E. Hirsch 1990; B. Nelson 1988).

The complexities of vision, strategy, and tactics also shaped each faction's use of religious rhetoric and by differences in their long-term strategies to achieve an eight-hour day in the campaigns of the 1880s. Before the eight-hour campaign of 1886, explicit religious ideological demands for eight hours increasingly disappeared from the newspapers and pamphlets published by the CTLA. This is not to say that skilled craft unionists never used religious language, however. Protestant religion, after all, remained a vital part of the culture of this more conservative branch of the working class. The *Chicago Boycotter,* for instance, continued its use of religious metaphors when announcing that "another sinner is on his knees, praying for remission of his sins. Nick Kuehnen, the scab cigar manufacturer of Davenport, Iowa is treating for peace" (March 9, 1886, 1). Or occasionally, the *Record,* the official publication of the CTLA, quoted biblical references to the day when God's justice would be restored on earth with the title "Not Yet" (June 28, 1886, 1). But the central arguments favoring shorter hours in the CTLA's papers, pamphlets, and the public addresses of its leadership show a marked shift away from religious rhetoric in the years leading up to Haymarket.

The Noble and Holy Order of the Knights of Labor was a new force in the eight-hour movement in the 1880s. Though the organization was founded by Uriah Stephens in Philadelphia in 1869, the first Assembly of the Knights of Labor (District Assembly 24) was formed on November 10, 1878, in the aftermath of the 1877 railroad strikes. The Knights maintained faith in the American political process and public opinion to secure shorter hours, despite their concurrent acknowledgment that employers resisted eight-hour laws that were already on the books. Formally opposed to strikes as detrimental to working-class interests, the Knights officially planned to fight for eight hours through the ballot, though rank-and-file members were more willing to use strikes and pressured the organization's leaders to provide support for them (Fink 1985; Weir 1996). Under the leadership of Terrance Powderly, the Knights reached out to many groups of workers previously organized only by socialists, including women, the unskilled, and immigrants, and in doing so the Knights were one of the most diverse factions of the eight-hour movement (E. Hirsch 1990).

The Knights of Labor made powerful ideological contributions to the eight-hour movement. Initially coming out of Chicago's native-born Protestant working class, the Knights subverted traditional discourse of the work ethic into a central tenet in their arguments for opposing the conspicuous leisure of the rich and supporting shorter hours for labor. Even as the organization became dominated by Irish Catholics, the language of evangelical Protestants remained intact and provided the basis for the Knights' social Christianity. The Knights claimed Jesus as their symbolic role model. "Christ must have been a true Knight of Labor, being a carpenter's son; He was the master of His father's trade. And this proves that all Knights of Labor should become Christ-like" (*Knights of Labor* [*KL*], August 14, 1886, 9). They espoused early Christian communities as the exemplars for solidarity among workers (Weir 1996). Also, like the Trades and Labor Assembly, Knights were staunch supporters of temperance and went to great lengths to keep anyone in the liquor trade out of their organization (Fink 1985).

For the Knights of Labor, the eight-hour reform remained "a religious movement," and attempts by Terrance Powderly to minimize religious language were met with resistance from rank-and-file members (*Journal of Urban Labor* [*JUL*], October 10, 1884, 7; Weir 1996). The Knights upheld the desirability of eight hours "for the soul" (*KL*, August 21, 1886, 11) and directed their religious rhetoric to challenge claims that workers, by desiring more leisure, were lazy and prone to intemperance. In response to these opponents, George Detweiller, *Knights of Labor* editor, pressed upon readers' minds that the Knights of Labor were hardworking and thrifty individuals, "the barefooted friars of earnest labor" (May 15, 1886, 8). The Knights deserved public support, not opposition, because they embodied the cultural ideal of industriousness, especially when compared to radical factions of the movement, using a biblical proverb to frame this distinction.

> Lazy people, old and young, are of an ancient pedigree. They were denounced by Solomon, when he said: "I went to the field of the slothful and by the vineyard of the man void of understanding, and they were grown over with thorns, and nettles had covered the face of it." No lazy man will be found among the Knights of Labor. . . . They will ever be found among the abettors of revolt and confusion; with strong hands and willing minds they work for justice, and gain for themselves equal rights at the ballot box and in the council halls of the nation. (August 14, 1886, 9)

Emphasizing their commitment to the Protestant work ethic separated the Knights from radical factions of the eight-hour movement. The work ethic, citizenship, and a life of faith were as inseparable as were laziness, freethinking radicalism, and atheism, and these religious themes played as well to Catholic audiences as to Protestant ones (Weir 1996; Craig 1992).

For Knights, religious language provided a foundation for building coalitions with clergy in addition to mobilizing members. Religious leaders were understood to be representatives of Christianity who ought to be living out the Christian ethos of loving one's neighbor and standing with the weak against the powerful. Although this was accepted in principle, in practice workers by the 1880s did not hold out much hope that clergy would turn against their wealthy patrons. Weir (1996, 75) observes that the Knights identified more with the order than their churches. Clergy were still too ignorant of industrial conditions and out of touch with the realities of class conflict. Nevertheless, religious leaders were invited to and appeared at mass meetings to voice their opinions on the eight-hour question. On the whole, the Knights maintained the strongest religious rhetoric of all the movement's factions.

For their part, by 1877, as noted in Bruce Nelson's (1988) comprehensive narrative, diverse radical organizations and trade unions operating in Chicago had morphed into the Socialist Labor Party. Its first and foremost demand was "eight-hours for the present as the legal working day and prompt punishment of all violations" (*Socialist,* September 14, 1878, 4). The SLP's English-language newspaper, the *Socialist,* went into circulation by September 1878. As editor of the *Socialist,* Albert Parsons understood that "eight-hours is the new great need of labor," arguing that it would solve the unemployment crisis and raise wages for all workers (October 12, 1878, 4). The SLP believed that trade unions would not, however, be able to put the eight-hour system in place without a labor party to enforce it. The SLP was a revolutionary organization and never detached reducing the hours of labor from a comprehensive abolition of wage slavery. In addition to the SLP, anarchists affiliated with Chicago's Central Labor Union. By 1886 twenty-three different unions were a part of the CLU. Most represented non-English-speaking, unskilled workers. Among the prominent unions in the CLU were mostly German and Bohemian members of the Furniture Workers Union, the International Carpenters and Joiners Union, the Cabinetmakers Union, and the Typographical Union No. 9.

Contrary to what one might expect from this radical wing of the labor movement, religious themes and rhetoric were common in *Socialist* editorials and articles (Burns 2010). Of course, socialists were often critical of organized religion, but they also saw in it the roots of their call for revolutionary justice for the working classes. On the front page of their second issue, the editors included "Precepts from Holy Writ," a set of biblical quotes for their readers to ponder (September 21, 1878, 1, 2). These included quotations from the book of James (2:2–6 and 5:1–4) in which the writer, in the first quote, warns believers against favoring the wealthy over the poor when they enter their places of worship and, in the second, warns the rich that their time is almost at an end and that God will punish them for neglecting to pay their workers. But these verses are not chosen at random. They reinforce the idea that the religion practiced by most Christians is purely spiritual and as such is a distorted form of Christian faith. For the readers of the *Socialist,* socialism was "practical Christianity," and as such the socialist movement should have the support of people of faith (January 4, 1879, 2). "In the name of God, I beg of you, Christians—subscribe for *The Socialist*—preach this doctrine in the church. Unless you also preach and practice the Man's doctrine, how can you expect to be saved by it? Did he not face His enemy, and was put to death for so doing? Will you call yourself a Christian and fear to walk in his footsteps for fear of the Money Kings? Go forth and preach the Gospel to every creature" (November 16, 1878, 3). But there was no optimism that such mass conversions of Chicago churchgoers to socialism would actually take place. Religion was an obstacle that kept the labor movement, and other movements before it, from advancing.

> From the beginning of history, the Church, no matter of what creed, was ever foremost in decrying and denouncing every earnest and honest reform that struck at the root of an evil, . . . declaring it in opposition to God and religion (which secretly meant gold), and in accusing the most unselfish advocates of such reforms of treason, of demogogism, of infidelism, and of all other isms that implied criminality. Although such reform questions were of a purely secular character, the Church, as secret handmaid of those who were gainers by some unjust and rotten system that needed reforming, always knew her place and duty. It was for this reason that CHRIST was hung to a cross, together with two thieves. . . . It is a matter of history that whenever the despoiled and oppressed began to understand GOD's command of love and justice, threatening defiance to the brute force of the ungodly oppressors, their gold had summoned the fraudulent skill of priestcraft to their aid. . . . The clergy are not taking position against the atheists and free-thinkers, but leaving GOD, the Great Creator of the universe and heaven, the place of salvation, undefended, jumping to the defense of the earthly treasures of their masters and their own pockets. (December 21, 1878, 4)

But despite such pointed accusations of churches and their ministers, socialists continued to employ religious themes in their eight-hour rhetoric.

Although the CLU shared many of the religious sentiments expressed by allies in the SLP, anarchists were much more critical of capitalist domination of society and of organized religion and its consistent role in opposing any effort at changing this state of things. The *Furniture Workers' Journal* saw the emergence of a new God in the new industrial order to replace the old one of Christianity:

> Science discovered the principle of "Free Competition" and it was proclaimed to be the new God. His laws are of iron cruelty. The old God at least recognized all mankind to be his children; though the masses were in fact but step-children, condemned to "eat their bread by the sweat of their brow." But the new God sayeth: "If thou, man, hast no means of existence, and the ruling class has no use for thy labor, thou hast no right to exist. Thou hast better let things take their natural course—and starve." He has disinherited thee, workman, he has taken thy rights and dignity from thee. Thou art nothing but the wheel of a machine. Today he is condemning thee to work 24 hours per day, and tomorrow he will throw thee in the street. His greed is insatiable, for he sacrifices fragile women and innocent children. He elevates the mighty and the reckless, and he grinds the weak ones to dust. And if the downtrodden and the oppressed cry out against such shameless tyranny, if they are not yet bereft of all human feelings; if they unitedly rise up as a power to demand improvement of their condition, this tyrannical God will howl for revenge against what he calls the "tyranny of labor." He orders the rebels, who oppose his laws of iron, to be persecuted by public and secret police, he sends them to the dungeon through the instrumentality of his servants—the judges. He employs the entire organism of the State, the legislature, and the executive power to make laws and carry them out, for the purpose of keeping down the workers and "persuade" them that the institutions of the world are just very nice and that they must remain as they are. But they will not remain so. (May 22, 1885, 1)

The anarchist themes were clear. Employers had no interest except accumulating as much wealth as possible. If workers or anyone else tried to fight back or resist employers, then employers used all of their power to crush resistance. But most important, employers used the institutions of society, including religion, to keep workers believing that the world was fine as it was and had no need for change. When ministers addressed labor's concerns, they usually reinforced rather than challenged radicals' assertions that they simply were too out of touch with industrial reality to merit worker attention. When, for instance, Rev. Thomas E. Green gave a sermon on the labor movement suggesting that employers should, as Christians, simply be more "merciful" to their employees, the *Alarm* dismissed his ideas as more "folly" from church leaders (November 8, 1884, 1). But such critical positions did not keep anarchists from trying to appeal to clergy (Burns 2010).

For socialists and anarchists, the morality of eight hours lay in its role in the social evolution of industrial conditions toward the "historic unfolding of the rights of man" and worker emancipation from wage slavery (*Alarm*, February 20, 1886, 2). This was the dominant theme of every radical voice in the eight-hour movement. These revolutionaries believed themselves to be furthering *true* Christianity by fighting for an eight-hour day (*Socialist*, November 16, 1878; January 4, 1879). However, it is important to note that not every revolutionary was willing to concede to the efficacy of making these religious appeals. Socialists also saw economic reform as a scientific enterprise and felt that involving clergy and religious sentiments in industrial conflicts would breed "more confusion than clarity" and risked disrupting worker solidarity with religious controversies (Burns 2010, 51).

The competition and activity of all three factions of the eight-hour movement and the repression they encountered from elites created an environment of mounting frustration, what Green describes as "seething discontent" (2006, 125) and class hatred for elites among workers in Chicago. A day did not pass without the press reporting on strikes, mass meetings, employer association activities, or religious opinions of the eight-hour movement. The public hysteria brought on by the national railroad strike of 1877 had subsided into widespread suspicion of any effort to organize workers or to institute industrial reforms. The mention of a mass meeting of workers brought terror to local business owners, some of whom closed their shops until any expected trouble had passed. Nevertheless, the *Chicago Tribune* diligently reported the proceedings of weekly (usually Sunday) meetings of local labor organizations.

Readers of the *Tribune* and *Times* also learned that male workers were not the only group to see the eight-hour day as the means to a better future. Women wage earners also began to mobilize, and the *Tribune* ensured that their activities were covered as well. In 1878 Lucy Parsons, wife of Haymarket martyr Albert Parsons, formed the Working Women's Union along with Aliza Stevens, a member of Chicago Typographical Union No. 16, Lizzie Swank, and Elizabeth Rogers. The Working Women's Union pressed for a reduction in the hours of labor for women and contributed an impressive pink float to the 1879 Eight Hour League Parade. Seven years later, in 1886, Sarah

Ames and Lizzie Holmes worked to organize sewing girls for the eight-hour campaign of that year as well (Avrich 1984). From the beginning, women worked to organize across the lines of class, race, ethnicity, and religion. They were welcomed into the Knights of Labor, and many radicals were members of both the Knights and anarchist and socialist unions (B. Nelson 1988; Weir 1996). Many middle-class women took an interest in organizing workingwomen in their shorter-hour fight and joined in their organizing efforts. Reporting on a meeting of the Working Women's Union in 1878, one *Tribune* journalist observed: "There were others among them who did not seem to be particularly oppressed by the grinding, crushing heel of capital. On the contrary, they were by no means poorly clad; there was an absence of anything on the woe-be-gone order in their faces, and no one could have seen them without coming to the conclusion that they ate regular meals and slept well at night. Mrs. Ellen A. Higginson, the organizer and president of the movement, was of this class" (July 29, 1878, 4). Whatever their class, under the auspices of their own associations, women began to raise the conditions of workingwomen before the general public and workingmen with the hope of achieving legislation to restrict the hours of women's labor. The eight-hour movement was truly universal in its appeal, "independent of all considerations of nationality, religion, or previous condition" as well as skill level and gender (*CT*, June 17, 1879, 4).

The Eight-Hour Protests of 1879

The spring of 1879 was a politically turbulent one in Chicago. It was an election year. Elites in the Citizen's Association successfully lobbied for a new law that would increase the size of the state's militia and prohibit any armed groups from marching in public. This was a direct attack on the Lehr und Wehr Verein, the Sharpshooters, and all the other worker militias in the city (Green 2006). The SLP nominated Dr. Ernst Schmidt, a German, to run for mayor. His unusual candidacy attracted the electoral attention of German merchants, saloon owners, and others who were not within the socialist constituency but who had felt under attack by the city's native-born Protestant business and political elite. Although Schmidt did not win the office, neither did the Republican candidate, making Carter Harrison, who also presented himself as a friend to workers, Chicago's new Democratic mayor (Jentz and Schneirov 2012, 225). Shortly after the elections, in May, new rumors of a fresh eight-hour protest were heard. The Trades and Labor Assembly called a meeting to discuss resolutions passed by the Trades and Labor Assembly of St. Louis concerning the formation of a national eight-hour movement. Union delegates representing workers who were in attendance adopted these resolutions, and July 4, 1879, was chosen for the inauguration of a general strike (*CT,* May 19, 1879, 3).

A procession and picnic at Ogden's Grove on the city's north side was held in mid-June, kicking off this new round of protest, with two thousand people and four brass bands and nine singing societies drawing crowds of supporters. Albert R. Parsons, head of the Socialist Labor Party, spoke earnestly for eight hours to become the rallying cry of Chicago workers. He promised no strike for the upcoming Fourth of July, as employers feared would take place. Parsons assured his audience that only when "the labor army was organized, no strike would be necessary because it would bring about capitalistic concessions," but at that moment the city's labor movement was not united enough to achieve its goals through striking (*CT,* June 23, 1879, 8).

As Parsons predicted, there was no strike on July 4. Only a small demonstration, washed out due to a rainstorm, followed in Ogden's Grove. Ira Steward was the chief speaker of the day, presenting to those assembled the "Second Declaration of Independence," the central tenet of which was shorter hours. Steward observed that "in the matter of this eight-hour question, you men of Chicago ought to be proud and thankful that you are leading the whole civilized world. No other place on this Continent I have no doubt at this hour can show a sight so grand and so bright as this mighty up-rising of the workingmen of Chicago for eight-hours" (*CT,* July 5, 1879, 2). Other eight-hour leaders addressed the crowds in German and Bohemian. The day generally passed without incident, leaving the press to conclude it a failure. Three weeks later, the city's cabinetmakers tried to lead a strike for an eight-hour day. After eight days, the men could not hold out against the Furniture Manufacturing Association, which was unanimous in its decision to shut down all of the factories under its members' control for a month before they would ever give into worker demands for shorter hours. The cabinetmakers gave up the strike and returned to work.

Employers, as before, remained galvanized against any attempt by any group of workers or any labor organization to enforce the eight-hour system. They organized their own hiring practices to ensure that none of their employees belonged to labor organizations, radical or otherwise. Following attempts by the workers to strike for shorter hours, furniture manufacturers resolved "that no member of this association will knowingly employ in his factory any communist, anarchist, nihilist, socialist, or any person denying the right to private property or recommending destruction or bloodshed as remedies for existing evils" (Bonnett 1956, 265). In their resolve, *all* labor reformers, not only those who claimed these radical labels, ran afoul of this resolution. Anyone—employers, workers, clergy, or middle-class progressives—who challenged employers' right to organize production as they saw fit could be labeled a communist or anarchist precisely because they were trying to interfere or limit employers' freedom. Further, employers had the right and even the obligation to use any means at their disposal to protect their property and economic freedoms. The intensifying polarization of employers against workers and workers against employers was setting the industrial stage for the great eight-hour strife of 1886 (Green 2006).

Clergy were not ignorant of the concrete connections between the wealth of the few and the poverty and related revolutionary spirit of labor. Their early opposition to the eight-hour campaign, unlike that of employers, had its own unique religious character. Their opposition was based on a concern over inappropriate uses to which workers might put leisure. Some clergy continued to cite more puritanical reasons for not supporting labor reform. Presbyterian minister Rev. C. H. Zimmerman, for example, argued that poverty was a condition that was predestined for some and that "it is often one's duty to bear it contentedly. . . . [W]e should ever be content with what God assigns" (*Interior*, November 8, 1883, 4). Zimmerman expressed this idea again in the *Interior* (May 24, 1885, 1). But more often, clergy criticized labor for resorting to strikes in an effort to compel employers to give them higher wages or shorter hours rather than patiently and peacefully negotiating with them. Equally problematic for some clergy was the perception that union workers used violence "to compel non-union men to unite in their strikes" (*NWCA*, June 14, 1882, 4). Although these were familiar frames in the religious press, they were not the only ones.

Clergy and the Protestant press expressed clear concerns about the actions of employers, the changing nature of work, and misguided consumerism that tempered what has come to be interpreted by scholars as Protestants' monolithic antilabor feelings. The majority of articles in the Protestant press that directly addressed capitalists laid the blame for labor unrest on *employers* as much as on wild-eyed labor agitators and anarchists. As the *Northwestern Christian Advocate*'s editors observed, "The strife which exists between capital and labor, and seems to grow louder, is brought about largely to the evil doings of capitalists" (July 5, 1882, 4). But they went further to analyze what was at the root of conflicts between employers and workers. The Protestant press was as prophetic in nature in their pronouncements as any statements from the Knights of Labor or the Socialist Labor Party. As Howard Crosby, writing for the Methodist press, warned:

> The present peril of our country is exactly here. The dangerous classes among us are those who are engaged in amassing colossal fortunes—the giants who tread ordinary men under their heel and care not for how much men suffer. They are absorbed by with their own greatness, lifted by their wealth out of all sympathy with the mass of mankind, and live as if the world belonged to them. The cries of want and sorrow are unheeded by them, and the appeals of charity and benevolence are spurned, the demand of cooperation in works for the public weal is slighted—while all their millions are poured into the channels of their own selfishness. (*NWCA,* April 11, 1883, 6)

Even the Episcopalian *Living Church*'s editors, who were rarely critical of employers, concurred with these ideas:

> The selfish use of wealth and power is felt, by the "working men" through whom this wealth and power are gained and enjoyed, as an outrage upon humanity; and the laws of religion and society by which men are rightfully protected in the use of that which they have gained, are executed. The law of sacrifice is a "higher law" not on the statute books, but the persistent disregard of it threatens the stability of all law. Riches and power must take note of this, or they will find that the conditions of their existence and enjoyment will be withdrawn. . . . Men must learn that they are stewards, not owners. (November 25, 1882)

Two years later, the *Living Church* reasserted these ideas, calling on employers to answer for their sins against their employees. "There are too many who should be made to feel that starvation wages and starvation rents mean to multitudes hopeless poverty and wretchedness, and perhaps enforced crime and immorality. What use to talk about people improving their conditions when the pittance they get for weary hours of labor is largely swallowed up by the exaction of landlords, who are as careful, perhaps, not to keep the premises in repair, as to have the pay forthcoming?" (January 19, 1884).

The Protestant press and ministers who preached sermons on these issues were unanimous that employers, on the one hand, claimed to be Christians but, on the other hand, did not apply Christian principles to industry. The fundamental social sin employers committed was to ignore their obligation to be good stewards of their wealth and power and to use them for the good of the entire community, including their employees. As a result, in the minds of some Protestant leaders, "it is not surprising though not defensible, that [workers] resort to violence to get what they cannot obtain by peaceable means" (*NWCA*, June 14, 1882, 4).

What, then, did these editors and ministers propose to address these sins? Employers needed to be "Christianized" and begin to implement Christ's teachings in their dealings with workers (*Standard*, April 16, 1885, 4; *Interior*, July 5, 1883, 4). Some, such as the editors of the *Living Church*, proposed that employers should provide education and services for the poor and sustain charities, schools, and churches that helped them (November 25, 1882, xx). The Methodist *Northwestern Christian Advocate* went further:

> The dangerous classes must be rendered harmless. But how can this be done? Only by righteous laws righteously administered . . . for our safety is the enactment of laws to defend the poor man against the rich oppressor. . . . There must be a limit to individual wealth if we are to be preserved as a republic. . . . Cease, ye men of pleasure and of business, cease from thinking only of yourselves. Give thought to the community in which you dwell. Do your public duties. Discharge your solemn trusts imposed upon you by your country, your conscience, and your God. (April 11, 1883, 6)

While the proposition to regulate the wealth accumulation of capitalists was not a remedy proposed by many Protestant leaders, it was an idea that gained sympathy in the years leading up to the Haymarket affair of 1886. Although Protestants did not endorse the eight-hour workday uncritically, Chicago employers were increasingly criticized for their unwillingness even to negotiate with workers and for their disregard for the stability of the community and for the Christian principles employers professed on Sunday mornings.

The Eight-Hour Campaign of 1886

By 1884 organized labor once again was ready to make a city and nationwide eight-hour demand. At their Chicago meeting that year, the Federation of Organized Trade and Labor Unions voted to inaugurate the eight-hour day on May 1, 1886, recommending that labor unions across the country work to enact or enforce eight-hour laws by that date. By the mid-1880s, it was apparent to most craft unionists and radicals, but not to the leadership of the Knights of Labor, that legislative attempts at securing an eight-hour day were doomed to failure. For almost twenty years, employers found ways either to circumvent laws or to use the courts and have them declared unconstitutional. Strikes became the accepted weapons of organized workers to secure the eight-hour day as the only way to meet the force of capitalists successfully. Yet the ongoing hope of the Trades and Labor Assembly was for a "cordial response" from employers. The assembly asked employers to recognize the validity and spirit of the eight-hour law already on the books (*CT*, December 21, 1885, 3; January 19, 1886, 8). In contrast, anarchist labor reformers, such as Samuel Fielden and August Spies of the IWPA, conceded their support for a citywide eight-hour strike in the interests of solidarity but only as a compromise and not an ultimate end to labor's bondage.

By the middle of the 1880s, Chicago's labor movement was growing quickly (Fink 1985). There were forty-five trade unions associated with the Trades and Labor Assembly and twenty-eight assemblies of the Knights of Labor (*Chicago Boycotter*, March 9, 1886, 4). Among Chicago's two radical groups, the Socialist Labor Party was represented in nineteen labor organizations, and the International Working People's Association members had affiliations in thirty-one, including the Knights and the Trades and Labor Assembly (B. Nelson 1988, 99). Green (1996, 126) recounts that 20 percent, or between five and six thousand members of the IWPA, were in Chicago. Organizations affiliated with the Central Labor Union also witnessed rapid growth among the city's Germans, Bohemians, Poles, and Scandinavians and claimed twenty thousand members (Green 2006, 126; B. Nelson 1991). For all of Chicago's workers, two themes regarding the eight-hour day remained constant: that overwork was an unjust, moral evil and that the capitalist class by their own sinful greed as well as through the introduction of labor-replacing technology was the objective root cause of the injustice. More specific religious ideologies reemerged with this new wave of protest, but now, as in the past, they were refracted through the movement faction articulating it.

Paradoxically, in the 1886 campaign, the CTLA, which represented the majority of conservative, religiously inclined, skilled workers, had ceased to frame the eight-hour workday in explicitly religious terms. Compared to the CTA in the 1867 campaign and even through most of the 1870s, the Trades and Labor Assembly had adopted frames that argued for shorter hours on systematically economic grounds. Eight-hour workdays, proponents argued, would increase employment for workers and increase production for employers. The CTLA explicitly stated, "With chimerical theories and visionary and impractical dreamers we have nothing whatever to do. Do not let it be understood that we have no thought or care for the future. By living in the practical present, we are laying the foundation of organized labor upon the fundamental principles of eternal justice, which will endure for all time" (*Chicago Boycotter*, February 1886, 2). Their individual and collective commitments to evangelical faith, temperance, God, and the respectability of organized religion were strategically privatized in the eight-hour campaign as religious rhetoric was pushed aside. Religious appeals became even less relevant in a growing movement rhetoric that understood respectful negotiations between bosses and workers to be the logical means for making eight hours into an industrial reality. The CTLA asserted that the eight-hour system would be achieved only through "mutual concessions" by both capital and labor "for the common good of all, for the peace and prosperity of our common country, and the perpetuation of our free institutions" (*Chicago Boycotter,* February 1886, 3). These appeals to the commonality of employer and employed and the willingness to negotiate conditions pointed to the emergent ideology underlying the "pure and simple" unionism institutionalized later in the labor movement under Samuel Gompers and the American Federation of Labor.

The Knights of Labor built on the same Christian images that have already been discussed previously. Their local and national newspapers, the *Knights of Labor* and the *Journal of United Labor,* framed the eight-hour movement as a movement of religious and moral revival for the working classes who, with more free time, could avail themselves of the opportunities offered by churches for spiritual improvement. The Knights saw overwork endured by workers as suffering akin to crucifixion (the "cross") and eight hours as their resurrection or at least their redemptions ("the crown") in this poem published in the *Journal of United Labor* (April 1884, 676):

> Raise you wages as you will. Still will fortune on you frown;
> To shorten hours, is, was, and will be, but the way to wear the
>   crown.
> Labor less and think the more! Which will be the greater loss,
> While higher wages we implore, Ever shall he bear the cross.
> If today our wages rise, We pay more for goods tomorrow;
> And we find with great surprise, no load is lifted from our sorrow.
> If we but reduce the hours, That's more work for every man;
> Goods won't rise—no earthly power can raise the hours, do all
>   they can.
> Long enough we've born the cross, We've raised the wage—they've
>   pulled it down.
> To us has always come the loss, Strike for less hours—and wear
>   the crown.

The Knights intentionally invited sympathetic clergy to speak at mass meetings organized to address the eight-hour question and to include the full texts of supportive sermons from local congregations in the newspaper.

Many of these sermons were given by prominent Protestant leaders such as the nationally known Episcopal bishop Henry C. Potter and local minister Rev. Heber Newton. These supportive clergy criticized employers and church leaders for not seeing the divine justice in the eight-hour movement and all other labor reform efforts. Other speakers, such as William Salter from the Society for Ethical Culture, in addressing the ethics of the eight-hour movement, charged that Protestant clergy were out of touch with the realities of overwork that most workers endured. "Some would say that there were worse things than working more than eight hours a day. Probably eight out of every ten clergymen would dismiss the subject with such a remark. No one could conceive an eight-hour movement starting in a revival center" (*KL*, March 1886, 3). Yet Salter went on to express optimism, resonant with the Knights, that churches and their leaders could be a force for change, alongside organized labor. The church, like the state, was paradoxically part of the problem and the solution to the labor question (Fink 1985). Salter expressed the Knights' belief that "three agencies whose cooperation could secure the desired effect—the government, religion and the combination of laborers themselves. One or even two of these combined, could secure the desired end." There was only one duty confronting Christians. They must support the labor movement. As the editors of the Knights' national paper saw it, "If the church is to continue to exist, it must deserve to exist. . . . It must nestle down with people and every humane movement" (*JUL*, July 1883, 529).

For the Knights, the eight-hour day was simultaneously a religious, economic, and political cause. Shorter hours set those idled by unemployment back to work, and the leisure time afforded to workers would raise their spiritual and moral condition through increased church attendance and education. The Knights, more than any other branch of the eight-hour movement, constructed a vision for a just future that was built on the joint efforts of workers, churches, and the state to reform the ills of the industrial system. Their religious language also resonated with both their native-born Protestant and their Irish Catholic members in ways that allowed for the Knights to unite in favor of the eight-hour cause on religious grounds, despite differences of ethnicity, gender, occupation, or skill level (B. Nelson 1991).

Bruce Nelson's (1991, 247) assertion that radicals in "the Central Labor Union rejected the symbols, trappings, and content of Christianity" oversimplifies the approach of socialists and anarchists to religion in the eight-hour movement. While organized religion was frequently attacked and irreligion "institutionalized" among significant numbers of radical leaders and workers in the IWPA and CLU, Christian religion, even among the irreligious, still permeated the culture of Chicago and consequently could not just be ignored or dismissed by reformers (Burns 2010; B. Nelson 1991; Green 2006). James Green highlights the complexity of the religious dynamic within the labor movement in the 1880s in asserting that American radicals "felt compelled to illustrate their secular complaints with sacred texts and to connect their vision of a truly free society with the Christian imagine of heaven on earth" and to "suffuse their speaking and writing with biblical parables and verses . . . used to chastise their oppressors and arouse the spirits of their followers" (2006, 111).

Radicals expressed their demands for shorter hours in religious terms in the lead-up to 1886. Socialists and anarchists claimed the spirit of Christianity in doing so, but, in contrast to the Knights, they saw little hope or point in relying on clergy to actually do anything practical. Radicals held the mobilization of the religious establishment to achieve eight hours with the same contempt that they did efforts to achieve it through legislation alone. Waiting for laws to be passed was a "tedious delay" and contributed to "a loss of faith in [workers'] own powers" (*Alarm,* August 8, 1886, 1). In anarchist ideology, the state and religion were one, "in origin, in object, in method of action, and in tomfoolery" (*Alarm,* June 13, 1885, 3). As representatives of organized religion, clergy were seen as ignorant, as willfully misrepresenting the cause of labor, and as willing to deal with economic questions only because they were forced to. In addressing the strategy of the Knights to engage the support of Protestant clergy, social revolutionaries in the CLU were not willing to accept the premise that clergy could do anything for labor.

> The preachers throughout the country have taken upon economic questions, because being the only vital issues of the day, they are absolutely forced upon their notice. Professing to be teachers of the people, they persistently ignore the only subjects which possess any real live interest for their charges until they are pushed under their very noses, and must be dealt with one way or the other. . . . Right learnedly do these would-be teachers discourse on Socialism, rights of labor, capital, etc. exhibiting a knowledge of social sciences that would shame a six year old son of a Socialist, or else exercising more willful, downright misrepresentation, than would gain a reputation for a champion liar. . . . Teachers of the people have no right to be ignorant; and standing where they do, keeping better men away from the multitudes, they are villains indeed not to tell what they do know. (*Alarm,* December 26, 1885, 3)

But radical labor leaders did more than make antireligious and anticlerical arguments to their own rank and file. Anarchist and socialist leaders regularly spoke to clergy associations in the city and discussed labor reform with them.

August Spies met with sixty Congregationalist ministers on December 28, 1885 (*Alarm,* January 9, 1886, 3). Their points to clergy were consistently the same. First, they argued, overworked men and women had no time to develop the moral values clergy so highly prized or to become Christians. Second, they pointed out that clergy were uninformed about industrial conditions. And third, if Christian clergy truly wanted to follow their founder, Jesus, then they must be willing to challenge capitalist churchgoers and support eight-hour reform. But from their direct experiences with clergy, radical reformers saw no reason to hope that religious leaders would accept these challenges. So, in contrast to mass meetings held by the CTLA and the Knights, no clergy were ever present at mass meetings held by the Central Labor Union or the IWPA.

Contesting the 1886 Campaign

Employers opposed the eight-hour movement on the grounds that eight-hour shops could not compete with those that maintained long hours. If Chicago reduced the workday, employers threatened to relocate their operations to towns or cities where they could operate as they pleased. The laws of supply and demand could not accommodate labor's demands for shorter hours, and such sentiments continued to be echoed in the *Tribune.* The entrenched position of employers and the fears of revolution among church leaders and the general public were exacerbated in light of newspaper reports that recounted the "bomb talking" of anarchist groups and the vitriolic attacks by radicals on "God, country, and private property" (Green 2006, 144). If, as Green (2006) describes, the Chicago press amplified perceptions of labor radicals as wild, dangerous libertines and drunkards, and anarchists launched speech after speech calling for the complete overthrow of the American industrial order, it is no wonder that the elite and middle classes expected the worst from the eight-hour movement, while many workers saw it as the beginning of the end for their oppressive working conditions. The battle lines were drawn, and there was little room for a middle ground in the minds of business elites.

The religious press and clergy expressed mixed opinions about the eight-hour movement. Some mouthed the logic of employers, claiming that the eight-hour demand was impractical as a local measure (*Standard,* May 27, 1886, 326). At their extreme, the religious press reflected the same animosity toward the movement that was shown in earlier campaigns. The *Interior* claimed the "eight hour excitement a delusion in the minds of the uninformed" (May 6, 1886, 1). The Episcopalian *Living Church* included the following observation of the eight-hour movement: "The whole movement is a senseless and useless agitation of mistaken men, fraught with no good for anybody and that it could only work harm by being successful" (May 29, 1886, 138). Still others built on long-standing prejudices that linked Chicago's immigrant working class with drunkenness and overall moral laxity, as the following editorial comment to an eight-hour supporter from the editor of the *Interior* indicates:

> Mr. Charles F. Seib wishes us to advocate the eight-hour labor rule and to send him a marked copy of our paper, in order that "we may know our friends." We judge from the name that Mr. Seib is a late accession to the citizenship of this country. If we should have the honor of being enrolled in the list of Mr. Seib's friends, it would probably become incumbent upon us to treat the whole circle to pretzels and beer. Mr. Seib probably does not know that those of us who have roofs of our own over our heads, a little laid by for a rainy day, worked from ten to sixteen hours and kept clear of the saloons. (April 29, 1886, 4)

However, the Protestant press also included many more observations that were more favorable to the eight-hour movement, rooting the cause of unrest in the unjust treatment of workers by employers. The Congregational *Advance* again criticized employer actions as the cause of the growth in both membership in radical labor organizations as well as strikes.

> It has been this continual oppression of the laboring man on the part of greedy corporations that has at last driven the workingmen into such organizations as the Knights of Labor and, and often into socialistic movements. Those men who grind the faces of the poor, if they did but know it, are lighting torches to burn their own dwellings. . . . It is a hard lesson for corporations to learn, but they will learn it after awhile that those who labor for them should be protected in their rights, should only be required to work reasonable hours and should have full pay for their services. (March 11, 1886, 152)

A sea-change in Protestant thinking was certainly in the making. The *Living Church* radically articulated what many socialist labor leaders had repeated when one of its contributors argued, "Christianity is a form of Socialism. . . . Does the Gospel really favor these ever-widening distinctions in society—millions for the few, and ever-increasing poverty for so many, an operation, whether of social or economic laws that lifts up the one and bears down the others? One thing is certain: If it not responsible for this condition of things, it ought not to *seem* to be so" (March 6, 1886, 741). The final point in the quote is equally as significant as equating Christianity and socialism. In asserting that the church should not be perceived as giving its approval on the widening of the gap between rich and poor and between capital and labor, the editors understood that their practical role in transforming Chicago into a fully Christian community and of being the moral arbiters of that community was in jeopardy of being perceived as too closely aligned with the wealthy. Likewise, the Methodist press articulated a similar critique and questioned whether it was time to reject the taken-for-granted assumptions of economic law entirely as another tool that employers have used to resist industrial reform.

> Great is political economy; greater still is the stupidity or heartlessness of its teachers of the laissez-faire school who say all working is for the best; starvation of redundant population regulates the labor market by checking the supply of laborers; let well enough alone. Yet we are occasionally told from the pulpit that we are nearing the millennium! We are making some progress, however. We are learning to distrust some of the teachings of the old political economists; to doubt some things in our industrial system of which that science, perhaps falsely so called, is simply the exponent. We have learned that the cry of overproduction is a *bete noir* with which employers frighten laborers into acquiescence in lower wages or half time. (*NWCA*, February 3, 1886, 8)

As the campaign of 1886 progressed, and class tensions continued to rise, the shared and taken-for-granted understanding of the eight-hour question and industrial reform generally among employers and Protestant clergy was fragmenting.

Campaign Outcomes in 1886

On May 1, 1886, divisions and animosities within the labor movement were unexpectedly replaced with solidarity and anticipation, as the promised general strike and demonstrations for eight hours were launched in Chicago and across the country (Green 2006). Membership in unions affiliated with the CTLA, the Knights of Labor, and the CLU soared, as workers saw a hope for the first time that they could reduce the hours of labor through their own united action (Green 2006). The immediate result was that 340,000 workers across the country struck to reduce their working day. Chicago alone witnessed 387 strikes in 1886, all for the reduction of hours. Nearly 80,000 workers were involved, and half of these workers only threatened to walk out in order to get their employers to promise reduced hours (*KL*, May 15, 1886,

11). But the events of the Haymarket bombing following the May Day campaign, which have been the subject of extensive analysis elsewhere, changed the eight-hour movement in fundamental ways (Green 2006; Avrich 1984; David 1958; Roediger and Foner 1989). But the 1886 eight-hour campaign also changed how the public and especially clergy viewed the labor movement generally and the eight-hour demand in particular.

On May 3, a meeting was called outside of Cyrus McCormick's Reaper plant where some 1,500 iron molder union workers had been locked out and an additional 4,500 others had gathered in support. When some 200 left to heckle scabs coming out of the plant that afternoon, an equal number of police arrived and opened fired on the workers, killing 2 and injuring numerous others. The next day, anarchist leader August Spies published a flyer demanding revenge and calling all workers to a demonstration to protest the police brutality of the night before. Much to the dismay of both business leaders and police, the anarchists received a city permit for the mass meeting from Mayor Carter Harrison, and 3,000 people gathered that night. As the evening progressed, it started raining, and by 10:20 p.m. only about 500 people lingered at the meeting. The mayor left Haymarket square shortly after this time. Living nearby, he had been there twice that evening to supervise the proceedings and was convinced that nothing dangerous would come from allowing the anarchist leaders to continue to speak. The mayor had instructed Captain John Bonfield to send the police and the reserve forces that had been called to duty home for the night. But after the mayor left the Haymarket square, Bonfield and Captain William Ward ordered his forces stationed nearby to disperse the crowd. In the brief foray that followed, a dynamite bomb exploded in the ranks of the police, killing 7 and injuring many more. The police opened fire and killed or wounded an unknown number of workers gathered there. News of the events reinforced elites' belief that the revolution seemed to have begun. Hysteria stirred up repression of radical worker organizations and newspapers, but the eight-hour movement as a whole came under attack from all quarters (Green 2006; Messer-Kruse 2011).

The verbal reactions from Chicago's pulpits and press were equally hysterical. Both condemned the labor movement in all its forms for weeks following the bombing. Erastus Snow, a contributor to the Presbyterian *Interior,* wrote: "The Knights of Labor is a misnomer; the Knights of darkness would be better. . . . These foreign ingrates instead of thanking God for the blessings and wages they never knew at home, turn traitors to both God and our government, and curse them both. A class of men who demand ten hours pay for eight hours work with '16 glasses of beer' is not a class we want here" (May 20, 1886, 2). Snow presents, in two sentences, a widely held perception that linked shorter hours with the presumed drunkenness, laziness, atheism, and anti-Americanism of immigrant workers in Chicago. To label the Knights (and all other labor organizations) the "Knights of darkness" sums up all of these ideological components in one word: *evil*.

Antilabor sentiments in the Protestant press also provoked reactions from its readership, who were appalled by the blanket condemnation of organized labor. Readers recognized that many of those in the labor movement were "excellent Christian men, and they adhere to the societies [unions] from an honest conviction that thus they may obtain redress from genuine grievances and positive acts of injustice" (*Living Church*, June 12, 1886, 169). This letter writer (signed A. P. Z.) goes on to recount life in a steel town in which workers were laid off for three months only to go back to work at severely reduced wages, due to the debts that had been incurred during their layoff. The writer asks, "Is this justice?"

Throughout 1885 and the spring of 1886, Protestant leaders criticized employers for the violence and unrest as much as they did workers. Employers mandated Sunday work and created such conditions in working-class communities that saloons were the only escape. Workers driven to extreme measures by factory owners who kept them overworked and underpaid came as no surprise to some clergy. The *Advance* went so far as to argue, in reporting on a strike for shorter hours by New York streetcar conductors, that the workers were "clearly in the right. . . . Street-car conductors have been subjected to one of the worst forms of slavery . . . compelled to work from twelve to eighteen hours, with only a few minutes allowed for their meals." Its analysis of the strike implicated employers no less than labor: "We believe that when strikers assume the form of a mob and undertake by force to interrupt traffic, they should be dealt with summarily, and punished as any other law-breakers; but we hold that all these strikes have their root in the injustice done the laborer on the part of corporations" (March 11, 1886, 152).

Ultimately, the dynamite bomb that exploded on May 4, 1886, did two things to and for the eight-hour movement. It marginalized anarchists and other radical activists within the movement. CTLA president Mark Crawford was reported to have observed that the eight-hour campaign had been a success until the bomb was thrown and "years of work neutralized and the movement killed" (Messer-Kruse 2011, 137). It also raised the anti-Semitic specter of a shaggy-bearded, hook-nosed radical, an archvillain, an evil force from which workers needed deliverance. Yet fear, stirred up by the bomb and ten years of intensifying conflict between capital and labor, did not only stir up repression of the labor movement. Public fear also generated dialogue. Like the railroad strikes of 1877, the campaign of 1886 and its aftermath drew serious public and religious considerations of workers' demands.

It must be said, however, that not all employers were opposed to the principles expressed by the eight-hour movement, although most remained cautious and suspicious of it. Edward P. Allis, of Alliance Iron Works, believed in the principle of eight hours as a sufficiently long workday, although he also believed that other conditions industry faced made such a general change unwise at the moment. Others, in the wake of the Haymarket events, reflected on the need for compromise and negotiation between capital and labor. The editors of the *Advance* reported on the views of employers outside of Chicago. Former Milwaukee mayor John M. Stowell of Cream City Iron Works, a factory whose workers did not strike, believed "in shorter hours or more pay for the workmen, and both as soon as may be. I believe in leveling up . . . meet labor with prudent concessions. Brawn has rights as well as brain. The contest should not be forced. A wise compromise is not only the dictate of wisdom, but it is becoming a necessity to save us from anarchy." Julius Goldsmith, vice president of the Brand Stove Company, took a similar view. "The solution of the labor problem must be sought in improved relations of confidence and mutual interest between employer and employee. It cannot be reached by force or law. . . . Labor organizations must be recognized by the employer, but on the other hand strikes, lock-outs, or boycotts must become a thing of the past, they being decidedly un-American" (May 27, 1886, 326). Others went further. Charles C. Bonney, head of the American Bar and president of the Citizens' Law and Order League, observed in an address at the Union Park New Jerusalem Church: "Let the echoes of the Haymarket bomb awake them to their duty. Not merely to spasmodic contributions to a charity fund, however noble and sacred, but to the permanent support of those safeguards of civilization without which accumulations of property rest on shifting sands" (1886, 35).

Reducing the hours of labor and recognizing trade unions were ideas slowly being embraced by some employers. In August 1886, three months after the Haymarket affair, even Andrew Carnegie expressed his opinion that "the eight-hour movement is not without substantial foundation. Works that run day and night should be operated with three sets of men, each working eight hours" (1962, 114). It is clear, however, that Carnegie, as an employer, was ahead of his time in expressing such beliefs about eight-hour reform as a means to improve industrial efficiency. Yet these employers built their sympathy on economic rather than religious or moral grounds, as well as on expediency. Eight hours could improve production as much by making it more efficient. But adopting the eight-hour system could improve relations with workers and inaugurate class peace on the factory floor, saving capitalism from "anarchy."

Protestant condemnation of employers for their greed and unwillingness to fulfill their religious obligations to employees was an important dimension of church-capital-labor relations that is too often left out of historical accounts of the labor movement. Clergy responded to real conflicts that their local churches and the city as a whole faced. Rev. R. Heber Newton, at his church on Forty-Eighth Street, used his pulpit to address employers in his own congregation:

> Dangerous classes, I do not find them in the slums, but in the chairs of political economy and the seats of enormous wealth, where brains and wealth unite in the chorus, "It can't be helped." Woe for us in our civilization if so it be. But my friends, it is a lie of the devil. . . . The duty of the pulpit is clear in such an emergency. It must speak with calm words on behalf of peace and with fearless words on behalf of justice. . . . One Hell's Mills is enough to turn thousands of workingmen into demons. (*KL,* May 22, 1886, 2)

Challenging employers in such direct terms from the pulpit was risky for clergy. Newton's sermon provoked loud comments from the congregation when several people left the church while Newton was still speaking, but Newton carried on to speak on labor's behalf.

Strikes, poverty and extreme wealth, growing sympathy for socialism and anarchism among laborers, and the obvious disregard for the basic religious holy day, Sunday, by employers required clergy to create their own oppositional understanding toward industrial conditions, steeped in Protestant tradition. So long as actual social conditions remained in harmony with the language of the work ethic, frugality, and temperance, as they had in the immediate postwar decade, Protestant leaders threw their support behind employers and characterized labor's demands as generally unreasonable. Social instability caused by chronic unemployment during the depression of the 1870s was exacerbated by industrial conflicts over hours and wages. While the bomb thrown in the Haymarket square in 1886 did provoke the hysteria of xenophobia of the clergy, that bomb was also the historical linchpin for instigating widespread sympathy for social reform efforts. As clergy awareness of actual living conditions of most of Chicago's working classes became widely publicized, a moral code that only condemned the poor for their poverty could not account for the fact that long hours, low wages, and no work contributed to the deterioration of Chicago and raised the threat of social revolution generally. Social reform and a new morality to regulate industry had to come from those who gained great wealth at the expense of others—employers themselves.

> We may cover the pages of our statute books with laws regulating strikes and inflicting severest penalties on those who organize resistance to the individual liberty whether of employer or workman; we may drill regiments and perfect our police; the safety and welfare of a State is not in these things, it is in the contentment and loyalty of its people. And these come by a different road. When capitalists and employers of labor have forever dismissed the fallacy, which may be true enough in the domain of political economy, but it is essentially false in the domain of religion, that labor and laborer alike a commodity to be bought or sold, employed or dismissed, paid or underpaid, as the market shall decree; . . . when the well-being of our fellow-men, their homes and food, their pleasures and their higher moral and spiritual necessities, shall be seen to be matters concerning which we may not dare to say: "Am I my brother's keeper?"; then, but not until then, may we hope to heal those grave social divisions. (*Living Church,* May 22, 1886, 124)

Whether they supported employers or supported workers, Protestants kept their aim at preserving the integrity of community life and harmony as best they could and condemned activities by either party that threatened it. That clergy had a part to play in social reform was never disputed. The goal was clear: to shape the social and political order in accord with Protestant Christian principles and to obviate the progression of industrial warfare. But how would this best be accomplished? On the one hand, it was clear for most clergy that their role ought to stay within the moral and religious realm. But these leaders also worked with the assumption that their moral teaching ought to be brought to bear in the lives of "all duly instructed Christians." As clergy confronted the limits of their "purely spiritual" influence on a just social order, it became clear that to win the alienated working classes back to the churches, it would be necessary to apply pressure directly to those members of congregations who actually could effect industrial reforms.

Protestant clergy, some uneasily and others more willingly, began to take an active, prophetic role in order to secure much-needed reform, certainly, but also to ensure that Protestant churches remained relevant institutions. The *Advance*, at a point when most Protestants attributed the lack of church attendance by workers to their moral inferiority, highlighted the possibility that the church could regain lost ground among the working classes if it took a stance more sympathetic with their needs:

> It is for those involved in the crisis before us, that we have invoked the interposition of the Church. We invoke it likewise for her own sake. If she can bring these contending hosts to terms, if she can gather to herself that part of them among whom she is almost unknown, it will be well for her as for them. Humanly speaking, there can be no greater triumph in store for her than the recovery of the laboring classes. They have hitherto gone far astray. Not understanding her, and we must add, not being understood by her, or by her members, they have regarded her with indifference, if not aversion. Could they be called back, could they be made to feel that the Church is their rightful place, it would be the beginning of a new era in Christian history. (February 8, 1872, 2)

Fourteen years later, this sentiment was echoed by the editors of the *Living Church*. "Our missions to the poor will fail as long as our missions to the rich are powerless. We shall reach 'the masses' by subduing to Christ and His law the conscience of those in whose keeping are the bodies and souls of the toiling millions. The Church of Christ is the only labor union wherein the brotherhood of all men can be realized, and the inequalities of human conditions can be reformed" (June 19, 1886, 185).

Clergy regarded themselves as central to bringing about social and industrial peace, despite differences in opinion over strategy. Entrusted with extending Protestant Christianity into all areas of social life, Protestant ministers actively engaged the labor movement and the eight-hour campaigns in their pulpits and newspapers and through their own direct involvement with labor reformers.

Through the 1870s and 1880s, through press and pulpit, ministers continued to act as spokesmen for employers and opposed the majority or organized labor's efforts to institute an eight-hour day in Chicago. But as the writings from the time illustrate, employers received two messages simultaneously from clergy: employers had the right to govern their industries as they saw fit, but the church, broadly defined, would oppose business practices that systematically turned out large numbers of able men onto the streets, depriving them of their livelihoods in order to accumulate more profits or refused to concede reasonable demands for industrial reform. When unemployment, strikes, riots, bombs, and mental and physical exhaustion threatened to completely disrupt the social order, Protestant leaders began to withdraw their support for employer interests. This is not to say that clergy as a group immediately championed labor causes, but over time Protestant clergy came to see the eight-hour movement as a vehicle for social harmony in the city. As labor continued to frame support for shorter hours in religious terms, clergy did the same, seeing the eight-hour day as a means to mobilize support for the temperance and Sabbatarian movements and to reinforce Protestant morality among an increasingly Catholic working class. As the eight-hour movement recovered from Haymarket, new waves of mobilization emerged to continue the fight to reduce the hours of labor for workingmen, for workingwomen, and for children. With these new mobilization efforts came new ideological contests between workers, employers, and clergy.

CHAPTER 5

A "New Consciousness" for Constructing a Morality of Leisure

The eight-hour movement and tumultuous events at the Haymarket square in the opening days of May 1886 represented the culmination of another major cycle of eight-hour protests in Chicago. Descriptions of those events ever since have been colored by analysts' particular viewpoints (Messer-Kruse 2011; Green 2006). Kinsley (1946, 83), for example, regarded the events of 1886 as labor upheavals resulting from "poorly paid and poorly organized [workers] . . . led astray by vindictive and emotional German Anarchists." Other scholars characterize Haymarket as a landmark of labor mobilization but the end of labor's power in the nineteenth century, spurring repression of unions and labor newspapers, not only in Chicago, but also in other industrial centers of the United States (Adelman 1976; Green 2006). Samuel Gompers pronounced that it "demolished the eight-hour movement" (Avrich 1984, 429) or at least rendered it largely impotent (B. Nelson 1988; Messer-Kruse 2011). These characterizations were not overstatements considering the extremes taken to shut down radical labor newspapers and close halls where radical reformers spoke, alongside police repression and employer offensives to reestablish ten-hour or more workdays in areas such as the packinghouses and building trades (Green 2006).

However, despite overt repression and dire forecasts for the movement, the story of its effects on the eight-hour movement is complex. Chicago eight-hour advocates took only a brief hiatus from organizing for shorter hours. Kinsley (1946) notes that the hanging of the four anarchists accused of instigating the Haymarket bombing was actually linked to a renewal of the eight-hour demand by labor. Schneirov and Suhrbur (1988) also argue that Haymarket increased membership in the carpenters' union, as anarchist carpenters rejoined their locals and renewed organizing for an eight-hour day in 1887. While the public fear and hostility directed at the labor movement were certainly a potent repressive force resulting in the virtual obliteration of many radical labor organizations and the Knights of Labor, too much ground had been gained to prevent reformers from reorganizing and reenergizing the movement.

The events of the 1870s and 1880s profoundly altered the political opportunities for the eight-hour movement in ways that limited it but also in ways that reignited public debate about the future of the industrial order (Green 2006). Political opposition to the eight-hour movement began to fragment. By 1886 Chicago political elites, fueled as much by a growing appreciation for the inherent justice of shorter hours as by a growing presence of labor-backed candidates as election competitors, increasingly supported implementing an eight-hour day. Mayor Carter Harrison had been a firm supporter of the eight-hour movement during his 1886 campaign. Harrison was ousted from his post due to elite assertions that he abetted the anarchist conspiracy by allowing them to organize and spread their plans for revolution and was replaced by Republican mayor John A. Roche with the support of the city's "law and order" business elites (Green 2006, 246). But within three years, Roche's successor, Mayor DeWitt Clinton Creiger, and the city council passed an ordinance granting the eight-hour day to all city employees, with overtime pay if more hours were worked. Although this law covered only a small percentage of workers, its significance for the broader eight-hour movement was twofold. First, local ordinances shaped workers' perceptions that political support for reform existed in principle and, second, even limited ordinances now set legal precedents for more comprehensive shorter-hours legislation.

A small number of business elites were beginning, however slowly, to adapt to a changing industrial landscape that included the presence of organized labor. The eight-hour system had already been in force for stonecutters since the 1860s and had gone on without challenge. In shops where other types of workers had been able to demand and enforce shorter hours, employers saw that reducing the hours of labor would not result in an economic apocalypse. As the 1880s gave way to the 1890s, arbitration was heard much more frequently as a solution to impasses between employers and organized labor. Prominent businessmen such as Cyrus McCormick and Marshall Field rejected the notion of bargaining with their employees on what they considered to be their right to conduct their business affairs free from interference. Nevertheless, finding ways to minimize class hostilities and prevent the production losses that inevitably accompanied drawn-out strikes and lockouts was becoming a priority for more and more employers.

Another factor shifting the public debates following the 1886 eight-hour movement was the emergence of a new awareness among Protestant clergy regarding the oppressive industrial conditions facing workers. In his *Death in the Haymarket,* James Green makes two observations about the effects of the Haymarket affair on Protestant clergy. Green asserts that Haymarket "traumatized many Protestant clergymen and church-goers . . . and exacerbated the hostility to organized labor." He also suggests that it "pushed many middle-class people and their ministers . . . into streetcar suburbia, where they could escape the lava of a social volcano that seemed ready to blow again at any time" (2006, 279–80). There was, however, a third response among ministers. Protestant clergy addressed class animosity and industrial conditions from their urban pulpits and in the Protestant press, spurred on by growing interest among their middle-class congregants (G. Smith 2000). This awareness did not create immediate or unanimous support for labor among Protestant clergy. However, as the nineteenth century drew to its close, more clergy used their moral authority to build a systematic critique of the new industrial order, calling both employers and workers to act more charitably and reasonably with each other based on an assumption that they shared interests in maintaining the class peace and prosperity of Chicago and in the living out of Christian principles. Strikes, reports on industrial conditions, and renewed attempts to limit the hours of women and children all gave clergy opportunities to use a "new conscience" to address the eight-hour question from the vantage point of Protestant theology, and it provided a motivating force for trying to actually change these conditions through coalitions with workers before Chicago disintegrated into class warfare and upheaval, as it had in 1877 and 1886.

Regrouping and Relaunching Eight Hours

In 1887 and 1888, Chicago's Protestant press, the Knights of Labor, and socialists and anarchists all continued to speak out on the eight-hour question and how clergy might support the movement. The Methodist *Northwestern Christian Advocate* in two separate articles in 1887 openly called for reducing the workday for laborers to eight hours, which, in one article, Rev. C. H. Zimmerman charged, "would give workingmen time and means for intellectual, social, and spiritual culture" (October 19, 1887, 3). In an earlier article, Zimmerman noted that if "all of us as consumers [who] take advantage in reduced prices for our goods . . . once realized that there is a hardship of great and crushing weight in the ten-hour day, there can be no doubt that the change would be made at whatever the cost" (February 9, 1887, 2). The Reverend M. Wolsey Stryker reflected a similar sentiment in a sermon at the Fourth Presbyterian Church. Stryker told his congregation to picture "the wage worker earning a paltry pittance and kept half-starving, while his employer piled up his millions, and these dollars were the price of human lives laid down on the altar of necessity." Stryker went on: "I would go to Hell's back-door to help this cause now waged . . . for fewer hours and better pay, and how much [more] Christian would it be for you to refuse to buy anything from the shops after 12 o'clock on Saturday to let these hundreds of tired toilers have the Lord's Day in which to read their Bible" (*CT,* March 14, 1887, 8). Clergy more and more linked the structure of industrial capitalism and the conditions experienced by workers that drove them to join the eight-hour movement. Ministers also began to describe how Christians could live out their moral values and help labor redeem time through an eight-hour day with their actions as consumers.

These ideas drew fire from parishioners, especially in wealthy congregations, who maintained that ministers should not meddle in industrial affairs. The Protestant press took this criticism head-on. The Congregational *Advance* joined the Methodist press in critiquing the attitude of those who saw religion as having no place in industry:

> Many a pew-door has had a sharp slam in the face of the minister, because he was trying to get a little bit of the ethics of righteousness and brotherhood into the moral life of the nation. Men have sometimes taken the position too, that religion and business ought to be kept separated. Trading, it is said is one thing, and worshipping God quite another. . . . But attitudes like this involve an entire misconception of both religion and business. No man ought to think of his religion as being a religion at all unless it is something he can take with him everywhere. (October 20, 1887, 664)

The *Northwestern Christian Advocate* made the point more directly by framing such an attitude as something other than true Christian belief in arguing that "a religion which does not control the actions of citizens as well as of the worshipper is not the religion of Jesus of Nazareth. Genuine Christianity will go with a man . . . to the shop or store as well as to the sanctuary (April 9, 1887, 3). In rare cases, some clergy went further than this, critiquing the wealthy and correlating Christ's teachings with socialism. Rev. Bird Wilkinson of Bethesda Baptist Church, pastor of what is described as a large congregation of the "elite of the colored population" of the city, was one such pastor:

Christ came to preach the Gospel to the poor. Christ would be called a socialist in Chicago today. . . . The rich man is simply a steward of God. But what stewards they are! They use their wealth to rob the poor. . . . It doesn't take the modern Christian long to get selfish. Christ went further than socialism. He preached and practiced communism. . . . The church has become as corrupt as society itself. . . . God intends that Christianity shall rule upon earth. The world may call it socialism; I will call it Christianity. (*Labor Enquirer,* August 27, 1887, 1)

But how best to bring genuine Christianity into eight-hour struggles remained a hotly debated point. There were those who believed that having "good men who believed in God" leading labor reforms would save the movement from the "suicidal and fatal . . . alienation of the wage-working classes from the Christian religion" (*NWCA,* May 11, 1887, 8). A few local clergy spoke at meetings organized by the CTLA and Chicago Knights and were verbally supportive of moderate efforts to achieve reform. But verbal support, while appreciated, seemed to workers far too timid a response to achieve such a monumental reform effort. The editor of the *Knights of Labor,* George Detweiller, characterized local clergy who gathered to discuss reducing the hours of labor as "the most impracticable set of noodles in existence." While clergy signed petitions and passed resolutions at the denominational level and through ministerial associations in support of labor reform, what eight-hour advocates really wanted was for the clergy to "come down out of the clouds and assist us to accomplish practical results in a practical manner" (October 29, 1887, 8).

But slowly the simplistic views of clergy were developing into relatively more complex considerations of shorter hours. Solutions for most Protestant clergy lay neither in the unregulated market nor in its radical overthrow. In a clear statement of what was the emerging Protestant middle way in addressing capital and labor, an article beginning with what seems to be another familiar criticism of radical labor ideology in the *Advance* quickly turns into a critique of the ideological excesses of *both* capital and labor.

What is anarchism? The fiendish folly of the Haymarket Square tells it all. . . . From excessive individualism there has since come to be a reaction in the minds of many to a foolish extreme of socialism. The thing that is needed is not to substitute socialism for individualism. . . . [I]t is necessary to "socialize the individual," so as to make each man feel, whether rich or poor, whether employer or employee, that no man lives to himself, and that everyone should consider the interest of others as well as of himself, then the solution of these industrial and social questions will begin to appear in sight. The truth is the modern "industrial community" includes all of us.

> No one-sided scheme of sheer selfishness will ever settle the trouble. Which is worse, socialism or unsocialism, may not be easy to say. The welfare of society needs neither the one nor the other. (May 19, 1887, 312)

In rejecting both unrestrained industry and revolutionary socialism and desiring to establish a spirit of "unselfish mutual regard," the *Advance* suggests there could be middle ground for practical solutions to develop, though the writer never suggests what those solutions might be.

Washington Gladden, among the leading voices of the rising Social Gospel movement, went further than only hinting at solutions and called for economic power sharing between capital and labor in the Baptist *Standard*. "The solution is in the power of the Christian employer. . . . All he has to do is admit his laborers to an industrial partnership with himself by giving them a fixed share in the profits of production to be divided among them in proportion to their earnings, at the end of the year. . . . This is not the ordinary cooperatives scheme, since the capitalist retains his larger rights; neither is it a method of socialistic distribution, being voluntary. It is rather an application in business affairs of what closely resembles the 'golden rule'" (January 6, 1887, 4). Others saw the labor problem as a "problem of unflinching acceptance by both parties alike of the infinitely fruitful law of Christ, every aspect and precept of which is holy, just and good." In offering up the opening of a Young Men's Christian Association clubhouse in New York City by Cornelius Vanderbilt as a laudable illustration of the point, the *Advance* was willing to "hail with eager approval and hope . . . every conspicuous exhibition of its happy operation" (October 20, 1887, 664).

From workers' perspective, however, such religious musings by clergy, and even their verbal support for the eight-hour day, were largely pointless without action. Labor's consensus was that trade unions themselves had done more for the workingmen in Chicago than all of the churches and clergy combined (*Inter-Ocean,* March 14, 1887, 8). The *Knights of Labor* was quite pointed in expressing its thoughts about clergy interest in finding solutions to the problem of the hours of labor. "You may as well sing Psalms to a dead horse, as to meet in your weekly assemblies and discuss the evil and propose remedies among yourselves. If you expect to accomplish anything you must come down to the dead level of commonsense and assist those who are trying to lift themselves out of the depths of despair" (October 29, 1887, 8).

The radical press, back in operation following the Haymarket repression, was equally put off by clergy asserting solutions for problems that they did not understand and for remaining aloof from the realities Chicago's workers faced. The chief difficulty with clergy was that they had forgotten their principal mission of mediating between the wealthy and the poor, "to be somehow the link between the high and the low, to give the miserable and downtrodden hope and contentment, to humble the haughtiness of the strong." Consequently, caught up in and distracted by their growing wealth, Protestantism was becoming the exclusive province of the elite. As the editor of the *Labor Enquirer* observes:

> We need not particularize the numerous things said about the Protestant denominations. They too fall under the general condemnation. . . . Some of our wealthy churches have forgotten this: They have become places for the fortunate few, where, as it were, crowds are deprecated. . . . Everything in and around them proclaim them to be exclusive ecclesiastical clubs for the accommodation of persons of $5,000 a year and upward. . . . It is all very nice, all very beautiful and aesthetic, all very correct and in good form, but the spirit of Christ, where is that? (April 16, 1887, 1)

Protestant obsessions with building grand edifices and providing more social gathering spaces for elites distorted the moral messages heard in most churches. Sermon after sermon quoted in the labor press, albeit selectively chosen for effect, reinforced an abstract spirituality that was disconnected and irrelevant to the actual problems that masses of workers faced. After detailing Thanksgiving sermon quotes from Protestant pulpits around the city, the editor of the *Labor Enquirer* remained disbelievingly speechless:

> Comment is unnecessary. Words are inadequate to express the feelings of the true philanthropist after reading or hearing the ebullitions of the bloated, surfeited devotees of the church on Thanksgiving Day. . . . [S]uch sermons are not only obnoxious and disgusting, but they present questions like these: Is it possible that these men are so far removed from the great mass of the people, and so blinded by church and class prejudice that they actually believe what they say, or are they all a set of hypocritical liars, bent on the destruction of humanity by persistently ignoring facts and propagating fallacies instead of using their positions and influence to educate the people in the true science of economics. Why not assist the people, helping to make opportunities for them to help themselves, instead of conniving at their robbery, persecution, and murder? (December 3, 1887, 1)

But the seemingly ineffectual work of passing resolutions supporting workers and criticizing employers was not without its costs to clergy. When the ministers of Punxsutawney, Pennsylvania, passed a resolution in sympathy with mine workers on strike against the Punxsutawney Coal Mining Company, a subsidiary of the Buffalo, Rochester, and Pittsburgh Railway, and censured the companies, mine owners went on the offensive against these clergy. The *Journal of United Labor* reported that "the corporation turned their poisonous fangs toward the church, and has since manifested every unkindness for the same. In one instance, orders were given to the 'Pinkies' to prevent one of the ministers from using the railroad track as a path from his church to his home, and caused the minister and a goodly portion of his congregation, including women and children, to wade ankle deep in mud rather than allow a 'time honored custom' of walking on their tracks" (April 17, 1890, 1). While shocking to clergy, this kind of attack came as no surprise to labor reformers, used to such animosity from employers, who believed clergy remained unwilling to risk their positions in elite churches.

At least some clergy were aware of the way they were perceived by working people, but rarely did they address it as candidly as Rev. Louis Osborne, rector of Trinity Episcopal Church, in a letter to the *Knights of Labor* that accompanied his check to renew his yearly subscription. Osborne, taking a moderate approach, reminded the Knights that the clergy were in a difficult but important place in the struggles between capital and labor.

> I know that radicals, even "loud-mouthed agitators" are necessary to the triumph of every good cause. . . . Our only knowledge of the founder of Christianity is from the New Testament. This tells us not that, he was a "loud-mouthed agitator," rather that "he did not strive nor envy, nor cause his voice to be heard in the streets." If it be wrong for a clergyman to misjudge an "agitator," is it less wrong for the agitator to utter stupid lies against a church and its ministers, which neither help the cause of labor nor religion, but only widens the breach between many good people, whose end and aim are the same, who might be friends and helpers of one another? . . . An honest, thoughtful, temperate plea for the rights of the wage-earners lands [the preacher] between the upper and the nether mill stones. The capitalists baptize him "socialist," the "agitator" brands him as a "weak-kneed old fogy." . . . Only extremists are wanted now, and in the Church, the State, the Labor Union, sober-minded, moderate counsels fall upon deaf ears. (November 3, 1888, 1)

Yet such a defense did not hold much weight among those who understood Christianity as a liberating force for labor.

> Their Christianity consists in going to churches, singing psalms occasionally, listening to eloquent sermons and trying to get the better of their neighbors during the rest of the time. . . . The doctrines of Christianity are acknowl-

> edged by professing Christians, but *they are not practiced*. . . . [T]hese glorious doctrines are as little liked today as they were 1,900 years ago. They were denounced as fanatical and revolutionary, and their propagators were murdered by law and sent into jail because they preached doctrine that proposed and rendered necessary a social reformation. . . . Christian doctrines are socialistic, revolutionary; they favor the organization of society on the principle of *equal duties and equal rights* and they call upon men not to accumulate riches and to do other things which employers of labor as a rule, and rich men generally . . . will *not* do. . . . They profess to be Christians and yet they declare that Christianity *cannot* and *must not* be reduced to practice. . . . And why? . . . They do not like true Christianity because it teaches the doctrines which today form the fundamental principles of the great labor movement of the world. (*Bakers' Journal*, December 1, 1888, 2)

The anarchist *Alarm* was more sarcastic in its standing criticism of the church as a principal obstacle that the labor movement faced:

> Working men continue to look upon the church as a chump-trap baited with insurance policies against imaginary dangers as long as it stands as the exponent of existing wrongs, and with nasal-twang seeks to divert our eyes from the land and exchange to the beatitude of sitting astride a damp cloud and playing "Old-Hundredth" on a Jews-harp. Give us access to what you claim your god gave us and in the increased responsibility which only liberty can bestow we will have more leisure to consider the acceptance of a complimentary ticket to your Christ's weekly soiree. (July 21, 1888, 2)

As a new phase of eight-hour protest began, labor reformers were more skeptical than ever of getting practical support from clergy just at a time when Protestant clergy were poised to take more supportive positions on reducing the hours of labor.

The Carpenters' Eight-Hour Strike

At the end of the 1880s, skilled craft unionists in the American Federation of Labor took over the leadership of the eight-hour movement. At its 1888 St. Louis convention, the AFL announced that the eight-hour movement would be inaugurated with a general strike on May 1, 1890 (*CT*, November 26, 1888, 5). But this revived movement also included a new strategy. The AFL would fight for an eight-hour day, industry by industry. AFL leaders, headed by Samuel Gompers, in contrast to many rank-and-file workers, steered clear of all "visionary" thinking about labor reform and focused on achieving practical economic reform for labor (Green 2006, 287). Convention delegates planned for mass meetings to be held on four days every year: Washington's Birthday, May Day, the Fourth of July, and Labor Day. But not all delegates agreed with this strategy to revive a general movement for eight hours, reigniting animosities and entrenched differences of strategy and ideology within the labor movement.

In debates within the AFL, socialist Thomas Morgan refused to endorse a movement whose tool was the strike unless it was "a strike at the ballot box," reflecting lingering suspicions about using more militant action without simultaneously ensuring support among politicians to pass enforceable eight-hour laws. Morgan was ideologically outnumbered by those in the AFL who believed this to be the best strategy to win an eight-hour day. Similarly, Terrance Powderly of the Knights of Labor, already weakened by the repression following Haymarket, was suspicious of another general strike for an eight-hour day. The *Knights of Labor* paper hinted that Powderly did not want to support any movement that would lead to a repeat of 1886. Chicago Knights, however, felt strongly that because the Knights of Labor platform demanded an eight-hour day, Knights were morally bound to stand by the movement (*KL,* May 18, 1888, 1). Radical labor unions affiliated with the Central Labor Union remained committed to direct action. They rejected Powderly's contention that strikes for shorter hours would only hurt the labor movement, attacking Powderly's call for an educational program to raise the consciousness of the public and of workers on eight-hour reform: "No Terry, the veneering is too thin. . . . If you could but understand that the polity of the movement is toward voluntary co-operation and not knife this tendency by betrayal into political camps, the original dream of the order would today be far nearer a bright realization. . . . But alas . . . Powderly's failure to comprehend this, his narrow provincialism, his 'creedal' affiliations, his irresolute femininity of character, his desire to pose as a harmonizer, and his insane overwhelming vanity, renders an educational campaign hopeless" (*Alarm,* April 7, 1888, 2). While the ideal of an eight-hour workday could mobilize workers, creating practical unity and solidarity across the three factions of the movement was a greater challenge.

Nevertheless, movement organizing among workers and attempts to gain support of the religious community went forward. The Presbyterian *Interior* noted that in working to establish the eight-hour day, a dual strategy to convince the public of the justice of the cause and to secure the voluntary agreement of employers demonstrated that the AFL was "directed with a wisdom and conservatism rare in such associations" (February 28, 1889, 1). More support came from Rev. W. E. Sillence from the Union Tabernacle

Congregational Church and Rev. Calvin S. Blackwell of the Central Church of Christ, who spoke at a mass meeting organized by the Trades and Labor Assembly in support of the eight-hour day (*Record*, February 28, 1889, 1). But while attitudes were shifting, Protestant clergy were still divided on the issue. When asked about the eight-hour struggle in Chicago, a presiding elder in the Methodist Church still feared that fewer hours at work would lead to more drunkenness and crime. Elder Trusdell argued that "a man who works from ten to fifteen hours will be tired enough to go home and stay there" (*KL*, April 20, 1889, 1). Such an attitude garnered the derision of the *Knights of Labor*, who called it "antebellum," comparing it to the logic held by many slave owners who saw long hours of exhausting labor the only way to keep a slave out of trouble (*KL*, April 27, 1889, 1).

Workers both desired the intervention of clergy on behalf of eight-hour reform as evidence of their embrace of authentic Christianity and recognized that clergy were also an obstacle to reform (Burns 2013). Thomas Morgan summed up this assessment of organized religion at a lecture sponsored by the Socialist Labor Party: "'We don't attack religion, that's alright; we don't jump on Christianity but on *churchianity*. We attack those men at the head who are but the tools of robbers and thieves.' Again the applause broke forth. 'If a man is religious at all,' said a man in the rear part of the hall, 'he can't help being a Socialist. Christ was one. T'isn't religion that seeks to down us, but the fellers in it'" (*CT*, January 14, 1889, 3). As protest to shorten the workday intensified, the lack of responsiveness from the city's clergy united many workers within the eight-hour movement in seeing organized religion as a hindrance rather than help, though some eight-hour reformers still hoped that Protestant leaders might be converted to their cause.

The city's preparation for the announced eight-hour campaign began, in 1889, with a Fourth of July demonstration and picnic at Cheltenham Beach in South Chicago. Six thousand people attended the AFL-sponsored event and heard Mayor Creiger, Samuel Gompers, Congressman Frank Lawler, and Henry Demarest Lloyd argue the benefits and justice of the eight-hour system. Mayor Creiger was especially well received, because the Chicago city council had recently passed its municipal eight-hour ordinance. However, the reporter from the *Tribune* noted that although Mayor Creiger "said not a word about eight hours . . . his presence . . . convinced his hearers of his sympathy with the movement." As president of the AFL, Samuel Gompers expressed, "ominously," as the *Tribune* saw it, his view that workers "must force [employers] by the power of their organization to submit to the inevitable" (*CT*, July 5, 1889, 1).

Henry Demarest Lloyd took the most hopeful approach of the three speakers, framing the eight-hour movement as part of the unfolding narrative of moral justice and progress, reminiscent of the speeches during the 1869 campaign:

> This is a new sound in the strains of the day—a strange chord in the songs of jubilee. The crowd is chanting choruses of the deliverance that has been, labor breaks in with the deeper tones and strikes the notes of a deliverance that is to be . . . seen from the right side, it is growth; it is revolution only when viewed from the side of evil, whose unjust privileges and vested wrongs are to be disturbed. . . . The labor movement is a distinct stage in the march of progress with a definite, clearly marked mission. That mission on its constructive side is to extend into industry the brotherhood already recognized in politics and religion and to teach men as workers the love and equality which they profess as citizens and worshippers. . . . The organization of workingmen is today the great harbinger of universal peace. . . . [I]t is the only important movement among the peoples against the continuance of the savage and monopolistic wars that disgrace mankind. (*CT,* July 5, 1889, 1)

Lloyd offered a twist in his speech and concluded with an indictment of the church for its silence and inaction on the matter.

> The labor movement is the most religious movement of the day, for it carries the Golden Rule into the market, and insists that the Gospel which men profess in their families they shall also profess and hold in their factories. . . . Why don't the workingmen go to church? Because they are ahead of the church. . . . Because the church steadfastly refuses to leave off repeating the glittering generalities and lacks either the courage or intelligence to apply the test and language of the ten commandments to the practices of men who sit in the high places in the congregations. Because it contents itself with admiring Nathan for telling King David to his face: "Thou art the man," but does not do the same to our nineteenth-century robbers and murders. (Lloyd 1909, 16–17)

The Brotherhood of Carpenters Union had been selected by the AFL to lead the eight-hour strike in 1890 (Schneirov and Suhrbur 1988). On April 7, six thousand carpenters and an unknown number of nonunion men walked out for a forty-cent wage increase and an eight-hour day. The size of the walkout amazed the union by including almost all local carpenters, and it even amazed Chicago contractors, who reported that the strike was bigger than they had anticipated (*CT,* April 8, 1890, 1).

Other workers threw their entire support behind the carpenters. A week and a half into the strike, ten thousand people gathered on the lakefront in solidarity. Twenty unions and three assemblies of the Knights of Labor marched in parade to the event, where labor leaders and others addressed the crowds. Lawyer James T. McShane addressed several key points in his speech that illustrated the change in thinking that was in the air regarding the eight-hour day. First, McShane noted that the gulf between rich and poor in Chicago was widening and that "there must be a leveling process sooner or later, and it is for the people of the country to say whether that shall come peaceably and quietly by increasing wages and reducing the hours of toil, or if it shall be spread like the thunderbolt of anarchy and carry death and destruction." McShane linked the eight-hour movement with peaceful change as opposed to violent change, not so much to disparage radical voices as to highlight how the resistance from employers made revolutionary upheavals inevitable:

> You gave your employers timely notice. They refused every overture and you were compelled to strike as a last resort. Strikes are evils, but sometimes unavoidable. If it was not for the fears of strikes the workingmen would not get many of the advantages they enjoy today. . . . The responsibility for the present strike was on those who refused to even consider the demands of the journeymen and placed them in the absurd position of refusing to negotiate with an organization while acting as an organization themselves. The strikers had repeatedly offered to arbitrate. The refusal of the contractors to do so showed their consciousness that their cause was weak. . . . The people of Chicago are awakening to the fact that a few men are paralyzing the industries of the city. Public opinion is being aroused, and your proposition to meet the contractors half way and their stubborn refusal will eventually crush them. The eyes of the world are upon you. This is the inauguration of the eight-hour movement. The workingmen of the whole country are with you. You are on trial. Let every man arise to the importance of the occasion. (*CT*, April 18, 1890, 1)

McShane saw that justice and the public were on the side of the eight-hour movement, which was reasonable in both its demands for reform and its strategies to achieve it. Reticent employers, unwilling either to consider shorter hours or to arbitrate, were the ones, in his words, "practicing anarchy."

Despite growing sentiments from Protestant clergy and the religious press that shortening the hours of labor was morally desirable, Protestants were still not united in supporting the carpenters' strike or the eight-hour movement generally. The *Interior* expressed a clear sense that eight-hour reform was limited by the forces of the market and had no clear religious mandate.

> The leading feature in the present contest is the eight-hour rule. IN THIS THERE IS NO MORAL PRINCIPLE INVOLVED. . . . This is not a question to be decided by resolution. An idle dreamer may long for a pot of gold, but the gold cannot be acquired by volition. . . . The truth underlying this question is this: the workman and his family each twenty-four hours consume or lay by the product of ten hours labor. If all producers agree to work but eight hours labor, then all producers must, per force, live upon the proceeds of eight-hour's labor, in bread, fuel, clothing, houses, furniture, education, pleasure, and recreation. There is no possible way of evading this law. It is as inexorable as gravitation. . . . In the sweat of our faces we must eat bread. If our work is poor, or but small in amount, we must eat poor bread—if it is large in amount or in value we may eat good bread and have abundance of it. (*Interior,* May 1, 1890, 4)

In contrast, three weeks later the Congregational *Advance* was prepared to discuss the desirability of the newly emerging theology of "Christian socialism," as a new way to talk about the practical application of Christ's teachings to labor reform.

> Christian Socialism, or whatever the phrase one sees fit to designate it by, bringing out into view the long half-hidden meaning in the example and word, and total gospel of the Son of Man, the world's Redeemer, replies: "Yes, precisely that; he that seeks his life shall lose it; inasmuch as ye have done it unto one of the least of these, ye have done it unto the Master; whatsoever ye would that men should do to you, do ye even so to them." These and other such divine utterances begin to be much more radical and many sided than was formerly suspected. . . . The true socialism begins with this, the hearty alliance of people who are conscientious and right-spirited in acting together, and so to effect for the good of all. (May 22, 1890, 390)

The national voice of Christian socialism came in the form of a new paper called the *Dawn,* first published in Boston in May 1889, designed to bring together the ideas of Christian reformers of all kinds regarding the many social and industrial problems that American society faced. Congregationalist pastor Rev. W. E. Sillence was the *Dawn*'s correspondent from Chicago until his death in 1891. Christian socialists called on all sympathetic Christians, as individuals, to "educate, agitate, and organize" and collectively to work for "gradual, scientific Socialist legislation" (*Dawn,* October 15, 1889, 1). Among the legislation advocated by the *Dawn* was the eight-hour workday, going so far as to claim that "the *Dawn* and the eight-hour movement are different manifestations of one movement, towards the realization of ethical democracy in trade" (May 1890, 35). Gathering a growing readership of progressive clergy, middle-class reformers and settlement-house workers, and educators, the *Dawn* and Christian socialism generally provided a context for the Protestant thinking regarding eight-hour reform to develop.

By May 1890, public support for the carpenters' eight-hour demand was spreading, and the united front of contractor resistance ebbed, as more and more builders gave in to the carpenters' demands. May Day drew an estimated fifty thousand people, equally split between workers marching in the parade and those spectators who were in the audience to hear the lakefront speeches (*CT,* May 2, 1890, 1). The *Tribune* observed that conditions in Chicago were more favorable for shorter-hour reform than had been the case in 1886 (May 5, 1890, 2). From the perspective of the press, this was due to two key factors. First, the eight-hour demand was made with a willingness on the part of the movement to use arbitration to achieve it, and, second, "there were no incendiary mottoes breathing hatred for capital, no banners bearing legends of hostility to law and order, no appeals to popular passion against schools, churches, corporations, and employers" (*CT,* May 2, 1890, 4; May 5, 1890, 2; Green 2006). Chicago's carpenters showed solidarity in their desire to win, and they had a broad base of support behind them. Within four days, the Carpenters and Builders Employers' Association surrendered, and within a month all the carpenters were back to work with an eight-hour day conceded absolutely (*CT,* May 6, 1890, 1). Moreover, on the heels of this victory, momentum for eight hours made another important gain. In 1891, when faced with strike threats by unions in the building trades engaged in preparation for the World's Columbian Exposition, Fair Board of Directors president Lyman Gage conceded an eight-hour day without a fight (*CT,* March 6, 1891, 2; March 7, 1891, 2).

But other groups of workers were not as successful. In April 1890, one thousand packinghouse workers, organized under the Packing Laborers' Union, prepared to strike for an eight-hour day on May 1, concurrently with the carpenters (*CT,* April 17, 1890, 2). The union faced the opposition of Philip Armour, the owner of the largest of the meatpacking houses, who claimed to support a universal eight-hour day but not one limited to Chicago alone, since local packers could not compete with other cities where the packing workers continued to work longer hours. Frank O'Neill, union president, observed that Armour would not compete with any other city, since he ran the packing industry all over the region (*CT,* April 28, 1890, 1). By May 1, the Packing Laborers' Union canceled its strike plan because they were not strong enough to mobilize the vast majority of packinghouse workers (*CT,*

May 1, 1890, 1). What became increasingly clear to Chicago workers was the principle that without the mass organization of workers, winning an eight-hour day would never succeed.

Chicago labor leaders continued the challenging work of organizing more workers in as yet unorganized industries, directly fueling the momentum of the eight-hour movement. The *Tribune* reported, "The carpenters' union has increased from 2,375 in May 1890 to 7,000 in May 1891. Architectural ironworkers 150–500, tin and sheet iron workers from 0 to 300, bookbindery girls from 0 to 100, sash, door, and blind workers from 0 to 1,500, cornice-makers from 150 to 700, machine woodworkers from 0 to 1,500, cement pavers from 0 to 100, ship carpenters from 0 to 300, carriage, wood, and iron workers from 30 to 300" (April 27, 1891, 9). By June 1891, 1,500 cabinetmakers walked out for shorter hours. Like the carpenters' strike of the previous year, employers initially refused to consider their demands. Employers from the Brunswick-Balke-Collender Company called the cabinetmakers' demands "absurd" and tried to argue that the workers quit only to have a holiday. The head of the A. H. Andrews & Company confidently recounted, "We are used to strikes. Our men are out. Their demands are preposterous. They presuppose the overturning of all our established rules of trade." Z. S. Holbrook, president of Carsley and East, went further and said that "no intelligent employer would consider those demands a moment. He would see every man in the cemetery first" (*CT,* September 2, 1891, 5). But just as W. P. Rend had predicted would happen in the coal industry, by October the cabinetmakers had won their strike. Smaller employers gave in to the demands of workers almost immediately, and all but these three large firms could not find men to replace strikers and so conceded defeat (*CT,* October 20, 1891, 3).

In the ensuing years, despite another severe economic downturn, workers kept up their demand for shorter hours. While an eight-hour day remained their chief goal, workers modified this demand as they saw fit based on what made sense to them in their respective industries. Chicago's west side shop clerks, who could work fourteen to fifteen hours, six days a week, began a concerted campaign to close shops earlier in the evenings and for two nights off each week (*CT,* January 9, 1893, 3; April 15, 1892, 3; February 13, 1893, A7). City boilermakers, carriage makers, and printers each adopted a nine-hour day as their target (*CT,* April 28, 1892, 7; January 23, 1893, 3; June 17, 1893, 2). Others continued to fight for national eight-hour legislation and for better enforcement of the existing Illinois eight-hour law (*CT,* December 20, 1892, 6). Emboldened by the public successes, more and more groups of workers were drawn into the struggle. It drew in more of Chicago's Protestant clergy as well.

Shifting Patterns of Labor's Religious Rhetoric

From the end of the 1880s through the 1890s, the religious message that the eight-hour day was a means to redeem time for Chicago workers underwent changes as a result of strike successes and failures as well as changing opportunities in the political realm. The craft-based faction represented by the Trades and Labor Assembly and the AFL replaced religious and moral language with completely secular rhetoric based on economics to mobilize solidarity around eight hours. AFL president Samuel Gompers offered responses to every economic objection raised by employers for not adopting shorter hours, but at no time did he suggest that the length of the workday was anything but an economic issue (*CT,* May 2, 1890, 1). AFL spokesman George Gunton (1889), in his eight-hour pamphlet, claimed that the eight-hour movement represented a phase of social evolution in the progress of modern society, but argued that shortening the workday would do nothing to disturb existing economic institutions. Gunton argued that presenting the eight-hour demand in humanitarian or religious terms actually alienated employers, who would adopt eight hours only when they perceived it to be in their economic interests to do so.

Likewise, Lemuel Danyrid, in another AFL-sponsored pamphlet, asserted that the eight-hour system should be instituted universally because economics, humanity, labor-saving machinery, and business interests demanded it. Danyrid's key themes consistently came back to improved production, improved consumption, and consequently improved earnings for employers. When discussing the "humanitarian" aspects of the movement, Danyrid saw the eight-hour movement as a struggle for "wider civilization," creating a "prosperous and contented people, with increased needs and the means to supply them" (1889, 10). This was social evolution in Danyrid's thinking. Workers would rise on the social scale and become new consumers within the industrial order once they were freed from overwork. His rhetoric was economic and pragmatic. Just as a six-day week became common practice without worry that workers were paid seven-day wages for a six-day workweek, the eight-hour workday should be established without any reduction in wages at all. Like Gunton, Danyrid saw no use for religion or for crafting religious arguments for what was only an economic question.

In the same year that Gunton's pamphlet was published, industrialist Andrew Carnegie (1962, 114) asserted that employers ought to organize daily production around three eight-hour shifts as a means to increase productivity and profitability. Carnegie drew on his reading of industrial history and the gradual shortening of the workday. Economically, Carnegie argued that production would increase and offset the estimated 16 percent increase in labor costs incurred from operating industry with three shifts of rested workers working eight hours each. Carnegie was revolutionary among employers in making this argument. His ideas, however, were gaining support. A widening circle of opinion that included proponents of scientific management, industrial statisticians, factory inspectors, and others began to put forward evidence that shorter hours meant greater efficiency and productivity for employers and improved health and safety for workers. The leadership of the CTLA and industrialists were speaking an increasingly similar *secular* language of economic productivity and efficiency that transcended union hall and boardroom.

If the eight-hour system was increasingly framed as a purely economic question for the AFL and the CTLA, the relationship between the labor movement and clergy and their churches still loomed large in public debates of the labor question. As Protestant clergy attempted to organize mass meetings to discuss the eight-hour movement, the tension between the clergy and labor remained palpable. George McNeill, himself an Episcopalian, in his *Eight-Hour Primer* written for the AFL, included an engaging give-and-take between himself and a clergyman. In the exchange, McNeill asks if the clergyman's parishioners practiced the gospel message to love God and one's neighbor and whether this gospel had any bearing on the relationship between capital and labor. The clergyman only replied, "They do the best they can. . . . The trouble is that such as you bring discontent to the masses of men, and array them against the church. . . . My dear sir, you must excuse me; there is no doubt that something is wrong, and we clergymen recognize the difficulty; we are not independent men. . . . [I]f I should undertake to defend the laborer I should lose my place, and have to take a smaller salary somewhere else" (1889, 7). McNeill's concluding thought is that although some ministers were beginning to advocate eight hours, this fearful response was more typical. Labor leaders encountered little to contradict their belief that clergy were unwilling or unable to be allies in the eight-hour struggle whether there was religious justification for it or not.

But despite the erosion of religious framing from the AFL's eight-hour arguments, its leaders remained in debate and dialogue with clergy about their relationship with the labor movement. In February 1894, William Pomeroy, vice president of the CTLA and a general organizer for the AFL, debated Rev. William A. Burch, pastor of the Hamlin Avenue Methodist Church, on the role of the church in the labor question under the theme "Stacks and Steeples" (1894, 1). Pomeroy asserted the continued commitment of workers to the teachings of Christ, "the carpenter, whose church was the world, whose pulpit was in the breasts of men; whose religion was humanity," as emblematic of the values of the labor movement itself. But for Pomeroy, without substantial changes in the attitudes of the clergy, the church would have very little positive effect on industrial reform.

> Speaking of the church as a whole, I am deeply impressed with the good which it could accomplish, should it forsake catering to the money lords, and demonstrate its oft-repeated and seldom exercised friendship for the masses. . . . Its chief supporters are men, who pray for "peace on earth, good will to men," and secretly subscribe to armory funds and equip military companies to call progress to a standstill. They give museums to posterity while the present generation is in need of bread . . . sermons about heaven, while earth is fast becoming a hell; panegyrics on Jesus, but small help for his "images"; charity on installments for the time being, while the future looms dark and dismal about the yawning grave of the republic. (1894, 7)

Converting Chicago clergy, much less employers, to become eight-hour supporters, while something to be hoped for, was not realistically to be expected. The relationship between the Protestant clergy and wealthy parishioners was too deeply entrenched. The clergy needed their patrons for salaries, building projects, and ministry support. The economic rhetoric of the AFL and its local federations and trade assemblies made them more acceptable to the mainstream press and gave them a shared logic in dealing with employers. Religious arguments did neither of those things and, in fact, threatened the fragile unity of Protestant and Catholic trade unionists.

The Knights of Labor, although facing organizational decline, consistently used religious language in discussing the eight-hour day. The Knights' universal vision of a moral industrial community stood in stark contrast to the AFL's vision of simply giving workers a stake in the capitalist system (Weir 1996). Christ's lesson for workers and for industrial society was to establish eight hours for one's vocation, eight for sleep, and eight for "devotion to the Deity and for charity" (*KL*, July 20, 1889, 9). Similar to how Pomeroy framed the way workers viewed Christ, Christ was still held up as an example, instructor, and teacher for the Knights (*KL*, November 15, 1890, 1).

On a practical level, the Knights challenged clergy to join them in the fight for shorter hours. This was the role of all of the biblical prophets. In both the Chicago *Knights of Labor* and the national *Journal of United Labor*, the message was clear and consistent. As a class, the clergy typically showed themselves to be on the side of employers. As a letter addressed to three Protestant clergymen—Rev. Dr. F. B. Mores of Calvary Baptist Church; Rev. M. C. Peters of

Bloomingdale Reformed Church, New York; and Rev. Dr. Sydney Corbett, Church of the Transfiguration, Philadelphia, all three of whom had taken public stands against the labor movement—stated, "Your sermons leave no doubt that you are for the classes against the masses; for the spoilers against the toilers; for the have-everythings as against the have-nothings; for the sweaters against the sweated." The letter went on to point out:

> Sermons by apologists of capitalism would be incomplete without the spice of a little rant about the dignity of labor. . . . One of you tells of a past time when men "worked long hours and were contented with them," and "fourteen hours a day and contentment," seem to be his conception of what ought to be the blissful lot of workingmen of America, while the rest of you appear to have about the same idea. It does not seem to occur to you that a man to fit himself for the duties of home and of citizenship—not to speak of yet higher duties—requires a little leisure. (*JUL,* September 25, 1890, 1)

For the Knights, because clergy catered their messages to employers, they indirectly contributed to the continuation of an unjust industrial system based on long hours of labor because they would not challenge the employers who sat in their pews week after week. Alexander Wright, frequent contributor to the Knights' newspapers under the name "Spokeshave," pointed out:

> If they were faithful to their mission they should surely be ready at all times to rebuke those who are found in possession of more than their just and equal share of the world, and to assist those who have been deprived of their share to regain it. . . . They are powerful enough in their condemnation of "sin in the abstract," but they seem to have entered into a sort of conspiracy or alliance upon "sin in the concrete." There's always, or nearly always a "present company excepted" proviso in their sermons when they speak of those things which might be expected to make some of the wealthier brethren feel uncomfortable. . . . Yet it seems to me that the preacher has no right to hesitate. . . . There are homes made miserable and broken up, men brutalized, women degraded, children growing up in ignorance and vice, and all because of an evil system, rooted and grounded in usury. . . . Yet the men who call themselves the messengers of the loving All Father have nothing to say in condemnation of this system. . . . It seems to me that the true preacher should go as Nathan did to David, and say: "Thou art the man." (*JUL,* February 6, 1890, 1)

Twice in the months that followed, this critique of the Protestant clergy by the Knights leaders was repeated. On both occasions, the paper warned that should church leaders remain on the side of employers, workingmen and -women would not simply ignore them, but actively oppose them.

> It seems to me that if the Christian Church would fulfill its mission it should devote itself to arousing the public conscience, not merely for the purpose of enabling men to obtain reward or escape pain hereafter, but for the purpose of having them arrange their social affairs so that equal and exact justice will not only be possible, but inevitable. . . . The people ask for bread, and they won't be satisfied with a creed; they demand a fish, and no confession of faith will be accepted instead of it. . . . [I]f the Church will not help right the wrong, they will have none of it. Nay, more than that, if it continues longer to make excused for the wrong and to say that it is part of God's plan for the governing of the world they will quickly repudiate it. They will not much longer be rendered patient of present wrong and robbery by promises of "mansions in the skies." Either the church must be true, or it will share the fate which has everywhere befallen the false. (*JUL*, February 13, 1890, 1)

In the second of the two articles, the writer underscores that workers are ready to listen to the clergy if they intend to preach true Christianity but not if they intend to only tell workers to hope for better conditions in the next life.

> The masses have not rejected and will not reject true Christianity; but this tinsel, brummagem, gilded commercialism . . . you seek to substitute for the religion embodied in the Sermon on the Mount, they will have none of it. . . . And you would lull the masses into contentment with their conditions here by promises of happiness in heaven. You would frighten them from asserting their right to enjoy the wealth they have created by threatening them with hell. The game is about up. The people are awakening. You can no longer get them to tolerate a hell here from which they have the means of escape by promising them a heaven hereafter. No, they will destroy the hell in which they now live by exorcising the devil of commercialism, who has created it, and all the threats and entreaties of all the priests of mammon who masquerade as ministers of Christ will not prevent the dawning of a better day. (*JUL*, September 25, 1890, 1)

When the Knights' organization collapsed in the early 1890s, their religious rhetoric went with it. Rather than trying to entice Protestant leaders to bring their moral authority to the eight-hour movement, the Chicago *Knights of Labor* expressed the sense that employers and employees understood best the issues at stake and could negotiate a solution to the problem of long hours without the church:

> That there is a better understanding between employers and employees on the demands of the latter generally and on the subject of the eight-hour day particularly no one will doubt who is cognizant of the facts. The employers

> have learned that in their demand for a shorter workday their employees are not governed by caprice not a spirit of tyranny or unreasonableness. They are earnest and honest in their purpose to benefit their fellow workmen and to give employment to the army of the unemployed. The employees have learned that in their opposition to the eight-hour work-day, the employers are not governed by a lack of sympathy or a desire to be harsh and cruel, but from a serious disarrangement of the business interests of the country. (February 1, 1890, 1)

Radical labor organizations continued to use religious rhetoric into the early 1890s. As in earlier campaigns for shorter hours, these radical factions of the movement, the Christian gospel, and the Bible together contained an "incendiary message" of justice for working people living a miserable existence of long hours and low wages under the capitalist system (*Alarm,* April 7, 1888, 2). Paradoxically, anarchists and socialists viewed religion as both a problem and a solution to capitalism in ways that were typical of the overarching ambivalence toward organized religion expressed by the other factions of the movement (Burn 2010; B. Nelson 1991). On the one hand, religion was relevant for its principles, in its demands for justice, and in its opposition to oppression of the weak by the strong. Support for eight hours demonstrated one's comprehension of the *moral* of Christianity without its organizational baggage. On the other hand, Christianity was perverted by religious leaders who used religion for their own purposes and to legitimate the actions of the industrialists in exchange for a piece of the economic pie. In doing so, clergy opposed new truths like those expressed by the eight-hour movement and diverted the attention of workers to a better life after death (*Alarm,* July 21, 1888, 2; *Labor Enquirer,* July 7, 1888, 2). Radical workers did not oppose religious beliefs as such as much as they opposed how they saw it lived out in struggles against pious Christian employers.

In practical terms, Chicago socialists joined with the other groups within the eight-hour movement calling for direct arbitration with employers, distancing themselves from public perceptions that they supported only violence as a means to achieve shorter hours. At the annual eight-hour march and mass meeting on the lakefront in 1891, Thomas Morgan made it clear that "it is not American to settle questions with Pinkerton assassins, Gatling guns, or standing armies. Argument, discussion, is the mode. We deplore acts of violence done by workingmen. We deplore the efforts of millionaires to crush us down. Let us argue the question. If we are unjust in our demands, we will withdraw them. We are however convinced we are right" (*CT,* May 2, 1891, 1). Politically, however, socialists hoped to elect more of their own to power and, by so doing, be able to legislate eight-hour reform directly. In a letter to the socialist *Chicago Labor,* Charles G. Davidson juxtaposed such a political strategy to the clearly ineffectual strategy of building coalitions with the religious community to realize the eight-hour goal.

> What reason have we to believe that the gospel will solve the labor question, hereafter, anymore than heretofore? Has not the gospel been preached for all ages, and is not the matter going from bad to worse? Would it not be safer for the masses to trust in the law-making power of the land—which so far has been the bulwark of Capitalism, because their tools have served their ends as law-makers—the laws to be made by men elected from the ranks of Labor, and to the effect that each and all should have a right to work and enjoy the full product of his Labor? Let us try this remedy and we may be sure of a glorious result. (March 10, 1894, 1)

Radical factions within the eight-hour movement embraced the idea that the core missions of socialism and Christianity were one and the same. Yet because Christian clergy refused to openly challenge employers to live out the equality and justice taught by Christ, there was no way for them to be effective partners in industrial reform.

> Gentlemen of the cloth, it is useless to cover over the corpse of a corrupt system with your various acts of charity. You know it is wrong, unjust, and un-Christ-like. Gold is the God of today and Christ is used as a mere puppet. Can you honestly believe there is one capitalist with a million dollars today who has anything in common with the religion of Christ—love for all. All his time has been spent in scheming and planning how to get up his fellow men to pile up wealth for his use and comfort, and yet you tell me, Doctor of Christ, these men are "brothers;" having all things in common? Nay, why do you mock Christ? . . . I think it is impossible for a person to be a Christian; a real live Christian, and not a Socialist; therefore, I contend that the Christians of today do not really desire to fulfill the teachings of Jesus Christ, or else they would join the ranks of Socialism, for the ethics of Socialism and Christianity are alike. Socialists do not find fault with you because you are preaching Christianity, but because you do not fearlessly practice it and help to remove the conditions which prevent you from loving every man as your brother from your heart. (*Chicago Labor,* September 8, 1894, 1)

Even the Christian socialist movement was viewed as one more illustration of how Protestant clergy were unable to understand the class dynamics at work within industrial capitalism. Christian socialism undermined its own significance as a foundation for action because it could not resolve the tension that Christian employers in church on Sunday morning would act as demons when they returned to business the rest of the week. As one writer for the socialist *Workers' Call* attempted to explain by century's end:

> The capitalist has two characters: as a human being he is our brother . . . but the capitalist has also another character, viz., his character as a capitalist. In this character he is not our brother, not a human being, but a fiend, a devil incarnate, a thief, robber, and murderer. . . . Christian Socialists ignore this double character of capitalists and say there is no class struggle between laborers and capitalists, meaning thereby capitalists as human beings; they are purposely and cunningly silent on the question whether or not there is a class struggle between laborers and capitalists considered as capitalists. This juggling with words, this playing with right and wrong constitutes the wickedness of Christian Socialism. It is socialism with the heart crushed out. It is Christianity in league with Satan; trying to worship God and Mammon. . . . It will do the Christian Socialists no good to cry peace, peace, peace, when there is no peace. The war is inevitable; the time is at hand when they must go over to one side or the other. Where will they be found when the test comes? (August 19, 1899, 1)

As with other groups of workers, the perceived gap between the beliefs and preaching of Protestant clergy, even those now claiming to be on the side of labor in the Christian socialist camp, on the one hand, and how they lived out such beliefs in practice, on the other, undercut any serious consideration of working with clergy to reduce the hours of labor.

The New Protestant Consciousness Unfolds

In the face of this increasing disenchantment with tepid Protestant clergy support for an eight-hour day, Christian socialists and proponents of the Social Gospel became driving forces in how Protestants framed the problem of overwork and its solution in shorter-hours reform. Recognizing shorter hours as the expression of justice and mercy required a new Protestant consciousness. In 1888 Henry Demarest Lloyd, prominent social reformer whose father was a minister in the Dutch Reformed Church, had addressed the Society for Ethical Culture of Chicago and called for the development of this "new conscience" to confront the great industrial questions of the city. In the "New Conscience," Lloyd heard "the 'still small voice' that was heard thousands of years ago, [which] has been commanding more and more attention, making tyrants quake, and compelling monopolies to reconsider the un-wisdom of their wicked deeds. . . . The 'New Conscience' looks at Chicago and New York and sees Cain in his palace and Abel in the slums; sees Cain well fed and richly dressed, and Abel in his rags, and asks as did the God of old, 'Cain! where is thy brother Abel?'" (*Advance*, February 9, 1888, 88). Industrial realities required clergy to alter previously accepted beliefs about the sinfulness of the poor, the evil of strikes, and the rightness of employers to do as they please.

But calling for this new consciousness was only the beginning. Even those who would later be recognized as leading names in the Social Gospel movement were cautious in fully supporting the eight-hour movement. Rev. Washington Gladden, in a sermon on the eight-hour movement published in the *Dawn*, was supportive of the movement but expressed reservations if the movement acted too precipitously. "God bless them for wanting it, I say; and God help them to get it! I hope that they will learn patience and prudence in pushing their campaign; that they will be wise enough to discern God's time, and never to force the season by premature demands; for the stars in their courses are fighting their battles; every circling year brings their redemption nearer" (July–August 1890, 147). Other clergy voices were not yet won over by the enthusiasm of either the Social Gospel or Christian socialism. The Presbyterian *Interior* and the Congregational *Advance* both expressed the old fear that workers could not be trusted with any increase in free time and would spend it in saloons or in other morally suspect activities such as dancing (*Interior*, March 17, 1892, 5; July 7, 1892, 8; *Advance*, May 3, 1894, 280). Dr. John Mills, pastor of the Second Presbyterian Church, Evanston, expressed schizophrenic sentiments of clergy who, on the one hand, believed the eight-hour movement to be a good thing in principle but, on the other, remained skeptical of any attempt to enforce shorter hours in practice. "While the public admires the magnificent work done by organized labor, and the splendid battle it has made, is making, and must make, it will scarcely see its own interest as consumer in the substitution of the selfishness of trade-unionism for the selfishness of capitalism. The forced reduction of the hours of labor to eight hours a day seems neither wise nor practicable. I know of no one in any walk of life who has risen to competence by laboring only eight hours a day" (*CT*, January 30, 1893, 8).

But despite this ongoing caution, the prophetic voices of prominent Protestant reformers such as Gladden, William T. Stead, Rev. Charles Stelzle, and local ministers working directly with wage earners such as Rev. William H.

Carwardine, Rev. M. M. Parkhurst, and others slowly penetrated Protestant thinking. Clergy needed a new moral discourse that redefined the Protestant overemphasis on a work ethic applicable to America's rural past but no longer supportable given the conditions of urban industrial production. Protestant eight-hour supporters built a rhetoric that maintained God's plan for all people of a life that balanced work and rest. Concentrated rest for a few and nonexistent leisure for many was the work of the devil. The social sin of overwork kept wage earners from personal salvation by driving them to despair, poverty, and the bottle. Work and salvation remained firmly linked in the Protestant mind, however, and work began to be seen as an activity that ought to uplift the worker and should not crowd out time for his or her spiritual and social advancement. The *Interior* reminded its readers that "too much labor tends to ruin and disintegration of mind and body. Too much recreation leads to the waste of the responsibilities of life. Happy is he who can find that ratio and generally preserve it" (July 13, 1893, 14). Rev. William D. P. Bliss, editor of the *Dawn,* elaborated to the fullest extent the nature of this balance and how reducing the hours of labor would achieve it:

> Man today is not free. Men are slaves, slaves of machinery, slaves of toil, slaves of long hours in factory and in shop. Manhood needs leisure. We are told of the right to work; we much also add to it the right to leisure. Manhood *implies* leisure. If we are ever to have men and not machines, heads and not hands, souls and not slaves, we much give opportunity to develop head and soul as well as hand and foot. Long hours in the factory mean short hours in the home, short hours in the library, and short hours in the Church. Short hours in the factory mean long hours in the home, long hours in the library, and long hours in the Church. We shall never prosper in America, Democracy will never bless, till our working men become men, not mere hands, and therefore must we limit the hours of manual toil. . . . This is the religious point. I hope that the time cometh, nay, even now is, when one of the Church's marching songs will be, "Eight hours for work, eight hours for play, eight hours for sleep, and eight shillings a day." I believe that to be as divine a song, as any processional we have sung tonight. (July–August 1894, 127)

In addition to a transformed view about the nature of both work and leisure, Protestant arguments in favor of the eight-hour system took on a hopeful, millennial tone. Eight hours symbolized "the first ethical economic step in the pathway of the wage-worker towards equity, the abolition of poverty, and the heralding of the kingdom of heaven on earth" (*Dawn,* May

1890, 20). This ushering in of God's kingdom on earth had its precedents in abolitionism, which was seen as the beginning of a new era for humanity as the institution of slavery crumbled.

For Protestant eight-hour advocates, there was a direct connection drawn between increasing leisure time for workers and making them better Christians. While clergy now granted the desire for more leisure to be a legitimate one, even to the point of arguing that taking time for physical rest was a Christian duty, the blame for social problems associated with overwork was laid squarely on the shoulders of the employers. "What have [employers] ever done to make their employees good Christians? When we remember how constantly these men have been kept at work on Sunday until the love of Church and everything holy has died in them, it is hard for us to expect them to conduct a controversy like the present on Christian principles, or to abandon it in obedience to Christian precepts" (*Living Church*, June 19, 1888, 151). Such beliefs were echoed by workers who claimed that they were unable to participate in the religious life of Chicago because of prolonged hours at work. The public's voice also reflected this idea. Rena A. Michaels, in recounting a woman's view of the question, believed:

> So long as men and women work ten hours a day for six days in the week, tired and exhausted bodies will give little chance for spiritual uplifting of the soul on the seventh. When the churches recognize this, and Christian men demand from their workmen but eight hours from a day's labor, the church will have taken one practical step toward the much discussed evangelization of our cities. . . . It is this sort of Christianity, Christianity with a soul in it, that will always reach men and women and convince them that after all it is a real thing. . . . Why the Masses Are Not Reached . . . [T]he minister goes often into the homes of the select few and writes sermons that are relevant to them. His sermons are hardly made for the man who spends his days amid the clanging of machinery or for the work-weary woman who has labored hard all the long days and perhaps listened all the long nights for an uncertain footstep. (*CT*, January 13, 1893, 26)

In engaging the new consciousness, clergy sought to maintain class harmony for the good of all, but this amplified the need to construct a critique of contemporary industrial conditions and conflicts that pointed out the problematic behaviors of both capital and labor. The Homestead steel strike of 1892 in Pittsburgh and the Pullman strike of 1894 outside of Chicago both drew clergy condemnation on attempts by labor forcibly to hinder others from working for whatever wages or under whatever conditions they chose.

Clergy echoed employers' claim that strikers violated the freedom of contract of replacement workers, and, in the case of the Pullman strike, Protestant workers attending these churches summarily left these congregations in protest (Carter 2010).

But a growing number, especially among the younger generation of ministers and those who had closer ties to working-class communities, voiced their protest that workers had the right to organize themselves into unions and to strike (see *Interior,* August 2, 1894, 968; Carter 2010). These ministers were quick to criticize employers for disrupting community peace and order by driving their employees to desperate measures in the interests of profit. The *Interior,* usually more willing to support employers' rights over labor's, in reflecting on the Homestead steel strike, makes this point clearly:

> While there are obligations which the employee owes to his employer, there are obligations to the employee equally binding on the employer. He does wrong whenever, by depressing the prices paid for labor, he unduly deprives the employee of the necessities and comforts of life. . . . [I]t is sometimes the duty of the capitalist to be content with shrunken profits to preserve the welfare of his men. . . . A man or company, controlling four or five thousand men, upon whose conduct the peace of the whole community is dependent may not lightly stir up a strife which may jeopardize the stability of the state. To purposefully excite to violence so large a mass of men is practically treasonous sedition. Whoever willfully disturbs civil and industrial peace is guilty of a crime against society and the state. (July 14, 1892, 3)

Although this was not the first time clergy claimed employers had duties to their employees, such sentiments were more assertive in telling employers to accept lower profits in order to be sure employees could earn enough to live on and not disturb the stability of the community. Articles in the *Interior* repeated this multiple times two years later in relation to the Pullman strike (see, for example, July 12, 1894, 871; August 2, 1894, 968). This is not to say that clergy voices were unanimous. Within the same denominational paper, including the *Interior,* one would read letters and essays condemning employers for being greedy and then condemning workers for being forgetful of how good their lives were compared to workers in Europe (August 9, 1894, 1000). Such mixed messages turned up in sermons as well. Preaching at the Second Presbyterian Church, Evanston, Dr. John Mills conveyed his support of the right and necessity of labor to form unions to level the playing field against organized employers but then chastised labor as "treacherous and cruel," because workers "foolishly struck when employers were carrying on work at a loss" (*CT,* January 30, 1893, 8). This frustrating combination of support and opposition for labor was entrenched even among ministers claiming the "new consciousness."

The Sweatshop Act of 1893

In the nineties, the focus of eight-hour reform efforts shifted from national strikes orchestrated by the AFL to local movements that aimed to shorten working hours for not only men but also women and children. Chicago again was in the spotlight. The *Tribune* noted that "Chicago is the labor center of the nation," with many independent trade unions moving their headquarters there. This notoriety meant the city continued as the epicenter for eight-hour protest. The *Tribune* predicted that "the great battle between organized labor and corporate capital in the United States will be fought out in Chicago" (January 2, 1893, 9). But while the newspaper was not optimistic that labor could win such a battle, the playing field was changing.

In January 1893, the first edition of the new *Eight-Hour Herald,* edited by M. J. Carroll, was published to support the local movement. In light of the recent success of the carpenters' union and the more open political climate, the Chicago movement found encouragement for increasing mobilization when Illinois representative Joseph A. O'Donnell of Cook County introduced another bill to establish eight hours as a day's labor "between the rising and setting of the sun in all mechanical trades, arts, and employments, whether public or private in nature" (*CT,* January 4, 1893, 2). O'Donnell's bill was extensive. It limited work to between 8:00 a.m. and 5:00 p.m., except when businesses organized production into shifts, in which case workers could work only one eight-hour shift in every twenty-four hours. Provisions were also made in the bill to assess progressively greater fines for each successive violation, to a maximum of five hundred dollars and between six months' and one year's imprisonment. Chicago employers resisted this new bill. The popular press called the bill an impossibility, believing that the hours of labor "must regulate themselves" and that the Supreme Court would "snuff it out contemptuously" as a violation of the right of wage earners to work as long as they wished (*CT,* January 5, 1893, 4). O'Donnell's bill never became law, but another legal attempt to shorten the hours for women and children emerged three months later.

In the early 1890s, more and more attention was being paid to working conditions in Chicago's sweatshops. Disturbing descriptions of sweat labor and the indifference of employers pushed municipal officers to conduct a citywide survey of the conditions within sweatshops headed by Florence Kelly of Hull House. In one instance, these investigations uncovered men who were working for fifteen hours a day, for one dollar in one case, and in another women working for sixteen hours a day for between thirty-seven and forty-four cents a day (*CT,* February 13, 1893, B7; February 20, 1893, 1). Such revelations caught the attention of the Protestant press. The Episcopal *Living Church* was appalled at the state of women's working condition. According to one shop superintendent: "We never think of taking precautions against disease. We get so used to the system that we never think of it." Another shop overseer testified that workers' "sanitary condition is nothing to us, except that the goods must come back unsoiled" (April 1, 1893, 6). This highly publicized report generated a recommendation that the Illinois Legislature ought to pass a bill regulating the conditions of labor within sweatshops. With the active support of Jane Addams and Governor John Peter Altgeld, on June 13, 1893, the Illinois Legislature successfully passed the Sweatshop Act of 1893, sometimes referred to as the Factory Law, which stated, "No female shall be employed in any factory or workshop more than eight-hours in any one day or forty-eight hours in any one week" (*CT,* June 14, 1893, 2). This was the first law to restrict child labor and limit the hours of women's work. The unique provision of this bill was its enforceability. Violations by employers were punishable by fines ranging from three dollars up to one hundred dollars.

In response, Illinois employers organized the Manufacturers' Protective Association as a defensive organization whose goal was to overturn the enforcement of the act. Harry Jacobson, secretary of the MPA, maintained the new law would not have been a problem if it had been enacted as a national regulation, but Illinois employers were forced to oppose it as a state law because it would leave them unable to compete with employers from other states without such regulations on labor (*CT,* September 30, 1893, 4). In the face of opposition from manufacturers, women labor reformers representing the Women's Alliance and the Women's Federal Labor Union challenged the MPA to a public debate over the merits of the new law (*CT,* March 3, 1894, 3). The businessmen did not accept the challenge.

The Women's Alliance went on the offensive and organized a public meeting on the Sweatshop Act a month later, where Bishop Samuel Fallows of the Reformed Episcopal Church, Clarence Darrow, and Thomas Morgan all spoke in favor of the law (*CT,* April 7, 1894, 11). Henry Demarest Lloyd addressed a second mass meeting of supporters and opponents of the law on

April 22, 1894. He criticized the freedom-of-contract argument and the idea that workers were free to choose the conditions of their employment as the root of all the industrial challenges of the nineteenth century.

> Our captains of industry began the century with the claim that they were free from this veto by the general good. They had but to utter the magic words, *laissez faire,* and all doors flew open before them as before the open sesame of the Arabian Nights. Under this theory they went on making contracts with little children and with women which turned the cotton factories of England into hells where the bodies and souls of thousands were consumed. . . . Then as now there were philosophers to protest in the name of individualism—preachers of Christ to defend those for whose profit this crucifixion of maternity was carried on. . . . [T]he more dreadful sin would be for us to leave our women and children to their "individual" and "sacred" right to be devoured by the sharp teeth of free contract in the sweatshops of Chicago. . . . In the name of common decency, establish some rules of the ring for this prize-fight. Let the state be the umpire, and let the rounds be only eight hours long. (1909, 115)

The state and courts did become the arena for this new battle between eight-hour advocates and employers. After a year and a half, thirteen members of the MPA were found guilty for violating the eight-hour provision of the Sweatshop Act, based on evidence from factory inspectors. W. C. Ritchie and Company, a paper box manufacturer in Chicago, challenged the constitutionality of restricting women's hours before the Illinois Supreme Court. As with previous employer efforts to undermine legal regulations on the hours of labor, W. C. Ritchie and Company argued their case on the grounds that an eight-hour provision abridged a woman's right to freely contract with her employer for as long a workday as she deemed appropriate to her needs (*CT,* April 21, 1894, 6). The Illinois Supreme Court ruled in the company's favor and repealed Section 5 of the act that shortened hours for women (*CT,* March 15, 1895, 1). Members of the Manufacturers' Protective Association were exuberant that the law's shorter-hours provision was overturned. Their attorney, Levy Mayer, was "highly gratified" to know that the court upheld their claim that women are "equal to men before the law and that her right to her labor, which constitutes her property, is as sacred and impregnable as the similar right of man" (*CT,* March 15, 1895, 1). The MPA used the Illinois Supreme Court decision to bring more employers into the association. Employers were careful to endorse the other portions of the law, especially those prohibiting child labor and regulating sanitary conditions, as public opinion was more unified in its support for these provisions of the law (*CT,*

March 22, 1895, 1). No further attempt to secure shorter hours for women occurred in Illinois until fifteen years later.

In this last high-profile battle, clergy were largely silent, with the exception of Bishop Fallows. In Pomeroy's "Stacks and Steeples" debate with the Reverend Burch at the Hamlin Avenue Methodist Church discussed earlier, Pomeroy countered Burch's criticism that the labor movement was hostile to the church with his own extensive critique of the church in relationship to this attack on the Sweatshop Act (*CT,* February 29, 1894, 9).

> Is the church the protector of women and children? A society of wealthy manufacturers has recently formed to purchase a verdict from the state Supreme Court declaring that most just law unconstitutional. They have retained the strongest legal firm in the state to handle their case. On the one side wealth and legal craft, seeing the re-enslavement of women and children. On the other, the labor organizations saying "hold your hand," with all the past record of the supreme court against us, we say hold! You are treading upon human hearts, and must be careful lest you feel the weight of human indignation. Where is the church in this controversy? How many sermons have been hurled from the pulpit against this threatened infamy, this huckstering of childhood, this immolation of feeble women on the altar of greed? "By their works shall you know them." Who are the members of this soulless manufacturers association? Prominent pillars of the church. . . . I charge the church as being tacitly guilty of complicity in the premeditated crime. . . . The church has guilty knowledge of this most damnable scheme and forgets to call down damnation upon the heads of the men who conceived of it. (Pomeroy 1894, 4)

Even with this clear opportunity to take a stand against long hours for women and children, the Protestant press and Chicago's clergy stayed out of the debate.

Eight Hours at the End of the Century

Between 1893 and 1897, as the country went into another economic depression, clergy were forced to confront the increasingly publicized grim conditions of labor in Chicago. Representatives of the *Standard,* during a visit to Hull House in 1896, met a Russian official of the United Garment Workers' Union, then on strike. He took them on a tour of the sweatshop district in the city and of the homes of the immigrants who lived around Halsted Street, between Thirteenth and Fourteenth Streets. The utter destitution of these workers left the Baptist reporters unable to believe their eyes, and, as they reported later, it was "no time for a denunciation of the evils of strikes, or for blaming the strikers for throwing away such wages as they were getting." It was only time for giving "these sufferers the help which, as men and women, they may ask from their fellow men" (April 4, 1896, 5). But giving "help" in the abstract was not enough. Workers were still waiting for practical support for eight-hour reform from Protestant clergy. Few clergy yet were as outspoken as Methodist pastor Rev. J. Stitt Wilson, who, at a mass meeting in support of Chicago garment workers who were then on strike for shorter hours, called for a pragmatic means for ensuring that the clothing the public purchased was made under humane and just conditions. "When we wear fine clothing we are conscious of the fact it is the product of the dungeons of the sweatshop district. What if the clothing in this room could tell its history? What a story of tears, misery, starvation, low waged, long hours, and abject slavery we would hear. We, the public, have a right to know where our garments are made . . . buy only clothing bearing the union label and to spread union ideas everywhere" (*CT,* March 30, 1896, 9).

While the growing recognition of desperate working conditions was forcing Protestant clergy to adopt a new consciousness toward organized labor and the eight-hour question, clergy as a whole were sympathetic, but even having a minister call for union labels on manufactured goods was a step further than most were willing to go, especially in such a public forum. Clergy were moving closer to labor but were not yet ready to launch themselves totally into the eight-hour movement. At the same time, clergy were finally beginning to see that employers would not give in to labor demands regardless of their moral arguments and that the labor movement needed to be able to fight with employers on a level playing field. Clergy saw themselves as mediators in the struggle for a more just industrial order achieved through reason, arbitration, and mutual respect between capital and labor. For Protestant clergy, this would be the fulfillment of the Christian mission. Baptist pastor Rev. J. J. Weddell summed up this idea in the *Standard:*

> Let it not be allowed that wild and visionary men taking advantage of the situation swing the labor movement into vicious and malevolent alignment. Let the Christian element prevail, and by kind offices, as in the recent successful efforts for arbitration, convince the workingman that his best friend is the Church of Jesus Christ, and so the bad chasm . . . between be bridged. Certainly in light of late events the laboring man cannot say that church and capital always go together. The church, in fact, is for both labor and capital in mutual and fraternal agreement, and the rich and poor meeting together. (January 4, 1896, 6)

But for the eight-hour movement, such niceties and optimistic pronouncements were not what the movement needed. Workers needed practical action and support, and if clergy would not or could not give it, the movement would fight on its own terms.

The AFL tried for one last national eight-hour movement to enforce the system beginning on May 1, 1896 (*CT,* December 9, 1895, 5). Since 1890 the economic downturn hit all trade unions hard, but the carpenters had experienced losses in wages and their hours increased again (*CT,* March 28, 1896, 7). The AFL planned for the carpenters and joiners to go out on strike and that all other trades would support their efforts. However, the AFL and its affiliates faced internal challenges of their own, undermining their full energies being directed to the eight-hour campaign. Socialist factions were battling for control of the AFL against more conservative craft union supporters (Foner 1982; Grob 1961). This national battle had local parallels. In 1895 the AFL was called upon to choose *the* legitimate labor organization in Chicago, either the socialist Labor Congress or the Trades and Labor Assembly. "Comparatively few people realize a crisis is at hand in the history of labor organizations in this country. That crisis will be reached when the relative strength of the two great factions (the 'socialists' vs. the 'strict trade unionists') in which organized labor is divided is tested by a vote for officers." The *Tribune* once again predicted a showdown that would lead to either violence and an end to the eight-hour movement or a chance for the eight-hour day to succeed.

> If the Socialist leaders get control of the American Federation of Labor there is a possibility of a repetition of the scenes of May 1886, when the worst strike Chicago ever experienced ended in the throwing of the bomb in Haymarket Square May 4, 1886. The Socialists and Anarchists killed the eight-hour movement in 1886, and they may do it again by precipitating strikes and riots when the critical time comes. If the conservative trade unionists element is in control of the American Federation of Labor after the convention there will be no chance of strikes until arbitration fails. The eight-hour movement will have an equal chance of success under conservative leaders. (December 9, 1895, 5)

After a week of ideological battles within the federation, Samuel Gompers was elected as president of the AFL. William Pomeroy observed a general sense among AFL delegates that "the hysterical era of the labor movement is passing and compact proactive measures are about to be inaugurated" (*CT,* December 10, 1895, 5). M. J. Carroll, of the *Eight-Hour Herald,* "was convinced from the opening of the convention that it would stick close to trades union ideas and have nothing to do with politics, socialism, or other ideas which have nothing whatever in common with the business of the American Federation of Labor" (*CT,* December 14, 1895, 2).

Following the AFL convention, Samuel Gompers and conservative trade unionists continued to distance themselves from the socialist wing of the eight-hour movement and all attempts to make eight-hour reform a political issue. Gompers's strategy consolidated around collective bargaining with employers, with the possible use of strikes against recalcitrant bosses only when necessary. Gompers declared:

> The eight-hour day is coming. . . . In my judgment a hundred thousand wage workers early in May will receive from their employers the concession of a shorter day. This does not mean a strike of half a million men. It does not mean a strike, a general strike, at all. These concessions have been made voluntarily, after application, discussion, and conference. . . . Socialism is dying out of trade unionism. Its advocates are leaving us to flock by themselves. The true trade unionist has no use for these blatant advocates of impossible frothings. Their teachings are vicious. The workingman is finding it out. (*CT,* April 25, 1896, 4)

Despite these political battles within the movement, either as strict trade unionists or as part of the growing socialist wing, Chicago workers continued organizing and striking for eight hours. Eight thousand carpenters and journeymen horseshoers struck for shorter hours. The carpenters took back their eight-hour day, and the horseshoers won a nine-hour day (*CT,* March 26, 1896, 2; March 30, 1896, 7; March 31, 1896, 12). Tailors and cloth cutters, representing between ten and twenty-five thousand workers, struck for eight hours (*CT,* March 14, 1896, 5; March 27, 1896, 5). In December 1897, the AFL debated a national movement for an eight-hour movement, to begin on May 1, 1898, to be led by the International Association of Machinists and the International Typographical Union (*CT,* December 9, 1897, 12; December 16, 1897, 5; December 19, 1897, 30). James O'Connell, president of the International Association of Machinists and vice president of the AFL, argued that the entire "existence of the labor movement depends on the international fight for a universal shorter workday" (*CT,* December 9, 1897, 12). Most delegates favored what was perceived as this more radical national action, but conservative leaders still tried, though without success, to convince delegates to delay action for a year (*CT,* December 17, 1897, 5). Both the machinists and the typographical workers won a nine-hour day in 1898 (*CT,* November 20,

1898, 4). And, in what was predicted to be a year that would "witness the greatest renewal of eight-hour struggle since 1886," the granite cutters at the Mount Waldo quarries won their eight-day in 1899 (*CT*, December 19, 1898, 7; December 29, 1899, 12). Finally, after seven years of struggle, the retail clerks' union reduced their hours from fourteen to twelve, with no Sunday labor (*CT*, December 31, 1899, 8).

The century ended with an increase in the numbers of organized workers who had achieved shorter hours in some form. Success was breeding success, as the *Tribune*, in its review of the year, noted. Nearly all of Chicago's unions would continue to demand shorter hours in the first decade of the twentieth century (December 31, 1899, 14). Chicago Protestants, when compared to the earlier eight-hour campaigns in the 1860s, 1870s, and 1880s, became more supportive of reform than they had even been, but there was still a wide range in how the Protestant consciousness was evolving regarding eight-hour reform. At one extreme, prominent Protestant voices continued to oppose eight hours, but they were becoming significantly fewer. On the other extreme, there were the proponents of the Social Gospel movement and Christian socialists claiming that the eight-hour movement was synonymous with the mission and teaching of Christ. Most clergy were well in the middle of the two. The new Protestant consciousness regarding the eight-hour day believed both capital and labor were guilty of excesses that disrupted the stability and peace of Chicago and were both therefore to be held accountable. Clergy increasingly condemned employers for driving their employees to desperate acts by refusing to arbitrate on industrial reform demands. Unions protected workers, and organized labor was now seen to be an important countervailing force to organized capital.

Labor's consciousness of the eight-hour day as having a religious and moral foundation too underwent a transformation in this period. Conservative trade unionists adopted the strategy of the AFL to fight for shorter hours on employers' terms. They developed rhetoric that was focused on the economic and production benefits that would accrue to employers that adopted the system. Practically, by organizing workers into strong trade unions, employers would be compelled to bargain and compromise on the question of hours. Such a strategy garnered public support for labor as well. Moderation would achieve more than the political or direct-action strategies advocated by the Knights of Labor, the Socialist Labor Party, or the Central Labor Union. Keeping eight-hour rhetoric secular allowed labor to speak a language that resonated with employers and minimized the risk of fragmenting a religiously divided labor movement.

For the Knights of Labor and the unions affiliated with the CLU, religious framing of the eight-hour day remained a significant part of the way these groups talked about reform. Workers affiliated with both groups and writers for their various newspapers articulated in various ways how supporting shorter hours embodied true Christianity. They used biblical narratives to underscore that God was on the side of labor in this fight and would eventually give the movement victory over their employers who opposed them. Most important, religious language gave these workers a means to frame a future social order based on cooperation and justice, the antithesis of industrial capitalism (Weir 1996; Green 2006). As the influence of the Knights collapsed, radical workers continued to operate within an ever-changing set of labor organizations. But for these workers, belief in a "radical historical Jesus" and critiques of clergy and their lack of practical support for shorter hours remained prominent features in their newspapers (Burns 2010).

Three decades of attempts to secure Protestant leaders as allies was generating too little practical assistance for achieving anything that labor wanted. In the first decade of the twentieth century, the eight-hour movement's strategy to build coalitions with clergy seemed more and more unnecessary at the same time as the new Protestant consciousness was about to be institutionalized into a pan-denominational social creed supporting labor rights. The debate over the relevance of clergy and of religious faith in capitalism would continue into the new century.

CHAPTER 6

Shifting Eight-Hour Reform from Consciousness to Creed in the Twentieth Century

On January 5, 1910, Charles Stuart, editor of the *Northwestern Christian Advocate*, posed this question: "Has the Church a Gospel of Recreation?" Jane Addams of Hull House contributed a feature article on the subject in that particular issue. The question itself embodied a half century of debate and struggle within Chicago's social reform circles about what it meant to redeem time for wage earners. For organized labor, creating a gospel of recreation to redeem time had been its moral mission from the beginning of the eight-hour movement. But many Protestants still balked at the very idea of linking the word *gospel* to the word *recreation*. The growth in popularity of Chicago's dance halls, amusement districts such as the Midway, nickelodeons, and other entertainment options continued to fuel Protestant concerns about the moral depravity that inevitably accompanied unregulated leisure among the lower orders (Duis 1998).

Nevertheless, in spite of ongoing employer opposition, the eight-hour workday was gaining widespread public support as a reasonable rather than revolutionary demand as part of growing progressive reform activism. Building a gospel of recreation as a foundation for reducing the hours of labor for workers required more than simply developing a new consciousness among a small group of ministers, and getting clergy out of the pulpits and into the streets on behalf of shorter hours remained a difficult proposition. Caught between the forces of organized capital and organized labor, Protestant clergy struggled to find a middle road that would allow them to support the eight-hour movement as an expression of their growing Social Gospel sensibilities but not let Chicago disintegrate into class war over the issue. As the movement unfolded in the early 1900s, Chicago workers, employers, and clergy continued to fight, rhetorically and politically, over the possibility that any "gospel of recreation" could redeem time and improve industrial conditions for labor.

High Hopes for Eight Hours in the New Century

The eight-hour movement entered the twentieth century with a more solid foundation than at the start of any of the previous three decades. Between 1900 and 1912, labor's strength grew tremendously, thanks to an upsurge in labor organizing and strikes to enforce demands for shorter hours. Chicago's workingmen and workingwomen, as machinists, woodworkers, stockyard engineers, railroad workers, bakers, laundry workers, store clerks, garment workers, bookbindery workers, printers, streetcar workers, and cement workers, all struck for the eight-hour or nine-hour day and faced renewed attacks from employers.

Business elites, as in the past, fought to block expansion of the eight-hour day using every possible means available in their own organized power (*CT*, May 23, 1903, 1). Packers, railway managers, and restaurant owners refused to grant any concession to union demands and refused any appeals for arbitration. Employers organized through their trade associations and through national organizations such as the National Manufacturers' Association or the Citizens' Industrial Association of America against labor unions, which were seen as "revolutionary and anarchistic menaces to the social and industrial system of the United States" (*CT*, February 23, 1903, 1). The president of the National Manufacturers' Association called the labor movement a "poison to the nation" and framed the AFL as an organization that "breeds boycotters, picketers, and socialists, and as the source from when proceeds such noxious emanations as the eight-hour bill" (*CT*, April 15, 1903, 7). Employers in the railroad, baking, and laundry industries were determined to go to war against labor's "exorbitant demands" for reduced hours (*CT*, May 19, 1903, 14).

But the industrial climate was changing, and employers were increasingly divided about holding a hard line in opposition to shorter hours. Employers were more and more willing to negotiate directly with union employees over the hours of labor. Within the first weeks of 1900, reports in the *Tribune* noted that local employers, such as Chicago lumber companies engaged in sash, door, and blind manufacturing, were signing agreements with their unions to grant eight-hour days without being forced to do so by a strike (*CT*, January 21, 1900, 14). After machinists went out on strike for a nine-hour day and a closed shop, employers compromised and granted employees the shorter day, though they refused to concede the closed shop (*CT*, April 2, 1900, 6). A year later, the Chicago Great Western Railroad Company also granted a nine-hour day to its machinists and so averted a strike (*CT*, April 20, 1901,

3). Strikes cost employers revenue, and it is clear that at least for some, it was more cost-effective to negotiate than to resist.

The benefits of shorter days and workweeks were being documented in the press. In Ivorydale, Ohio, employees at the Proctor and Gamble Company worked shorter hours and shorter workweeks. The company's general manager, Mr. Brown, noted that he found as much work being done as before the hours were shortened and that this has "produced a great change in the character of the employees. They are more self-reliant and better workmen, exercising greater care in the faithful performance of their duties" (*Interior,* January 17, 1901, 81). As a result of campaigns for the Sunday closing of shops and a half day of work on Saturdays, employers and shopkeepers were observing improved morale and productivity in their workforces. In July 1903, the *Tribune* reported that two hundred thousand workers would be enjoying half holidays on Saturdays, shortening the workweek, if not necessarily the workday. H. G. Selfridge, speaking on behalf of Marshall Field & Company, reported that "our 5,000 men and women and boys and girls feel better for the short vacation at the end of each week end" (July 4, 1903, 3). Such observations reinforced findings from medical and scientific research on the negative impact of fatigue and overwork that were circulating at this time (Rodgers 1978, 106; Rosenzweig 1983). Marshall Field & Company, in addition to half holidays, added recreation rooms, a gymnasium, and reading rooms for employees to use during their leisure time (*Living Church,* February 14, 1903, 563).

These instances of reducing the hours of labor at both the Proctor and Gamble Company and Marshall Field & Company were discussed in the Presbyterian and Episcopalian press and were used to showcase the application of the Golden Rule to business, in the first case, and "applied Christianity," in the second. But these links to Christian practice in business were made by contributors to these religious newspapers, not by the businessmen themselves. Perhaps this is why the papers included them. In fact, the *Living Church* observed that the average businessman "is too often prone to consider Christianity something apart from his business, the two revolve in different grooves and seem not to come into contact." While the writer conceded that adopting reforms "pays," he was certain, from a religious viewpoint, that "if all this was done to grind out greater profits, it would surely fail. It pays because it pays to do right" (February 14, 1903, 562). Within the new Protestant consciousness, there is no reform without religion. The idea that eight-hour reform could be adopted and succeed purely on the grounds of raising levels of productivity and therefore profits, as Andrew Carnegie had asserted in

1886, contradicted this logic in the religious press. Contrasting sharply, the attitude expressed by the manager from Proctor and Gamble framed why the company adopted shorter hours. From his perspective, "The ethical premise of the question did not concern the corporation. What they have done and are doing is merely good business practice and sagacity" (*Interior,* January 17, 1901, 81). Consequently, whether employers opposed shorter hours or incorporated them into the organization of production, profits and productivity were what mattered most, not "doing right" in a religious sense.

The labor movement possessed a sense of optimism in the future of the eight-hour movement. More workers were being organized. In one case, the Patternmakers' Union reported that 225 of 300 (75 percent) of pattern workers in Chicago were members of the union seeking a nine-hour day (*CT,* January 29, 1900, 3). In 1903 Chicago was the "trade union capital of the world," with more than 243,000 trade unionists (Montgomery 1979, 57). Unionized workers meant a stronger movement to fight organized employers. Montgomery further recounts that the Chicago Federation of Labor (CFL) used sympathy strikes to widen the impact of labor's power, even forcing International Harvester to adopt a nine-hour day for its machinists. Politically, too, the labor movement seemed on the upswing. A law limiting child labor to eight-hour days and forty-eight-hour weeks went into effect in 1903 (*CT,* July 1, 1903, 7). The AFL perceived the eight-hour movement to be growing stronger in light of a bill coming before Congress in 1902 that would require every contractor and subcontractor with government contracts to limit the workday of their men to eight hours and imposed a five-dollar penalty for every violation (*CT,* November 22, 1903, 4).

Protestants showed signs that their new consciousness was gradually taking hold across denominations, though ministers were still cautious about actively taking sides in capital-labor conflicts. Occasionally, individual preachers such as Rev. Mr. Beaton, preaching to a combined service of the Fullerton Avenue Presbyterian and Lincoln Park Congregational Churches, argued that the economics of eight-hour and all other labor reforms remained fundamentally religious questions, a point that eight-hour reformers from the ranks of labor had been making for almost forty years. Beaton felt that the only true solution to labor conflicts was for employers and workers to see "the man in the other . . . another way of saying the aims of organized trades unions are Christian at heart and bottom" (*CT,* September 29, 1902, 15). Others, such as Rev. Dr. Bruce Brown, addressing the annual congress of the Disciples of Christ, saw labor unions as "the best representatives of the industrial reform movements. I am a believer in the principles on which they are founded" (*CT*, March 23, 1904, 16). But these unguarded characterizations of trade unions and their reform goals were not typical. The more common approach by ministers was the more circumscribed observations of leading Congregational preacher Dr. Frank W. Gunsaulus, pastor of Central Church, who drew parallels to contemporary labor reformers and John Wesley.

> Wesley stood in England when the labor problem was most hopeless the greatest labor reformer since Jesus Christ, and talked to men on the docks and at their work about Christ and his laws. Talk as you will, these problems can never be settled by law. You may expect your president to arbitrate, but the question will not be settled until it is settled according to Christ's law—there will never be any peace until the heart of the one power is in touch with that of the other, and each touched by the finger of Christ. (*CT*, June 8, 1903, 2)

For Gunsaulus and many other clergy, permanent changes to industrial conditions, including eight-hour reform, would not come through arbitration or legislation. Instead, only when both capital and labor were "touched by the finger of Christ" would real change take place. But what this looked like in practice, Dr. Gunsaulus never said.

When Protestant clergy preached or wrote about industrial conflicts, they continued to build on an earlier frame that identified both capital and labor as wrong in some things and right in others. As Dr. John M. Driver, pastor of People's Church, Chicago, preaching at St. James Methodist Episcopal Church, pointedly observed: "When the trade unionists were weak they begged for arbitration and denounced employers for denying it to them. Today these same trade unionists refuse to submit to arbitration and denounce those to insist upon it. . . . What is the matter? Employer and employee, wage earner and capitalist, are equally guilty, equally selfish, equally regardless of the public weal and each other's highest interests. . . . Nothing but the gospel of Jesus Christ enthroned in the hearts of men, the hearts of the poor and rich alike, can settle this question" (*CT*, June 15, 1903, 2). But while clergy no doubt felt that they were being evenhanded in these statements, the labor movement was still more likely than employers to receive censure from the pulpit for its part. Two months earlier, Dr. Driver recounted his view: "The most dangerous foes of organized labor are in its own ranks. . . . [Driver] combated the idea that capital is the enemy of labor and deprecated the 'artful denunciations' of 'corporate greed' often heard from the pulpit. The workingmen, with work exceptionally plentiful, with wages exceptionally high, with only eight or nine hours a day required, and double pay for overtime, are made to believe that they are desperately abused and in constant peril of being utterly destroyed by organized capital. All such teaching is pernicious and perilous" (*CT*, April 27, 1903, 11). Even the supposed friends of the eight-hour movement were prone to chide labor more than praise it. Bishop Samuel Fallows, who generally expressed sympathy for the movement, in preaching at St. Paul's Reformed Episcopal Church, similarly pointed out that the problems faced by unions often came from within themselves. "Unionism," Fallows states, "is upheld [by clergy and the religious press] as the salvation of labor, but not the methods of those who, claiming to be union men, brutally attack their nonunion brethren and attempt to subvert the fundamental principles of human society" (*CT*, July 27, 1903, 8). Likewise, for two weeks running, Dr. W. A. Barlett of First Congregational Church preached the paradoxical position that he "long felt sympathy for unions" but now saw them as a form a slavery that forced workingmen to do things against their will and conviction (*CT*, June 8, 1903, 2; June 15, 1903, 2).

The Baptist *Standard*, which also tended to express a wider support for shorter-hour reform efforts in this period, still was more likely to see the labor reformer himself as more problematic than employers who were in their pews. The paper expressed its concern that representatives from the labor movement who, the paper notes, "have not the slightest claim to the name Christian" have been invited to Chicago churches "to discuss the question from the point of view of the man who sees in the church an institution that should make the problem of living an easier one for him, in some ways, but who at the same time refuses to recognize that the church of the Christian life has any claims upon him. He can tell what a Christian should do and be, and thinks that his employers ought to be such a man, but does not admit that he should be the same sort of man himself" (August 11, 1900, 3). And although the *Standard* concluded this observation with the familiar idea that there should be no distinctions made between employers and employees in churches and that the job of the ministry was to denounce the sins of the wealthy as well as those of the poor, at no point in this article were Chicago's employers indicted for their "sins."

Methodist leaders expressed concern that neither capital nor labor employed Christian principles in resolving their conflicts and disrupted the entire community as a result. Methodist bishop S. M. Merrill, in an article printed in the *Northwestern Christian Advocate*, maintained that "the observance of the Golden Rule or the recognition of the ethics of the gospel in social and business life would obviate the evils of our time, and go far toward establishing the right of peace and good will in the land. . . . Mobs and strikes and unlawful agreements and combinations, whether in the assumed interest of labor or of capital, are as incompatible with law as they are with good morals or religion" (June 7, 1905, 11). But beyond offering the Golden Rule as a solution, Methodist clergy had little to say about how to achieve both reform and create "peace and goodwill" in the city.

Such overemphasis by clergy on union violence did not go unchallenged from within the Protestant camp. Dr. John H. Grey, head of the Political and Social Science Department at Northwestern University, challenged clergy's characterization of trade unions as violent in a presentation to a Bible class at the First Congregational Church in Evanston. He argued that assertions of violence by clergy may be true, but "in view of the number of deaths and physical injury to working people for which industries are responsible, it is out of place to lay such emphasis on the small number of cases of violence. . . . [To do so] merely emphasizes the minor evil as the greater one. . . . Under the competitive system, where employers are driven hard and competition is severe, the pressure to drive workingmen is correspondingly keen. As a result of this and the concentration of wealth and energy certain great evils grow up" (*CT,* March 2, 1903, 7). Richard Ely, nationally known economist and social reformer, in an article on the value of the religious press to the labor movement, chastised this attitude of clergy, calling it a significant "weakness" in the Protestant press. Ely pointed out, "Consequently, we sometimes find this condition of things: the editor of a religious weekly will be in favor of the wage-earning classes and the labor movement in general, and in the abstract, but against them almost invariably in particular, concrete instances. This causes irritation, ill-will, bad feeling. It avails nothing to say, 'I am in favor of labor organizations,' and then take an attitude of antagonism towards those things which are necessary parts of labor organizations." But this passive-aggressive approach by Protestant clergy and the Protestant press was impossible to shift.

Clergy increasingly agreed that industrial conflicts over hours put the community's well-being at risk, a point largely ignored by both employers and workers who, from the perspective of the clergy, were more concerned about their own interests. Dr. Polemus H. Swift, pastor of Wesley Church, observed that "strikes are like war—the victor suffers with the vanquished and the innocent suffers more than either the victor or the vanquished; and so costly is a great strike that it is sane only as a last resort" (*CT,* June 8, 1903, 2). Rev. Clarence Abel of Trinity Methodist Church expressed a similar opinion: "In one sense strikes are a hopeful sign of progress. . . . They have been costly but have played an important part in the elevation of the common people.

. . . It is time this nation was asking itself if it ought not to be getting past this stage of violence and brute force in adjustment of industrial relations. . . . We need, on both sides, to be educated unto a seeking for what is right and just rather than for what is expedient from our own point of view and careless of the interests of the other man" (*CT,* June 8, 1903, 2). Swift's and Abel's sentiments were shared by many more clergy and reported on in both the secular and the religious presses. But as clergy tried to speak on behalf of the community's interests in the conflicts around the workday, they were left with simplistic rhetoric that told labor and employers to not allow their conflicts to disrupt social life. They offered no concrete directives rooted in their faith traditions to improve either the relationships between bosses and workers or the industrial conditions for labor.

But in these early years of the new century, clergy latched on to one concrete idea—that active arbitration between the two sides represented the embodiment of Christian brotherhood that is "necessary in bringing about a fruitful and lasting peace" (*CT,* March 26, 1900, 7). Arbitration, a catchword of this decade of eight-hour reform, and supported by groups such as the National Civic Federation, was something practical for clergy to support as a means for resolving industrial conflicts (Montgomery 1979). The Protestant Episcopal Church, at their 1901 General Convention, institutionalized this idea by creating the Joint Standing Committee on the Relations of Capital and Labor, composed of three bishops, which included Bishop Charles Anderson of Chicago, three priests, and three laymen. In creating the committee, the Episcopal Church confirmed its mission as "a mediator and peacemaker between those who are in strife" and that the committee would investigate the aims and purposes of labor organizations and the causes of industrial conflict and would act as arbiters "to bring mutual conciliation and harmony" to employers and their workers (Protestant Episcopal Church 1901, 192). Other Protestant denominations adopted similar committees and commissions emphasizing the need for churches to be better educated on the labor movement and its reform efforts as well as offering their services to mediate labor disputes. Rev. Charles Stelzle, a regular speaker in Chicago, was appointed the head of the Presbyterian Department of Church and Labor. Baptists formed the Committee on Social Service. The Methodists created a Federation of Social Service. And Congregationalists established a Labor Department. Despite their good intentions, the usefulness of these denominational organizations was limited. In the three years after the creation of the Episcopal committee, for example, their report noted they had no requests for arbitration, nor had they had any time to study the causes of labor disturbances (Protestant Episcopal Church 1904).

Yet even though the eight-hour movement and the strikes that accompanied it were addressed more regularly in both pulpit and press, and Protestants were becoming more willing than in the past to concede that unions were workers' only protection against organized employers, other ministers continued to preach that unions were dangers to workers and the community at large. Catching attention and criticism at a meeting of the members of the CFL, a newspaper report was recounted that the Reformed Presbyterian Church adopted a resolution at their 1902 national convention in Pittsburgh regarding "membership in most of the labor and trades unions, as at present organized and controlled, as dangerous" (*CT,* June 3, 1901, 2). In the same meeting, a report came forward that a Chicago minister "likened trade unions to spider webs, in which the unwary worker becomes entangled." For many Protestants, unions and labor reform represented immoral and unjust intrusions into the operations of business.

How did the eight-hour movement and employers respond to any of these statements by clergy? Chicago workers by this point had been surveyed by Protestants to explain their views of both the clergy and the churches in industrial reform. But their clearest response came in their consistent absence from Protestant churches. The views of labor were definitive and detailed. The Protestant press bemoaned the fact that workers "look upon the church as more or less their enemy, or at least out of sympathy with their struggles" (*NWCA,* September 12, 1900, 8). In a report delivered at a meeting of the Federated Churches of the Westside at Western Avenue Methodist Church, Rev. Roy B. Guild outlined that workers believed that Protestant churches were for the rich and unwelcoming to the poor, and their ministers were afraid to support labor reform because it would upset their congregations. The low numbers of workers in churches was linked to long hours that required some unions to meet on Sundays or Sunday work itself, which kept workingmen and -women in shop and factory, a point argued again and again by labor. Samuel Gompers emphasized this point in an article that he was requested to write for the Presbyterian *Interior.* Gompers stated that more people would be working on Sundays as it was if labor had not organized to fight it (March 17, 1904). But the most telling observation in Guild's report came from two men who simply stated that "the laboring men generally did not understand the church and also that the churches did not understand unions" (*CT,* October 3, 1902, 7). A lack of mutual understanding was the Achilles' heel that continually got in the way of effective coalitions between Protestants and the eight-hour movement.

While working people consistently reflected personal devotion and religious sensibilities, surveys of local workers repeated that they did not take seriously clergy statements about unions or eight-hour reform. When Gompers appealed to Presbyterians to support shorter hours, he emphasized that workers wanted practical action.

> The workingmen want light—the light that will throw sunshine into their homes; not merely spiritual sunshine, but light that will give them better comforts in their lives today. They are tired of praying for the "sweet by-and-by" all the time and enduring the bitter now. They want something here. . . . They want the Church to preach more the charity that advocates and fights for laws upon our statute books (and the enforcement of those laws), which will prevent the employment of young children, and secure improved conditions in unsanitary workshops, factories, mills, and mines; better lien laws; liability of employment for "accidents" to workmen due to negligence, greed, or parsimony of employers; the abolition of "truck stores"; less burdensome hours of work and at a fair wage, and other improvements in the conditions of labor too numerous to mention here. (*Interior,* March 17, 1904, 339)

In the case where the Chicago minister compared unions to spiderwebs, the CFL adopted a sarcastic resolution to send a telegram to the man's ministerial association asking that prayers be said to ask God for success in achieving the eight-hour day. And when Rev. Charles Stelzle and other clergy proposed sending clergy as fraternal delegates to the CFL and other union bodies nationally, their voices reflected forty years of frustration in appealing to clergy to support eight-hour reform (*CT,* March 9, 1904, 4.). A *Tribune* reporter, covering the meeting, recounted that "half of the men in the hall wanted to answer the minister at the same time" (March 21, 1904, 1; *Chicago Record Herald,* March 21, 1904, 1). The reporter quoted responses from several men, Robert G. Wall, J. J. Linehan, and L. W. LaVine, each carrying clear suspicion and ridicule:

> If we let the ministers come here, as I hope we will, it will not be because we need their sympathy but because they need ours. There is no class of citizens so thoroughly out of touch with the workers as the ministers. Let us help them learn.

> The Christian ministers want to come here to spring some new doctrines. Others would follow the Presbyterians. The day is fast approaching when those fellows will have to organize to protect their wages.

> It will mean the disruption of the movement if we admit ministers here. Our sessions will be the scenes of fights on creeds. Ministers think the

> workingmen are getting too free, and they way to get in here to try to bring them back.

Many wage earners held strong religious beliefs, but they saw less and less practical use to actively court the assistance of clergy.

Not only were ministers "out of touch" with workers, but trade unionists also feared sectarian divisiveness that would undermine their movement by allowing ministers to join their organizations. In seeing the threat to unity from too closely aligning the labor movement with any single religious tradition or with religion in its entirely, Chicago labor was no different from labor movements all over the world. The socialist faction of the labor movement in Europe had, by 1900, already clarified its position toward religion both within and outside of the movement.

> Opposition to the priests must not be identified with opposition to religion. The principle, that religion is a matter of every man's own conscience, must remain ever sacred. There is genuine religious conviction, even if we do not show it. . . . If we are to succeed in reform agitation among our farmers, we must take an utterly different attitude toward religion. . . . People who think they have supped up all the illumination of the nineteenth century with their own little teaspoons and regard every man of religious convictions as a Blackbeard should keep away from social movements in this country; they had better keep away from all reform movements perhaps. (*Interior,* December 6, 1900, 1522)

In Chicago socialists adopted the position that socialism "has nothing to do with any man's religion. It concerns itself with the material questions of fuel, food, clothes, shelter, education, and entertainment of the working class. . . . [T]o point out to the working class how to get possession of these things which their labor produces in such abundance and how to get leisure time to enjoy them is the mission of the Socialist Party" (*Comrade,* July 1904, 218). Because the labor movement included workers from many different religious traditions, sectarian divisions among Protestants themselves and between Protestants and Catholics, Christians and Jews, and believers and nonbelievers were simply too pronounced to risk inflaming. By 1908 the Socialist Party adopted a platform that specifically ruled religion to be a private matter, irrelevant to the work of the movement (Craig 1992, 112). The labor movement found it safer to leave religion to individuals and fight collectively for eight hours on more secular grounds.

And what of the consistent accusation from all factions of the labor movement that the Protestant clergy were not actively doing anything practical to help achieve shorter hours? In some ways, such an accusation was unfair. Clergy were clergy, not community organizers or lobbyists. Their time was occupied with the day-to-day operation of their churches and seeing to the needs of their congregations. There were Protestant ministers whose names are now synonymous with the Social Gospel movement, such as Rauschenbusch, Gladden, Stelzle, and many others, who were engaged with industrial reform. However, these men were more likely to be spokespersons for particular theologies and courses of action that others implemented than the individuals who actually did the work. Most ministers, regardless of tradition, had neither the time nor the energy to engage in the difficult work of industrial reform on a consistent basis.

In Chicago's eight-hour campaigns of the early 1900s, three instances of Protestant clergy doing something more than just speaking about shorter hours stand out. In the first case, Rev. C. H. Doolittle, the pastor of Central Baptist Church who also worked as a machinist at the Troy Laundry Machinery Company, confronted a threatened strike at his shop for shorter hours and higher wages (*CT,* May 23, 1901, 3). The pastor-machinist, on hearing the news, walked to his workbench, knelt down, and offered a long prayer that his employers would grant the demands of the other men. After praying, Doolittle asked a blessing of the other 150 fellow workers and told them "to be more conservative" and outline a plan of action that included forming a committee, headed by himself, to meet with the manager, Mr. Wilcox, and the supervisor, Mr. Richardson, to present their demands. After discussion and compromise over the amount of wage increase, the head of the company accepted the men's demands for a nine-hour day. Doolittle's lesson was to settle all strikes with prayer, but the story also shows that while prayer could resonate with frustrated workers, it was the action of organizing a committee and confronting and negotiating with employers that won these workers their nine-hour day.

In the second case, the Methodist press reported on the activity of Rev. George L. McNutt, a Presbyterian minister, who with his wife and two sons went to live among the working people in an undisclosed city neighborhood. He learned firsthand the experiences and consequences of long hours of labor and why workers showed antipathy toward Protestant churches. In his narrative, McNutt recounted:

> Men and boys, ten years old and over, work in factories usually eleven hours a day one week and eleven hours a night the next week. Add an hour for the day or the midnight dinner, an hour to come and go, eight hours for sleep—how much time is left for home-love, neighborhood fellowship

> and civic duties? Sunday is their one free day—a merciful godsend. Ought I to denounce their getting together as neighbors on Sunday, as in itself a Sabbath desecration? They are too tired, mentally stupefied, to listen to a sermon. To open a library would be a love's labor lost, and then some people would want it closed on Sunday. (*NWCA*, April 4, 1900, 2)

Once he experienced the realities of overwork, McNutt, like the countless other workers, demanded change. Although few clergy went to this extreme, the stories of these pioneers were circulated among Protestant churches with the encouragement to engage in the practical work of reducing the hours of labor. McNutt's experiences also underscore the ways in which the social distance between clergy and workers intensified the mutual suspicions between them.

And in one last case, three local clergy, Dr. Frank Gunsaulus of Central Church, Dr. W. M. Lawrence of Second Baptist Church, and Father E. A. Kelly of St. Cecilia's Catholic Church, formed a board of arbitration to help settle a stockyard strike against Swift & Company Packers in 1903 (*CT*, March 21, 1903, 3). The steam-engineer workers demanded an eight-hour day and a raise in wages to 37½ cents. This clergy-based arbitration board was noted to be the first of its kind to resolve a labor dispute. After two months of deliberations, meeting with both the packers and their steam engineers, the clergy arbiters clearly seemed pleased with the experience and the outcome. The clergy offered their recommendation to both workers and employers:

> We recognize the fact that we are selected as a board of arbitration because we are not engaged in commercial relations, and by reason of our profession as religious teachers would view the matters submitted to us from the standpoint of justice, unaffected by business or political associations. While we are not confident that our decision will be satisfactory to both parties, and perhaps to neither, yet we wish to express our appreciation of the confidence reposed in us. . . . The principles of personal liberty should not be subverted. Therefore, the union, while it may show to every man of its craft that it will be beneficial to join its membership, should not, however, attempt to coerce anyone to come into its ranks, nor interfere with him for not doing so. Every man should be gauged by his ability to give satisfaction to his employer by performing any honest day's work, and the employer should recognize this by guaranteeing to such a man his position so long as he thus fulfills his duties.

That the decision of these ministers would satisfy neither the packers nor the engineers is a monumental understatement. When the steam engineers met to discuss the verdict of the clergy arbitration board, the *Tribune* reporter noted that "all were sarcastic, though none of them doubted the ministers had done their best in handing down what one of the men termed 'the worst that ever happened.' 'It's fierce' . . . 'It's the limit' . . . 'What does this give us?—Simply a lot of good advice.'"

> They asked for 37½ cents an hour—the standard scale of the city and got 30 cents. They asked for the eight hour day—the regular day in practically all of the downtown stores and factories—and they got a twelve hour day. Some little conciliation was offered to the engineers by two recommendations from the board which, however, neglected to demand that they be fulfilled. These asked the packers to arrange their business that the eight hour day can be put into effect and that they make their engine rooms large, well ventilated and sanitary.

And for their part, the packers were reluctant to talk about the decision on the grounds that they had accepted the board and agreed to its findings. "'We will have no more ministers in our [negotiations],' declared Business Agent Neil McCallum, and the others nodded in assent" (*CT*, April 28, 1903, 7).

Too many passive-aggressive resolutions and not enough practical action were the twin criticisms that the eight-hour movement left at the doorstep of Chicago's Protestant churches. Workers were better equipped with their own organized force and the changing legislative and judicial tides to achieve shorter hours for themselves on their own terms. Employers had no need for the open support of clergy to provide religious justification for their business decisions and operations. Organized labor and organized capital would negotiate the implementation of the eight-hour system for themselves. Protestants were left to determine how best to confront the eight-hour system and the larger demand to redeem time for working people through increased leisure and recreation.

A Test of Faith: The Methodist Book Concern and Eight Hours

By mid-decade, the boom time for unions became a period of retrenchment. Teamsters, garment workers, women bookbindery workers, and stockyard workers all faced significant strike defeats, and less than 25 percent of all strikes in 1904 and 1905 were successful (*CT*, July 23, 1905, 8). In 1904 Chicago witnessed ninety-two strikes in the first nine months of the year, including the massive strike among packinghouse workers and the numerous sympathy strikes by other groups of workers in support (Barrett 1987, 176). However, by year's end, the packinghouse workers were defeated, union locals collapsed, and union membership dropped from thirty-four thousand to sixty-two hundred (Barrett 1987, 180). Labor's strength to set the terms of work ebbed. But a new eight-hour demand was about to be issued by the printers across the country that, for Methodists in Chicago, would be a test of their developing social faith.

The printers' eight-hour strike in 1906 was significant as one of the last prolonged eight-hour strikes in the prewar period. Unlike the carpenters' strike in 1890 or the general strikes of 1867 and 1886, the printers' strike drew Protestant churches directly into the struggle. The publishing house for the *Northwestern Christian Advocate* and the Methodist Book Concern publications, alongside secular employers in the industry, refused to grant eight hours to employees (*ITU Circular*, no. 48, May 26, 1906). The International Typographical Union still appealed to churches for assistance in achieving shorter hours, "thereby acknowledging their kinship, as does a son who continues to ask bread from his father who give him a stone" (Addams 1960, 142).

In October 1904, a vote was taken among more than two thousand Chicago union printers in the International Typographical Union, Local 16, unanimously declaring an eight-hour day would go into effect on January 1, 1906, as part of a general strike in all unionized printing offices across the United States and Canada. Its objective was to reduce the workday from nine to eight hours with no wage reduction and to win a closed shop. Meetings with the United Typothetae, the publishers' association, yielded only a concession for a nine-hour day over the subsequent three years, at the end of which employers would "consider the advisability" of reducing the workday still further. Such inaction by employers only heightened the printers' frustration. The International Typographical Union, compared to other large labor organizations, was characterized as being "composed of the most intelligent and conservative class of labor," which realized "the wisdom of conducting a strike upon a high plane" (*NWCA*, September 20, 1905, 4). By September 14, 1905, with one million dollars in ITU strike-fund coffers, union men voted unanimously to strike for eight-hour contracts, and 30 contracts to that effect were secured by the following day (*ITU Circular*, May 29, 1905; *ITU Circular*, no. 19, September 15, 1905). A month later, the ITU assured its members that 322 eight-hour agreements had already been secured, covering some twenty-two hundred job printers and seven hundred newspapermen in Chicago (*ITU Circular*, October 14, 1905).

Employers in the United Typothetae planned to defeat the eight-hour demand with "foot, horse, and artillery" (Prescott 1905, 345). Publisher Henry

W. Cherouny, who claimed to support neither the printers nor the employers, expressed concern that the Typothetae's resistance was based on what he saw as "the antiquated notion that the rights of property vest them with the power of absolute government in their workshops" (1905, 540). But antiquated or not, both ITU Local 16 and the Typothetae prepared to fight over the eight-hour day, and both were optimistic of victory. John MacIntyre, secretary of the Typothetae, reminded employers, "Our cause is absolutely right, our position in the matter is fair, and we must and will protect ourselves against any and all claims to interfere with the management and running of the business. No one should allow himself to relax in his efforts. Greater care is necessary now than at any time in the past, and I urge the members to keep wide awake locally and to keep in touch closely with this office, so that they may be kept posted as to all that is going on in the national field" (*UTA Bulletin,* no. 50, November 19, 1905). Another eight-hour war was set in motion.

Problems emerged for the Methodist denomination when the union men working for the Western Methodist Book Concern walked off the job to secure shorter hours and a closed shop several months ahead of the January 1 deadline. At first the tone of the Book Concern seemed conciliatory at least to the eight-hour demand. H. C. Jennings, publishing agent of the Book Concern, reported at the Methodist Rock River Conference regional meeting, "We are not opposed to the eight-hour day, but do propose to do business with an open shop" (*CT,* October 5, 1905, 8). After four days of deliberation at the conference, Rev. D. D. Vaughn, pastor of the "stockyards" Methodist church and chair of the Committee on Capital and Labor, admitted that "labor can look to the church for support in the eight-hour day movement but the church has the right to be divided on the open shop question." Vaughn maintained the typical approach of clergy, promising to be evenhanded in its assessment of the conflict but also forthright. Vaughn noted, "The church will not flop either way. We will tell what we think of the rights of both trade unionists and employers. Something will be shot. If anyone is in the way they will be hit. It is their fault, not ours. We want to adopt the Christian attitude, an attitude of absolute fairness to both sides. I hold that if the employers were fair and honest we would need no unions." When asked by the secretary of the union local, John C. Harding, who the union could look to for support if not the church, Vaughn replied:

> They can look to the church for support in the eight-hour day. The men who work in closed shops are also worthy of our consideration. There is a

> question here upon which the church is divided but as far as this conference is concerned I believe it is approaching unanimity. Let us make the book concern office a model. Let us put it above everything else. . . . Let it be a place where fairness is the watchword. The labor question is growing into a great one and the attitude of the church is yearly becoming more intelligent. (*CT,* October 8, 1905, 3)

Vaughn, speaking on behalf of the Rock River Conference, was clear the Methodist denomination would support the eight-hour demand, but Vaughn wanted to use this conflict as a test of whether the church as a whole might employ its own advice to employers and organized labor for settling industrial disputes.

Though the denomination supported the printers, there remained major obstacles for the denomination's publishers in addressing the strike demands. The Western Methodist Book Concern had recently joined the United Typothetae Association. Like other manufacturers' associations, the UTA promoted its interests in the printing trade (*NWCA,* October 10, 1906, 3). Only when faced with the strike did the Typothetae take its stand opposing both eight hours and the closed shop. Many Methodist clergy resisted the demand for a closed shop as dictatorial policy from labor. Others highlighted its benefit as a guarantee to consumers that products with union labels would be quality goods produced by working people who were decently paid and worked under fair conditions. The closed shop, however, represented a greater problem to the Methodist Book Concern than did the eight-hour day even when its necessity was understood, as in this observation from Rev. David Morgan: "Let us pray that the day may come when both employer and employee can meet as brothers, and when both will be willing to throw away their weapons of warfare and settle all disputes by the Christian principle of arbitration; but until that day comes the working man must protect himself as best he can and with the best equipments he can find, which to him is a strong union and a closed shop" (*NWCA,* October 11, 1905, 9). But the Book Concern felt the pressure from the Typothetae to resist the printers.

Matters became more complicated for the Book Concern when Local 16 faced an injunction by Judge Jesse Holdom, at the request of the Typothetae, holding that attempts to force employers into eight-hour contracts or to operate a closed shop were illegal and would be considered a conspiracy. The injunction determined: "The union and its members . . . are at present engaged in the unlawful enterprise of endeavoring by unlawful means to force upon the complainants an unlawful contract of closed shop, an eight-hour day, and using threats, intimidation, the picket line, bribery and the boycott as a means to the end. Such an enterprise is, in the highest legal sense, unlawful and, in some of its elements of force and violence, criminal" (*NWCA*, October 25, 1905, 1). The union denied any use of violence or force, but the judge declared that the picketing had "annoyed nonunion men" and considered it an aggressive act. The injunction was upheld despite Local 16's attempts to nullify it.

The Western Methodist Book Concern rejected the injunction as an untrue and unjust characterization of the union's actions. But verbal distancing from Holdom's ruling did not placate striking printers. Local 16 supported a resolution of the CFL "calling on the Methodist Church to remember its statement supporting labor's right to organize . . . and attention of the Methodist Episcopal Church is also called to the fact that the Methodist Ministry of Chicago denounced the injunction as well as the Book Concern, their own property" (Chicago Federation of Labor 1905, 5; *CT*, December 18, 1905, 3). In addition to appealing to the Methodist Church to intervene on the printers' behalf, the resolution also declared a boycott of all products of the Western Methodist Book Concern until all of the printers went back to work. The ITU listed the Methodist Book Concern on the union's unfair list, the only denominational publishing house to be so listed (*ITU Circular*, no. 48, May 26, 1906).

Methodist members of Local 16 also took an active role in appealing to the church to act. A number of striking printers wrote letters to the editors of the *Northwestern Christian Advocate* and to its publishers to correct perceived misrepresentations of the strike, its demands, and the union itself. One such union member, C. M. Mack, went so far as to enjoin the Methodist newspaper editors to heed the warning of the biblical prophet Malachi (3:5, RSV), that God "will draw near to you for judgment; I will be a swift witness against the sorcerers, against the adulterers, against those who swear falsely, against those who oppress the hireling in his wages, the widow and the orphan, against those who thrust aside the sojourner, and do not fear me, says the Lord of hosts" (*NWCA*, November 1, 1905, 5).

The strike against the Methodist Book Concern caught the attention of other Protestants, most notably the Episcopalians. The *Living Church* took the position that it was wrong for a union to force employers to pay ten hours' wages for eight hours' work. "Whatever the outcome, every student of economics must deplore the short-sightedness of the demand; every lover of justice must cry out against its injustice; every friend of the workingman must hope that he may not succeed, lest success be to him inevitably the ultimate loss of opportunity to earn his living in the vocation which he has chosen and for which he has fitted himself" (January 13, 1906, 372). But this sentiment that had been argued frequently by opponents among the clergy and in the religious press for decades now elicited responses from readers that condemned the paper for not supporting the ITU.

Though the Book Concern did not agree with the Typothetae either in its descriptions of the union or in the principles set out by the injunction, the Book Concern would not give in to the union because it considered particular aspects of the ITU dangerous to the religious life of its members. The union faced sharp religious criticism for the oath of allegiance sworn by all members, which required that a union man's "fidelity to the union and [his] duty to the members thereof shall in no sense be interfered with by any allegiance that I may now or hereafter owe to any other organization, social, political or religious, secret or otherwise" (*NWCA*, November 1, 1905, 6). Despite attempts by the union to explain what such an oath "really" meant, it was interpreted literally by Methodist clergy, harking back to the days when Protestant and Catholic leaders condemned the Knights of Labor and other fraternal organizations as secret societies that required oaths of allegiance. This clause of the oath drew more than verbal criticisms from church leaders. One Catholic priest, Father M. J. Ward, went so far as to refuse absolution to any printer taking the oath, to expel such a person from the church, and to deny him a Christian burial after his death. In such cases, a printer's choice to join the union had consequences both in this world and in the next (*Workers' Call*, September 19, 1903, 1).

By January 1, 1906, ITU Local 16 printers were more and more successful in their strike. The *Tribune* observed that after eighteen weeks on strike, the eight-hour day was in effect in three-quarters of the book and job printing shops in the city, affecting twenty-four out of thirty-five hundred workers in the printing trades. The ITU Local 16 president, Edwin R. Wright, addressed "one of the largest labor demonstrations ever held in the city, saying that the outlook is bright. . . . Most of the employers are on our side. . . . We have plenty of financial resources" (January 1, 1906, 8). Only forty-eight shops held out against the eight-hour day and open shop, and while the Typothetae predicted a general lockout of printers in hundreds of small offices, the lockout never happened (*CT*, January 3, 1906, 3). But the Typothetae did its best in the holdout shops to replace any workers who were enticed by ITU members to walk out. The Typothetae also circulated an anonymous letter accusing the union of reckless use of strike funds for "office furniture and their own personal desires," an accusation denied by Local 16 officials (*CT*, January 3, 1906, 3).

As the strike wore on, the union's struggle to enforce a closed shop at the Book Concern began to edge out the eight-hour demand for dominance as an issue and in the debates among Methodists (*NWCA*, April 15, 1906, 5; April 18, 1906, 10). The closed-shop principle violated Methodist sensibilities of openness and judging individuals by performance and character. The Methodist Church was clear in its support for the work of labor unions and even sympathetic to their demands for economic justice. As noted earlier, clergy understood the "free-rider" problem that organized labor faced, that is, an open shop allowed nonunion workers to enjoy the benefits accrued by the struggle of the union without having to make a commitment to that struggle. But the Book Concern's position remained that it was obligated to follow a superior call to ensure the rights of all workers were respected so long as performance and character quality were both high, regardless of union membership.

In October Jennings & Graham and Eaton & Mains, the two publishing agents of the Book Concern, released their official and final position on the strike to the Rock River Conference of the Methodist Episcopal Church and published it on the cover of the *Northwestern Christian Advocate.*

> We have never been opposed to the principle of the eight-hour day in the Methodist Book Concern, East or West. But heretofore considered by us the conditions relating to it have been such as made it impossible for us to introduce it. After having given the entire question very careful consideration we have reached the conclusions: First, that we inaugurate an eight-hour day in all departments of our business, the same to go into effect at the beginning of our next fiscal year, November 1, 1906. Second, that we conduct the business of the Methodist Book Concern, East and West, on the principle of the "Open Shop," choosing our employees on their merit as workmen . . . permitting no employee to be discharged except for reasons of incompetency or irregularity of habits. . . . Third, that on the date of the announcement of the above plan we will formally withdraw our respective memberships from the United Typothetae of America. We have reached the above conclusions because we believe in the justice due all men, and while not unmindful of our business obligation, we desire, as always, to be responsive to the demands of that Christian spirit which should govern our administration of the great educational and benevolent trust committed to our hands by the Church. (October 3, 1906, 1)

The choice between loyalty to religious principles or to business interests put the Book Concern in a position that misrepresented its true attitude toward organized labor, requiring it to pull out of the Typothetae. It was the eight-hour question that decided this break with the business association.

The Book Concern was convinced that a shorter workday would eventually be established throughout the country. Jennings & Graham and Eaton & Mains decided that the Book Concern could in good faith institute this policy, and so, in order not to embarrass other employers in the association, they withdrew their membership (*NWCA*, October 10, 1906, 4).

Nevertheless, the CFL complicated church-labor relations by continuing the boycott of the entire Methodist denomination because of the open-shop policy that remained in force in the Book Concern. The federation circulated three hundred thousand posters that stated that the Book Concern was unfair to labor and did not deserve sympathy or support. The boycott extended to cover any business or professional person who supported the Methodist Church in any financial way (*NWCA*, January 30, 1907, 3). This boycott, however impractical, simply exacerbated the alienation between Methodists along with other Protestants and the labor movement. Rev. George H. Bennett of Chicago observed:

> We see the sorry spectacle of organized labor as such seeking to boycott and drive out of business a concern which officially and publicly grants the workday and the wages to its employees in accord with the primary object of the original organization of labor. Of course the only result of the proposed boycott, if persisted in, will be to make Methodists feel that they are being persecuted for their faith and to open a gap in trade union ranks between those who feel that they are Christians first and trade unionists afterwards and those whom the socialistic drift of trade unionism has made indifferent to religion. Nor is the result in any doubt. (*NWCA*, January 30, 1907, 7)

Striking printers went so far as to send pickets to Methodist revival meetings being held in Chicago. The job of these pickets was to act as "exhorters" and to pray for the conversion of the souls of the publishing agents of the Methodist Book Concern, which remained unwilling to grant a closed shop. David Thompson, editor of the *Northwestern Christian Advocate*, thought these pickets could have a profound effect on the labor movement if they happened to "catch the spirit of the meeting itself and are brought under conviction and are converted" (February 13, 1907, 4). Thompson continued to reiterate the position of the Methodist Church that while it supported eight-hour reform, it could not support the closed shop.

The union men at the Western Methodist Book Concern achieved the eight-hour day with the full support of the Methodist Episcopal churches in Chicago as well as the publishers themselves. As 1907 closed, the pressmen and bookbindery workers would follow the printers in striking for an eight-hour day, and, once again, smaller publishers who were less able to bear the economic costs of a prolonged strike, moved quickly to compromise, while larger firms resisted (*CT*, September 30, 1907, 4; October 1, 1907, 6).

Despite the verbal statements accepting the eight-hour day, when Rev. Dr. H. C. Jennings addressed a meeting of Methodist clergy in Cincinnati the following December, he claimed that "the greatest tyranny on earth is the tyranny of an unsanctified labor union." Jennings went on:

> In some places there is a belief on the part of the workingman that the church is prejudiced against him. This is not so. This idea has originated largely from the hoarse mouthings of anarchistic agitators and from those who spend $1,000 a year in saloons and not a cent in church. . . . Why brethren I could tell you things that have happened in this Book Concern within the last fifteen months that would open your eyes. The Saturday nights' work is not half so hard on the workingman as is his Sunday night's carousing. . . . If the workingman does not go to church it is because the workingman does not want to go to church. I don't see that he goes to church when he gets his Saturday half holiday for recreation then he does when he has to work all day Saturday. It's the whiskey bill that the workingman pays that is his ruination. (*CT*, December 24, 1907, 4)

Jennings's speech provides an important view into how far the Methodist social conscience penetrated the thinking of those who were denominational employers. The Book Concern used supportive language regarding the eight-hour day but revealed its ongoing antipathy not just to labor's demand for a closed shop but to the very idea of organized labor. Jennings did not believe shorter hours would result in more workers attending church, a point in which he may have been justified, though not for the reasons he gave.

The printers' strike at the Book Concern pushed Methodists to evaluate if and how well their religious approach to the eight-hour day and support for organized labor could be put into practical action. In this rare instance, at least in the case of shorter hours, workers saw Protestant leaders take definitive action. Although this test of faith was not the last Protestants would face, it prepared the way for the Methodists to become the first denomination to produce a social creed of labor reform goals that included reducing the hours of labor.

Shorter Hours for Women in Changing Times

While city printers and Methodists debated courses of action regarding shorter hours at the Western Methodist Book Concern, other political opportunities shaped the eight-hour movement and the ways organized labor, employers, and Protestant leaders fought over eight-hour reform. The view that shorter hours of labor were good for both workers and employers, with the government stepping in to "establish a rule of the game," was heard frequently in the press, among workers, and among a growing number of employers (*CT,* June 2, 1907, E3). In an apparent turnabout in rhetorical strategy, James W. Cleave, president of the National Manufacturers' Association, charted a new campaign of class peace. Withdrawing from a one-sided strategy of using all resources in the association's power to oppose organized labor, Cleave maintained the association would address what it saw as the dangers within both organized capital and organized labor.

> We propose to combat the tyrannical employer as earnestly as we do the despotism of the labor union boss. We intend to fight the vices and follies which have crept into many labor unions but not into labor unionism itself. In our own publications, in daily and weekly newspapers, and from platform and pulpit we plan to preach the gospel of peace between rich and poor, between capital and labor, between the captains of industry and their employees. In these ways, so we believe, we can make strikes and lockouts fewer in number and far less disastrous than they are now and help workers even more than we do employers.
>
> As a necessary preliminary to their moral transformation, the unions would be compelled to rid themselves of the ignorant, corrupt, and autocratic leaders who afflict most of them and who are responsible for nearly all the vices and follies from which labor unionism now suffers. Good results would be many and immediate. . . . [M]embership of the unions would be largely increased. . . . [E]mployers would glad treat with organized labor in disputes of all kinds. . . . [P]ublic respect would be given unreservedly to labor unions. With unionism as a principle we have no quarrel. We are only hostile to the reactionary and un-American practices which have become common in many labor organizations.
>
> The employer's position gives him the opportunity to be more oppressive if he is inclined that way than the worker. It was oppression on the part of some employers that caused labor to organize in the first place, although unionism would have come ultimately with the development of industry. There still remain arrogant and rapacious employers. . . . We must teach them that they are not only unjust to their employees and blind to their own interests, but that they are largely responsible for the Sheas, the Schmitzes, the Debses, the Haywoods, and all the others who aim to strike down the present social order and put the lowest stratum of the population on top. In short, we much teach Americanism to both capitalist and worker. (*CT,* October 6, 1907, E7)

In this lengthy excerpt, there is a transformation beginning to take place in which some employers recognized that unions had their place in the industrial order. Cleave articulates a desire for conservative unionism but never identifies specifically those specific labor demands and practices that were "reactionary and un-American," as opposed to those that were reasonable and would benefit boss and worker. Another change that is significant is that Cleave blames "arrogant and rapacious" employers for the emergence of radicalism. Employers never used language that suggests their own business practices were "unjust" or that, in resisting reform, they were "blind to their own interests." As with the Western Methodist Book Concern, employers' verbal acceptance of unions or labor reform in the abstract did not inevitably mean they would do so in concrete struggles. Nevertheless, that the president of the National Manufacturers' Association adopted this approach suggests that business elites were modifying their language in ways that resonated with the public sentiment that industrial reform was inevitable. The tide was turning against employers, and if they did not clean house for themselves, then others, whether unions, the courts, the government, or churches, alone or in combination, would do it for them.

On a national level, the politics of the eight-hour day was changing too. President Theodore Roosevelt issued an order to punish all violations of the eight-hour law that had gone into effect a few years earlier. Government contractors proved unwilling to enforce the eight-hour law and, when challenged by unions, claimed it was "not their business" (*CT,* July 20, 1906, 4). Commissioner of Labor Charles P. Neill was sent by Roosevelt to Chicago to investigate charges that contractors involved in government public works projects at Fort Sheridan and on improvements along the Chicago River and along the harbor were violating the law. Neill identified several cases, initially resulting in one contractor being fined five hundred dollars, another fifteen hundred dollars, and a third given a jail sentence for persistence in violating the law after due notice (*CT,* October 6, 1906, 6). By 1908 labor stepped up pressure to extend the eight-hour law to cover all government employees (*CT,* May 5, 1908, 6).

More eight-hour strikes unfolded in 1906 and 1907 by railroad workers, including engineers, switchmen, firemen, trainmen, and conductors (*CT,* December 13, 1906, 8). These strikes were accompanied by a bill sponsored by Senator Robert LaFollette that would limit periods of labor among railroad men to not more than sixteen in any twenty-four and would forbid workers from going back to work without having eight to ten hours' rest; any violation would result in a penalty of five hundred dollars (originally proposed to be one thousand dollars). Supporters of the proposed law pointed out that shorter hours would minimize the number of accidents on the railroads due to lack of sleep among workers (*CT,* January 8, 1907, 7). This bill advanced as the Railway Act and became known as the Nine-Hour Law because of its provision that train dispatchers could not work more than nine hours in any twenty-four and would go into effect March 4, 1908. Roosevelt himself was a staunch supporter of the Railway Act and wrote letters to persuade legislators to approve it (*CT,* March 5, 1907, 6). The *Tribune* favored the act "for the protection of the traveling public" (*CT,* February 14, 1908, 8) and gave no credence to railroad owners' claims there was not enough time to reorganize their operations, stating that "many of them have done nothing, hoping all along for some relief from the law. . . . They will have to face the situation and make the best of it" (*CT,* March 4, 1908, 8). When eight-hour strikes were threatened by dredgemen, tugmen, tug firemen, and steam-shovel men employed on the Great Lakes and also by telegraphers, Roosevelt sent Charles Neill back to Chicago to attempt some resolutions of these conflicts (*CT,* March 7, 1907, 6; August 15, 1907, 2).

But while the U.S. government seemed to be setting legal precedents for federal eight-hour reform, there were other forces limiting any moves forward. In statements that left President Roosevelt "deeply disappointed," the Judiciary Committees of the U.S. House of Representatives and the Senate concluded that the federal government had no authority to regulate women's and child labor, that such legislation would be declared unconstitutional, and that individual states had the responsibility to decide how best to protect women and children. Nevertheless, Roosevelt charged the U.S. secretary of commerce and labor to investigate and report on the conditions of women and child workers in the United States with special reference to their hours of labor and other working conditions with the hope to "arouse the public conscience" (*CT,* February 7, 1907, 6).

Amid shifting sentiments among employers and a changes in politics, Chicago women's groups, settlement-house workers, women in the Socialist Party, and the Women's Trade Union League (WTUL) took the lead in eight-hour reform by focusing on long hours among workingwomen (Tax 1980; Payne 1988). Once the provision limiting the hours of work for women to eight hours that was a part of the 1893 Factory Law had been declared unconstitutional by the Illinois Supreme Court, no further legal attempt to shorten women's hours had been attempted. Employers had been especially hostile to organizing efforts among women, and the Illinois Women's Alliance, which had been active in the 1880s and 1890s, collapsed along with its organizing efforts (Tax 1980). However, with the turn of the century, women exercised a stronger leadership presence in reform efforts of all kinds and rekindled the fight to reduce working hours for women. Margaret Dreier Robins, wife of economist and labor reformer Raymond Robins, was a vocal advocate for women's hours. Robins became the president of the WTUL in 1907. She challenged traditional ideas about improving the lives of workingwomen through charity, arguing shorter hours were the only way to truly change them. Speaking at a meeting of the Catholic Women's League's Philanthropy Department, Mrs. Robins observed:

> Charitable societies, made necessary because of poorly paid employees, really benefit employers in the end. . . . A girl cared for by some charitable organization does not care to remain there long. Often she leaves before she is well. She returns to the factory and is surrounded by the same insanitary conditions. Who gets the benefit of her added health and vitality? Why the employer. When we try to get improved sanitary conditions and shorter hours for our women workers the courts decide that our action is unconstitutional and therefore illegal. . . . A woman who works from ten to eighteen hours a day has no time to improve her condition. She is too worn out to protest. . . . These industrial conditions exist because of the ignorance of the public. We can only remedy the conditions when we have public opinion so strong that nothing can stand in its way. (*CT,* October 21, 1906, 4)

The Chicago branch of the WTUL launched a new campaign for a reduction in the hours of women in 1908, in the middle of a depression that had gutted many women's unions (Tax 1980). While the campaign would use political pressure as well as strikes, workingwomen also developed less traditional methods to build solidarity and to persuade employers and legislators to act. The WTUL formed an "eight-hour chorus" under the directorship of May Sprague from the Maxwell Street Settlement House and featuring solo performances by Mary McDowell and Margaret Dreier Robins. Mary McDowell asserted, "There is nothing that takes the poetry out of the souls of women so much as long hours and piece work" (*CT,* April 13, 1907, 7; April 17, 1908, 10). But while singing built enthusiasm among workingwomen, the tactical focus of the women's eight-hour campaign was political action, the watchword of significant portions of the labor, progressive, and socialist movements in this period (*CT,* September 6, 1908, 3; Payne 1988; Tax 1980).

On March 30, 1909, Senator W. Clyde Jones introduced a bill on behalf of the WTUL and the Chicago Waitresses' Union No. 484 that would limit women's workdays to eight hours and the workweek to forty-eight hours. The women were directed by lawyers and encouraged by the press to compromise and ask only for a nine- or ten-hour law, on the premise that it was the principle of a limitation on work rather than the question of working a specific number of hours that was at issue (*CT*, March 21, 1909, 4; April 23, 1909, 10). The waitresses' union refused to consider anything but an eight-hour bill, however, and the Jones bill went forward as such. The Illinois Manufacturer's Association (IMA) fiercely opposed the bill, going so far as to submit petitions of signatures of women workers who opposed eight hours to try to discredit the Hull House women involved in the fight. In the hearings, however, it was stated that in most shops where petitions were circulated, employers had posted threatening signs stating that wages would be reduced and women workers would be replaced by men (Women's Trade Union League 1909).

Senator Jones submitted a substitute compromise bill to amend the original eight-hour bill. The act that emerged from the Illinois Legislature mandated no more than a ten-hour workday for women and applied only to women working in any mechanical establishment, factory, or laundry (*CT*, May 6, 1909, 2). This amended bill did not limit the hours of work for the waitresses' union members, and John Fitzpatrick, president of the CFL, saw it as "a weak compromise" and thought the women should have stuck to their original demand (*CT*, May 31, 1909, 7). Women in the WTUL, however, saw it as a first step in achieving enforceable limitations of women's hours of labor by the state. In their leaflet on the struggle, *The Eight-Hour Fight in Illinois by the Girls Who Did the Work*, the WTUL asserted "Those working people who criticized this bill because it did not go further were the best friends of the overtime and sweatshop employers of Illinois, even though they were ignorant of their aid and comfort to the enemies of the working people. In the great struggles of labor it has been the shrewd device of the exploiters of labor to defeat a possible good by demanding an impossible best. We expect this sort of trickery from the enemies of organized labor but it seems hard when our friends used it to defeat our common cause" (1909, 18). Mary McEnernery of the Bookbindery Women's Union accepted ten hours as a victory for her union where women worked fourteen to sixteen hours a day.

The ten-hour law victory immediately came under attack from employers. Philip Armour appealed the application of the decision to thirty women employed in its ham-stitching department who worked eleven hours per day on the grounds that the ham department was not a factory (*CT*, July 23, 1909, 4). John M. Glenn, secretary of the IMA, announced at a meeting of the Garment

Manufacturers' Association that the IMA would file an injunction to stop the state factory inspector, Edgar T. Davies, from enforcing the ten-hour law (*CT,* August 31, 1909, 7). W. C. Ritchie and Company again appealed to the courts to stop the enforcement of the law. Ritchie contested the 1909 law as unconstitutional on the grounds that it violated a woman's right to freedom of contract and injured the families of workingwomen who were dependent on her work and wages, just as the company had done in 1893. Judge Richard S. Tuthill granted the injunction barring the enforcement of the new law by the state and declaring the law unconstitutional (*CT,* September 12, 1909, 6; *Living Church,* October 2, 1909, 774). Other employers from across a variety of industries, including cloak and suit makers, confectioners, candy makers, and even the Calumet Baking Powder Company, followed Ritchie & Company's suit and petitioned the courts to prohibit the state inspector and the district attorney from prosecuting them for violations of the law (*CT,* October 19, 1909, 7).

Tuthill's decision was condemned by women in the WTUL, the press, clergy, and other community groups who believed that the measure ought to be enforced and began a campaign to overturn the injunction (*CT,* September 13, 1909, 6). The CFL enlisted the support of Chicago churches and clergy in the fight. Clergy were asked to set aside one Sunday for preaching sermons urging the constitutionality of the ten-hour law. Once again, organized labor called on clergy to take a clear stand on the practical issue of a ten-hour day for workingwomen:

> Let the preachers and the church come out and tell us where they stand on this great question, said Delegate Philips. There can be no greater religious question of the present industrial age than this, and I would suggest that every clergyman in the city, of whatever denomination, respond to the cry of the women of Illinois for justice.
>
> Labor has a right to demand that the churches take a stand on this question, said Delegate Charles Curtiss of the printers' union. We also demand it as a right that the churches aid us in making the hard life of the working women of Illinois a little easier. If their religion amounts to anything they will do it. Let them show us. (*CT,* October 18, 1909, 10)

But in each of these quotes, there is a tone of skepticism along with hope that Chicago's Protestant leaders would act. A few days after this appeal, the Illinois Baptist Convention sent a letter to the CFL, endorsing labor's fight on behalf of the Ten-Hour Law (*CT,* October 21, 1909, 4). In the following weeks, more than a hundred letters from pastors of leading churches in Chicago and across Illinois were received by the CFL, offering support for the efforts to establish legal limitations on women's working hours (*CT,* December 10, 1909, 8). Two Baptist pastors, Rev. Melbourne P. Boynston, Lexington Avenue Baptist Church, and Rev. Johnston Myers, Immanuel Baptist Church, both approved of the movement to keep the law, and the Rev. John T. Stone of Fourth Presbyterian Church promised to preach a sermon on the issue. Unfortunately, there is no record of these men taking any further concrete action, nor were they asked what it was they felt they could do practically.

With public pressure exerted clearly in favor of the law and with the submission of studies demonstrating the negative impact of long hours on the health, productivity, and moral well-being of women in industry, the Illinois Supreme Court ruled that the ten-hour law was constitutional and enforceable under the auspices of "the police power of the State" (Beckner 1929, 204). The women's ten-hour law was perceived by its supporters to be the first step in winning a legally enforced eight-hour day for women.

Eight Hours and the Protestants' Social Creed

Within the shifting economic and political terrain shaping the eight-hour movement generally, Protestant leaders were moving toward a clearer articulation of their views of industrial reform generally and shorter hours for workers in particular. A younger generation of clergy ensured the Social Gospel penetrated Protestant denominations, which quickly formed committees and commissions to weave together a theology and set of practical steps to redeem time for workers (Curtis 1991). New groups of Protestant reformers, such as the Christian Socialist Fellowship, also emerged by mid-decade, joining older organizations such as the Christian Social Union, founded by Richard Ely in 1891. The CSF, like its counterparts, called for the application of Christian ideals to solve the many problems industrial society faced and for solidarity among all people of faith on behalf of workers. The CSF published the *Christian Socialist* newspaper, edited by Rev. E. E. Carr and his wife in 1904 (*Christian Socialist,* August 15, 1907, 5). But while the CSF contributed to the thinking of the left wing of progressive Protestants, it was the work of denominations themselves that set in motion more comprehensive changes in the how Protestants approached eight-hour reform.

By 1908 the changing dynamics of capital-labor conflicts and the gradual adoption of arbitration as a solution to the labor question were prompting denominations to change the titles of their committees from "capital and labor" to the less antagonistic "industrial relations" (Rock River Conference of the Methodist Episcopal Church 1908). Methodists created the Federation for Social Service, which brought together clergy and laity to supplement and further the "responsibility of the Church to meet the social problems of the day with a Christian answer." The federation's plan was to publish leaflets and books that addressed industrial problems and to create local federations to address local concerns. The federation's mission would create the basis for practical action among Christians resulting from being better informed on economic and social conditions (*NWCA*, April 1, 1908, 13). Within two years, Methodists at the Rock River Annual Conference, in calling attention to the work of the federation, advanced the need for the church to support eight-hour reform: "The limits placed upon the mental development by the introduction of machinery and the factory system have created a need for more leisure for those who toil with their hands, and we affirm our conviction that the marvelous success of modern industrial and economic enterprise makes urgent and possible the granting of an eight-hour labor day" (Methodist Episcopal Church 1910, 98).

Episcopalians organized the Commission on Christian Social Service in 1908 to build bridges with the labor movement and to attract wage earners back to the church through concrete action. Rev. Frederick Edwards, rector of St. James Church, Milwaukee, noted that "there could not be a true theology without a true sociology. . . . I am not saying it is the bounden duty of the rector to get up on Easter Day and preach a sermon on the need of a new drain in the fourth ward, although I have known situations where the preaching of such a sermon would have been about the best proof that the Church could have given of a resurrection" (*Living Church*, May 23, 1908, 131). The commission made a clear statement recognizing that workers were sympathetic to the teachings of Jesus Christ but were frustrated by the many ways clergy did not live up to them. Like the Methodists, the Episcopal commission urged "all Christians to study the existing social and economic problems in light of the Gospel of Jesus Christ; to join in every movement for the advancement of the interests of labor, and in particular, such movements as seek to obtain fairer wages and shorter hours of labor." In addition, the commission "strongly recommended" priests and congregations work to secure a Saturday half holiday for the employees of retail stores (Diocese of Chicago 1909, 50).

Presbyterians had established their precedent-setting Department of Church and Labor in 1903. Rev. Charles Stelzle, in working closely with organized labor, eventually became a fraternal delegate to the AFL in 1906. Stelzle organized a mass meeting of workers to coincide with the Presbyterian

General Assembly in Kansas City in 1908, drawing fifteen thousand workers, thirty vice presidents of various trade unions, and the treasurer of the AFL, John B. Lennon, who was also a Presbyterian. Stelzle's remarks highlighted the importance of the labor movement and the churches working together to change society. "A pure labor proposition, no matter who the speakers, has never attracted so vast a multitude. Here is a lesson for the workingman. There probably have been greater religious meetings in the history of the church, although the occasions have been rare, but this was undoubtedly the biggest meeting in the history of the General Assembly. There's a lesson for the Churchman. It's the combination of church and labor which makes such things possible, and therein lies our hope—the hope of the church and the hope of labor" (*Interior,* June 25, 1908, 840).

Individual denominations, calling for church and labor to collectively transform society, found a new structure for building real unity around this goal through the creation of the Federal Council of Churches of Christ in America, in Philadelphia, in December 1908. The new Protestant federation included Methodists, Southern Methodists, Negro Methodists, Episcopalians, Mennonites, United Brethren, Negro Zion Methodists, and Baptists as delegates (*Standard,* December 1908, 8). At its first meeting, the Federal Council issued its own Social Creed, articulating the shared understanding among Protestants regarding their unique role in shaping the economic and moral life of communities and a forthright statement mandating that all Christians support concrete industrial reforms to change the conditions endured by the working classes across the country. In its opening statement, the writers of the Social Creed expressed the pressing need for the church to act:

> The Church now confronts the most significant crisis and the greatest opportunity of its long career. In part its ideals and principles have become the working basis of organizations for social and industrial betterment which do not accept its spiritual leadership and which have been estranged from its fellowship. We believe, not for its own sake but in the interest of the kingdom of God, the Church must not merely acquiesce in the movements outside of it which make for human welfare, but must demonstrate not by proclamation but by deeds its primacy among the forces which seek to lift the place and better the condition of human life.

This creed was more than just a statement of belief that labor reform was a good idea. It mandated deeds as well as words. The Social Creed stated it was the *duty* of all Christians to join workingmen and -women in their struggles to secure "the gradual reduction of the hours of labor to the lowest practicable point, and for that degree of leisure for all which is a condition of the highest human life," and also "for a release from employment one day in seven" (*NWCA*, December 16, 1908, 14).

Individual Protestant denominations quickly endorsed the Social Creed and used it to create new groups to address the fourteen individual mandates that the creed included. The Presbyterian Church formed the Committee on Social Problems (General Assembly of the Presbyterian Church, USA, 1909, 47). This committee was made up of five ministers and five elders and reported to the General Assembly "regarding the great moral questions arising out of the industrial and commercial life of the people . . . and the application of the Gospel to the acquisition and use of wealth, to the relations between employer and employed, and between capital and labor, and to the existence of unnecessary poverty in a land where there is more than enough for all." A year later, the General Assembly recommended the creation of a Bureau of Social Service to oversee the work of its several related committees, including the Committee on Social Problems and the Department of Church and Labor (General Assembly of the Presbyterian Church, USA, 1910, 232).

The Episcopal Diocese of Chicago's Commission on Christian Social Service took seriously the charge to apply the gospel to questions regarding the acquisition of wealth. Considering the great wealth represented by those in the pews of the city's Episcopal churches, it is perhaps surprising to hear the pointed critique and mandate for resolution in its 1910 report.

> Every Christian man must ask himself this question: have the men and women who have been instrumental directly or indirectly in producing the wealth which I enjoy been benefited by its production and received their fair share of it? If he does not know, it is his duty to find out, and if he cannot answer yes with a good conscience, it is his duty as a Christian man to see to it—at whatever cost to himself—that every dollar of his income is honestly made and honestly administered in such a manner that the contributors to that wealth and the community in general are benefited thereby. Many a man sanctions corporate acts which in his individual capacity he disapproves. He is willing to share in gains which he knows to be unjust when judged by ethical standards, to sanction—at least by his silence—methods which he knows to be unfair. Can a Christian man as a member of a corporation profit by unchristian methods of business and remain guiltless? Can he at the same time serve God and Mammon? That is the question. There can be only one answer for a Christian. At whatever cost to himself he must stand for righteousness and refuse to be partakers in other men's sins. (Diocese of Chicago 1910, 53)

At the 1910 General Convention of the Episcopal Church, the Joint Commission on the Relations of Capital and Labor was equally forthright in its embrace of the Social Creed's support of shorter hours for labor, noting that "no business interests, no profit, however great, can warrant the deliberate deterioration of human life. Such a principle has clear implications. No Christian employer can find valid ground for conducting an industry which requires, or even permits, the regular employment of men for twelve hours a day seven days in the week at a wage which necessitates the work of women and children that the family may live" (Protestant Episcopal Church 1910, 537). The commission, which included Chicago bishop Charles P. Anderson, observed that many Episcopal dioceses were slow to take up labor reform and some remained afraid.

Baptists founded their Commission on Social Service in 1909 with a survey of congregational activities related to "applied Christianity," social settlement work, outreach to workers and the labor movement, involvement in political movements, and the degree ministers preached on social and industrial reform (*Standard,* February 20, 1909, 8). Chicago Baptists were supportive of the Social Creed and saw it as the basis for a "new Baptist consciousness" that emphasized social service along with education, evangelism, and organization. As the *Standard* observed:

> The most vital and absorbing of all is its reference to social service. What is called "a social self-consciousness" has deeply affected the attitude of the masses of men toward the church. . . . [T]he reason that should concern us most is the charge that the church has failed to apply the teaching of Jesus to the social conditions of men. . . . It is absolutely certain, the social gospel of Jesus must prevail, and this social gospel teaches that there must be just treatment of our brother man, just laws, just wages, just surroundings, before men can be said to live the gospel of Jesus. (January 11, 1911, 6)

The Baptists, as well as other Protestants, understood that evidence of one's religious conviction grows out of how they treat others. But it could also be argued that this new Baptist consciousness included recognition that workers would not be attracted back to the churches until their industrial conditions were reformed. Baptists emphasized the importance of work and the need for education to help train workers in the proper use of leisure, once it was obtained.

> The gospel of work is second only to the gospel of salvation, the one is an essential part of the other. . . . There is no question that an eight or nine-hour work-day is amply sufficient for the production of all the necessities

> of life, together with the legitimate luxuries, and that the men ought to have the extra time for social and individual development. But when you come to turn several hundreds or thousands of men out with one or two extra hours of time on their hands, you are simply bidding for disorder and carousing, unless at the same time care is taken to institute efficient propaganda looking to the training of the men in the wise use of the free periods. (*Standard*, July 8, 1911, 5)

In some ways, the new Baptist, and broader Protestant, consciousness was not dissimilar from the old one in its suspicion of unregulated leisure. Nevertheless, it was indeed new in seeing that between the gospel of work and the gospel of salvation comes redeeming time for labor.

One more test of Chicago's new Protestant consciousness came in the form of the United Garment Workers' strike for shorter hours in 1910, a strike that included almost forty thousand workers, many of whom were women. Within two months, a quick settlement had been reached, guaranteeing the ten thousand employees at Hart, Schaffner, and Marx union contracts, a minimum wage, and a nine-hour day. Katherine Coman of the Chicago WTUL pleaded for support from the city's Protestant clergy:

> The synagogues of the city have turned their tithes into a relief fund and are maintaining a commissary station from which six hundred families are fed. The radical Jews are issuing meal tickets for single men and women at a cost of $3000 a week. Father O'Callaghan of the Paulist Fathers and Father Hishen have appealed to their congregations for aid, and each church has contributed $100 to support the strikers. Several Protestant churches devoted the Thanksgiving Day offering to the same cause, but as yet the Protestants have not contributed in proportion to their numbers and wealth. This is a great opportunity. There can be no more effective demonstration to these strangers in our midst of the depth and sincerity of Protestant Christianity than the generous response to this, their first appeal for help. (*Living Church*, January 7, 1911, 337)

A few Protestant clergy heeded the call for support, and the Strike Committee reported funds collected from local churches (Women's Trade Union League 1910, 48). Second Presbyterian contributed $11, while St. James Episcopal gave $3.60. The Methodist Federation for Social Service hardly did much better with a reported contribution of $7. Episcopal bishop Charles P. Anderson held a special service in January 1911 at the Cathedral of Saints Peter and Paul for a just settlement to the strike. As the WTUL described the occasion, "A very beautiful labor liturgy was used for the occasion and the Bishop took a strong and unequivocal position on the rights of organization for the working people, stating that he believed in organized labor, and, as a rather large employer in his official capacity, employed it. Bishop Anderson stated that the manufacturers were occupying the untenable position of denying the right of organization to their employees, while themselves belonging to the strongest kind of organization" (Women's Trade Union League 1910, 26). But despite these gestures of support, the strike had limited success. Only a third of the striking workers achieved an eight-hour day, and the remaining thirty thousand workers called off their strike by early 1911 without any concessions made by employers and without further pragmatic help from Protestant clergy.

The eight-hour day was increasingly an inescapable part of the industrial terrain for employers, workers, and the clergy. On the eve of the printers' strike in Chicago, employer H. W. Cherouny prophesied: "The eight-hour day will come, if not now, certainly within the next ten years. The movement for its introduction is prompted by the spirit of our age; that is, by the universal opinion of people in regard to the means of securing their temporal happiness. No single trade, no Church, no State can build a dike against the wave of popular volition rolling toward this beacon fire, which is enkindled by the ever yearning human heart" (1905, 539). The history of Chicago's eight-hour movement illustrates the tenacity of workers to keep up their struggle over nearly a half century of opposition and slow gains. It also illustrates the vulnerability of workers, as internal divisions over craft and industrial unionism, socialism, anarchism, gender, and ethnicity hampered, but never extinguished, hopes for an eight-hour day. The slow progress of workers, however, kept the issue of hours before the public. Labor militancy, repressive actions by employers, the widening gap between rich and poor, and, above all, the demand of labor reformers that church leaders address industrial conditions pushed Chicago's Protestants to find a solution to these crises. And the churches responded.

In 1867 no Protestant clergy stood with the several thousand city workers to celebrate and enforce the first eight-hour legislation. In 1902 observers remained unwilling "to formulate in definite terms the attitude of the church towards the labor question" (*Standard,* August 30, 1902, 5). Yet a decade later, in 1912, Protestant clergy had adopted a new approach to the eight-hour movement. As the Baptist *Standard* noted: "Christianity is awakening to a sense of responsibility resting upon it, and its message is even now being emphasized, and will be more faithfully applied. Men everywhere are catching the vision, and a better and happier day shall doubtless soon be ushered in" (March 16, 1912, 13). Moreover, the Protestant gospel of work, employers' gospel of wealth, and a new gospel of leisure and recreation could be expressed equally through shorter hours for labor.

> Surely the glad tidings of work stand second only to the gospel of salvation. Bondage of any kind is a curse; worry and anxious care tear down the human tissue; but work is the key to life and happiness. The Father has seen in one of his highest manifestation as the Creator—the master-workman of time and eternity. "My Father worketh even until now and I work," says the Christ. And one of the dominant conceptions of the kingdom is that of labor for the Master in the service of our fellows. We all like to daydream of what heaven is like; one dream more or less will not harm and it may help. Heaven, dreamed a red-blooded man one day, is that condition of affairs where there is perfect balance between the individual capacity and preference for work and production. That is, when that day shall dawn upon which all labor is congenial to his talent, free from anxious care and worry, then shall come the first day of heaven-land, for then shall we be following hard in the way of the loving Creator whose joy is to sustain and bless his created beings. (*Standard,* July 8, 1911, 5)

But what effect did the adoption of a new creed and the new, more supportive relations between the church and labor have on the eight-hour movement in the twentieth century? Clergy involvement in labor reform assisted organized labor by rallying public support for shorter hours on religious and moral grounds. Church support was important to a movement dependent on the pressure of public opinion to succeed. These coalitions, while never completely successful, built a foundation of knowledge about industrial conditions that was separate from the general public hysteria surrounding many labor demonstrations. But in many ways, Protestant support for an eight-hour day did not have the impact that clergy hoped it would. Too often, social Christianity was led by the middle class and appealed to them, leaving the class-based social chasms between religious activists and the labor movement as wide as ever (Phillips 1996, 219). The alienated working classes of Chicago were not attracted back into the Protestant fold. To many among the rank and file of labor, such a transformation represented too little, too late from church leaders.

In the industrial chaos following the Civil War, labor reformers invoked the moral power of religion to argue for a reduction in the hours of labor. But in the twentieth century, as industrial conflict became an accepted part of industrial life, best solved by arbitration and collective bargaining, religious language was set aside in favor of economic arguments that more effectively convinced employers of the reasonableness of the eight-hour system. The vision of redeeming time through a transformation of the entire industrial order was reduced to winning shorter hours for workers as a part of that order, not in opposition to it. Organized labor and employers increasingly spoke a common language based on the logic of the capitalist market and sought only to situate workers within it. Religious values had no place in the industrial landscape of the new century. The cultural resonance of religious rhetoric could not, by itself, sustain alliances between clergy and wage earners, nor did it move employers to concede shorter hours to workers. Clergy and labor, two would-be partners in reform, inevitably talked past each other. Labor came to rely more on the courts and legislation than the church for its industrial salvation. This is not to say that the eight-hour movement never again framed its demands in religious terms. But the contributions of the religious community, in rhetorical or instrumental terms, were useful only as practical resources for winning particular battles with employers, not as ends in themselves.

CONCLUSION

Religion and the Trajectory of Labor Reform Movements

> The labor problem is a religious as well as an economic problem, and it is one in which the church should be deeply interested. . . . The church is composed of all classes of people, as is the state. It therefore should not and cannot take sides with one class as against another, but take its position with reference to great principles which make for the good of all. Like the state also, its position should be one which would be a worthy example for others to follow.
>
> —*Northwestern Christian Advocate,* October 10, 1906, 3

> So much for our treatment of the church. We clung to it as long as we hoped to make it useful. Disappointed in that, we have tried to expose its paltering and hypocrisy on this question, broadly and with unflinching boldness, in hopes to purify it and bring it to our aid. Our labors with the great religious societies, with the press, with the institutions of learning, have been as untiring and almost as unsuccessful.
>
> —*Labor Enquirer,* July 21, 1888, 1

Time, faith, and labor are three aspects of contemporary American life that continue to generate discussion, debate, and, at times, explosive social conflicts. Time is something none of us seems to possess in sufficient quantities, and, in an era of multitasking, it seems completely incongruous to discuss the idea of redeeming time in ways that create separate spheres of work and leisure. Technology structures time, so many never completely leave work, and for increasing numbers of people, being on call around the clock is the new normal. But even in our own time, critical voices from many directions, including religion, increasingly encourage us to unplug and reclaim nontechnologically mediated time for family, friends, and self. But in the twenty-first century, few voices suggest that in disconnecting from technology that we work less. The rhetoric of the eight-hour movement that argued shorter hours would increase employment opportunities for the jobless is not even a part of current economic or political debates over how to increase jobs in the face of the chronic and now seemingly permanent states of unemployment created for many American workers during the recession of the past decade.

Nevertheless, the desire to redeem time by nineteenth- and early-twentieth-century workers and the evolution of arguments rooted in faith and morality to support such a desire resonate as much today as they did then. Attempts by labor reformers to draw religious leaders into alliances to redeem time for workers, and the desire of the religious community to address contemporary economic problems, also hold lessons for us today. Since the late 1980s, the labor movement has strategically called upon the religious community for support in strikes, union organizing drives, and living-wage campaigns. Religious activists from many traditions also have mobilized on their own terms on behalf of workers' rights. But this analysis of the role of Protestants in the history of the eight-hour movement illuminates the complexities involved in bringing religion into industrial struggles, past or present, which is summed up in the two quotes that begin this chapter. What are the implications of this portion of Chicago labor history for understanding religion, the labor movement, and their combined impact on our understanding of economic justice and the nature of work?

Following the Civil War, Chicago clergy remained convinced that the well-being of the community rested firmly in the hands of Christian industrialists, a class whose moral standing was unquestioned due to their business success and regular attendance at Sunday church services. In contrast, the industrial problems sweeping the city were identified with the "dangerous classes," the "drinking classes," and the "tramps, sloths and thieves" who made up the city's working classes. Consequently, the Protestant solution to the social problems that were intruding more and more into the lives of respectable Chicagoans, such as intemperance, Sabbath desecration, and most of all class hatred and labor strife, was the regeneration of the souls of individuals from those classes most prone to these vices: Chicago's workers.

But by the twentieth century, Protestant leaders embraced a new social consciousness regarding eight-hour reform and its role as a mechanism for resolving the labor question and creating a more just industrial order. The editor of the Methodist *Northwestern Christian Advocate* expressed the understanding that by this point most clergy shared: that the labor question generally and all discussion of eight-hour reform were religious questions that concerned all people of faith. What seems to be a platitude is really a revolutionary shift for Protestants. This new consciousness laid the foundations for a new and specifically religious discourse to parallel a growing progressive civic discourse about the adverse effects of industrial expansion on city life and the need for concrete solutions. Church leaders employed religious doctrine and biblical injunctions against employers resisting efforts to increase leisure for workers rather than using them, as they had in the 1860s and 1870s, against workers themselves. Protestant Sabbatarians and temperance reformers allied themselves with eight-hour advocates in struggles to reduce the hours of labor because of the religious and moral gains they both hoped would be achieved by doing so. In the most dramatic move of all, Protestant denominations adopted the Social Creed that mandated support for shorter hours for labor and the creation of a six-day workweek as a duty for all Christians.

However, a persistent theme that emerged over and over again in their preaching and writing was that Protestant church leaders felt constrained from exclusively taking the workers' side against employers in their own communities. One practical reality contributing to this sense of constraint was that the city's employers and other upper- and upper-middle-class Chicagoans filled the pews of Protestant churches. In this narrative, as in many similar histories of industrial conflicts in other communities, clergy were not free to speak their minds from the pulpit without risking their jobs. When Rev. William H. Carwardine spoke out against the desperate conditions prompting the upheaval of the Pullman strike in 1894, he was promptly dismissed from his post, accused of being an anarchist and socialist, and "exiled" from the town of Pullman (Cawardine 1973, vi). This was an obvious point to workers who charged clergy over and over with cowardice when they needed, as did Jesus, to call employers who were also parishioners to repent for their industrial sins. And even when they were the most outspoken in preaching about the rights of labor to wealthy congregations, their good intentions did little more than cause business elites such as J. P. Morgan to "squirm uncomfortably" while listening to these sermons while pushing other employers to leave their congregations entirely (Weir 1996, 83).

But clergy also held a theological understanding that churches were composed of people from across the class spectrum and that the moral improvement of all the city's citizens, across class lines, was the central mission of the church. Clergy initially opposed shorter work hours because of fears about inappropriate and immoral uses of leisure time for workers. Drinking, gambling, and other sinful activities were presumed to preoccupy the lives of workingmen and -women, in which case overwork was deemed to be morally legitimate to prevent individual temptation and to maintain the unraveling of community life. When clergy condemned strikers or extolled the virtues of long, hard work to subordinate social classes, they spoke and acted out of their social positions as the moral leaders of Chicago. Clergy did not, however, hold employers blameless in industrial conflict and laid the responsibility for urban disruption at their feet. As direct knowledge about industrial conditions and the burdens of working ten- to fourteen-hour days reached clergy through the press in the 1880s and 1890s, their polemics against workers and the eight-hour movement were increasingly replaced by denunciation of leading industrialists and city officials for corrupting the morality of workingmen and -women by long hours and Sunday labor. The eight-hour day became an issue alternatively opposed and championed by Protestant leaders who wanted to bridge the gulf between social classes, not to polarize them further.

This theologically informed mission to work toward class integration led clergy to support arbitration and reconciliation as means for bringing workers and their employers together. Clergy occasionally recognized that workers had the right to defend themselves through strikes, given their relative powerlessness compared to employers. But verbal support, as it was expressed in sermons, speeches, denominational resolutions, and the press, for labor's efforts to redeem time through the eight-hour system remained the standard approach for Protestant clergy. By 1912 Protestants recognized the moral legitimacy of the eight-hour movement, but creating a more unified urban community remained the centerpiece of their support. Reform and reconciliation rather than political resistance and revolution always won the day with clergy.

But labor wanted more. The perspective of Chicago labor reformers expressed eloquently and directly by Wendell Phillips at the start of this chapter was taken from a collection of his speeches published in 1888. Phillips pointedly asserted that the adoption of a new consciousness by Protestants was too little, too late. He underscored both the longing of workers to join forces with clergy to transform society as well as their frustration at the reticence of Protestant clergy to take any practical action to assist workers in achieving the eight-hour day. Later in this same speech, Phillips referenced the church's position on abolitionism before the advent of the eight-hour movement. He critically observed that "if the church changed its policy and made abolition a possibility, it was after it had used every effort to make abolition an impossibility" (*Labor Enquirer,* July 21, 1888, 1). So while workers believed that eight-hour reform could be achieved with the aid of the religious community, experience taught them to expect most clergy and religious organizations to be unwilling or unable to provide substantive aid.

But impatience with local clergy inaction did not deter workers from challenging overwork on religious grounds. Labor reformers and workers within the eight-hour movement believed that shorter hours would redeem time by integrating a morality of work with a morality of leisure. Religious language incorporated older themes regarding the importance of hard work with newer themes focused on the moral necessity of leisure for workers to fulfill their obligations to their faith, their families, and their communities as well as to take advantage of expanding opportunities for education and other means of self-improvement. But as the struggle to close the World's Fair on Sundays showed, workers increasingly wanted to enjoy leisure for its own sake, for fun and entertainment on the one day of the week that more and more workers had off.

Tactically, workers had few expectations that Protestant clergy would do much to help them, and they looked to their own strength and solidarity to press for shorter hours with increasing success. From 1886 onward, as more shops worked under the eight-hour system, hard evidence that demonstrated shorter workdays were economically viable slowly offset the negative opinions of employers toward reform. Employers' attitudes changed too, and organized labor found sufficient strength to make their points through their own organized efforts and strikes. Appealing to the religious foundations of eight-hour reform and to clergy for assistance was increasingly unnecessary and irrelevant as movement strategy. In any event, employers were not convinced to shorten the workday by arguments rooted in religious morality. Redeeming time for employers meant maximizing efficiency and improving profit margins, nothing more.

Although religious and moral language punctuated the labor press and speeches, eight-hour reform was remade as a secularized economic and civic issue. Redeeming time involved an accommodation to capitalism and industrial production instead of resistance to it. Religious language could no longer penetrate the market in ways that shaped the decision making of business elites. Faith was a private matter and had no place in the logic and functioning of industry, especially as a basis for regulating the workplace. Consequently, even though churches sent delegates to labor conventions and were applauded for their resolve to support industrial reform, the eight-hour movement needed church leaders to solve what were now purely economic problems of rationalized production. Ironically, this shift in the rhetoric and strategies of eight-hour reformers coincided with Protestant leaders stepping forward to formally lend their institutional support to their movement. Protestantism and eight-hour reform in Chicago were fated to be like two ships passing in the night. The cultural resonance of religious rhetoric by itself was an insufficient basis in legitimating the movement's goal. Rhetoric needed to be tied to action. If religious appeals moved neither employers to reduce the hours of labor nor clergy to use their moral authority to pressure them to do so, the movement would choose other rhetorical strategies that would.

Religious Cultural Resonance

Religion has long been shown to play significant roles in movements for social change both in the past and in the present. There are those movements that are among the most familiar U.S. examples such as the civil rights movement of the 1950s and 1960s, the movement for peace in Central America during the 1980s, and contemporary movements for and against abortion rights, environmentalism, and lesbian, gay, bisexual, and transgender rights. Outside the United States, people of faith and religious leaders have played prominent roles in the fight to end apartheid in South Africa, in the liberation movements across Eastern Europe, and in social conflicts across the developing world. Beliefs about how best to organize social and political life and the social relations between groups with varying degrees of economic, political, and cultural privilege, derived from Christianity, Islam, Judaism, and many other traditions, have been necessary factors for mobilizing collective action. Religious language, imagery, and symbols contribute moral imperatives that drive people to challenge existing power relations or to support, as movement outsiders, those who do (C. Smith 1996a). These aspects of religion contribute, as Barrington Moore once observed, "the infusion of iron into the human soul to give it the power to judge and to act" (1978, 82).

But while history has highlighted the importance of religion in social change, less attention has been given to how the role of religion as a feature of social movements changes as a result of the changing dynamics between religions, a social movement, and its target elite over time. Nor have many of the historical and sociological works done on religion and social movements focused attention on movements attempting to generate economic or industrial reform and change as opposed to movements seeking political or other kinds of cultural reforms. The story of redeeming time in Chicago illustrates how the internal dynamics of an industrial reform movement and its engagement with its external environment, especially with the religious community, shape what happens to religion as a part of collective action.

It would be easy to think about the religious rhetoric within the eight-hour movement in terms of the cultural resonance that religious language had for Chicago workers, as others have done before. For instance, Gutman (1966), in his classic analysis of religion and labor activism, argues that religious belief was a taken-for-granted starting point for American workers in the nineteenth century and was used to challenge industrialization and offer alternative interpretations to counter the religious meanings of industrial change promoted by employers and clergy (Calhoun 1982). The nineteenth century witnessed numerous other political movements that were driven by religious ideas, from abolitionism to temperance to educational reform. Even when religious language, imagery, and narratives seem vague and disconnected from a specific movement's goals on the surface, in cultures of religiosity there is no collective action apart from religious belief (C. Smith 1996b, 140).

The religious dimensions of the fight for the eight-hour day are illustrative of the much more complex role served by religious rhetoric in industrial conflicts. Protestant beliefs underlying moralities of work and leisure permeated the culture of life in nineteenth-century Chicago. Clergy constructed their responses to the principle of shorter hours around them. Workers also constructed religious understandings of the eight-hour system out of this common religious language. In contrast, there is no evidence that churchgoing employers in Chicago ever employed religious language either as a mobilizing force in manufacturing associations or to frame specific conflicts with labor. As was seen again and again, employers used their own moral discourse, rooted in laissez-faire capitalism, productivity, and profit accumulation as the key logic for weighing all changes within industrial production.

Shared religious understandings of industrial conditions and community life are only a beginning for movements seeking to mobilize the religious community as an ally. Differences in how those beliefs were interpreted by clergy and workers as well as differing understandings of their implications for economic life meant that efforts to transform religious ideas into practical reform efforts would face serious obstacles. Workers and clergy spoke different religious languages even when they used the same words. And like the biblical story of the tower of Babel, when these groups were not able to communicate through a shared language, alliances and shared efforts collapsed. The eight-hour movement had to find a new language, one that would resonate with employers and entice them to adopt the eight-hour system. Doing so became a higher priority than maintaining religious frames as part of the movement's strategy.

Chicago workers actively incorporated a religious understanding of industrial relations to build religious arguments in favor of shorter hours. Eight hours was a religious issue, ordained by God, and, therefore, anyone who claimed to be a person of faith was morally obligated to support reform. But workers were not theologians. They wanted more from clergy than just tacit agreement to shared moralities of leisure. They also wanted action and instrumental support to change industrial conditions in ways that were consonant with their understanding of transforming Chicago into a moral economic community, and it was over this shift from talk to action that workers and clergy were most at odds.

Changing Conditions

A key point often overlooked by historians and social scientists that examine movement rhetoric is that the ability of religious language to actually mobilize support is influenced by local conditions and contexts. Conditions change over time as a direct result of local struggles over industrial reform between challengers and the challenged (Piven and Cloward 1979). Movements therefore adjust their rhetoric in ways that further communication and access to elites, not limit them. Consequently, unfolding movement campaigns can solidify a movement's commitment to some forms of rhetoric, on the one hand, or shift its commitment to rhetoric more likely to resonate with target elites and achieve movement goals, on the other (Babb 1996). Independent of the cultural significance of religious beliefs among Chicago's working classes, the use of religious rhetoric rose and fell within the eight-hour movement based on how much they were perceived to heighten movement power and success when faced with the intransigence of elites.

A specific series of events unfolded in Chicago that had an impact on how the eight-hour movement understood its mission, ideologically and instrumentally. First, legislation did not yield an enforceable eight-hour day for workers, as reformers had expected. Second, despite persistent appeals for clergy action from the movement, there was little substantive practical action and support forthcoming from Chicago's Protestants, generating cynicism and frustration among workers. Third, the general strikes of 1886 and the industry-specific strike of 1890 were successful as a result of union strength and solidarity. Fourth, *economic* evidence from eight-hour shops (again, slowly) liberalized business attitudes in favor of shorter hours. Fifth, and finally, public debates over labor reforms following Haymarket (slowly) increased public sympathy for workers' *political* rights to peacefully protest and to collective bargaining. Together, these events shifted the perceptions of eight-hour reformers. Why look to religion as an effective tool for change when the organized strength of unions, pressure from the courts, and employers' willingness to accept some degree of reform were getting the movement closer to achieving the eight-hour day?

But whether to see religion as a means to gain shorter-hours reform was not only a question that concerned workers in the eight-hour movement. Protestant clergy too were compelled to address industrial conditions, and their understanding of the eight-hour question was shaped by these evolving local conditions. In addition to the labor upheavals that rocked Chicago across the last decades of the nineteenth century, two specific crises in particular confronted Protestant leaders in the late nineteenth century. First, clergy were worried that workers continued to be alienated from Protestant churches, removing their moral influence from the labor movement. Second, the steady growth of immigrants from Catholic countries threatened to eclipse the cultural hegemony of Protestantism. The desire to offer relevant moral leadership to new industrial circumstances and to maintain cultural dominance pushed Protestant leaders to engage the eight-hour issue on their own terms.

With the development of the new Protestant consciousness, a shorter workday was championed by clergy in the hope it would demonstrate to the working classes that Protestant ministers were on the side of struggling workers and so combat the entrenched suspicion that many workers expressed about clergy. The eight-hour system also became central to the Protestant belief that with fewer hours of labor, workingmen and -women would have the time and energy to engage more in the religious and civic life of Chicago. Finally, eight hours became an important issue for Protestant leaders who believed their mission in social life was to act as a social conscience in urban communities, actively championing industrial policies that promoted social harmony between classes and minimized urban disruption.

But while changing social conditions from outside and within their churches encouraged clergy to verbally support workers, structural features of their social positions *as clergy* kept them from becoming full activists in the struggle. Clergy from Episcopalian, Presbyterian, and Congregationalist traditions typically led congregations with the largest segment of religiously inclined employers and their families. These clergy were also least likely to support eight-hour efforts prior to 1890, either in their rhetoric or in their actions. Methodist and Baptist clergy, in contrast, had comparatively fewer ties to large manufacturing interests and were more likely to be supportive before 1890. The strength of Sabbatarianism in these two denominations in particular encouraged this support.

Although such patterns among Chicago Protestants support previous research on the ideological and political ties between nineteenth-century industrialists and clergy, paradoxes abound that challenge the often taken-for-granted assumption that clergy supported only employers. For instance, the editor of the Congregationalist *Advance* applauded the eight-hour movement of 1867, one of the first to publicly offer moral approval to reform, but then made no further reference to the eight-hour day until 1886. While the Protestant Episcopal Church embodied wealth and privilege, it was the first denomination to organize clergy and laity to join forces with labor with its Church Association for the Advancement of the Interests of Labor in New York City, and by the end of the century the Episcopal bishop of Chicago led the denomination's Industrial Relations Committee. Presbyterians characterized the eight-hour movement as "delusion in the minds of the uniformed" in 1886 but were the first denomination to create a denominational department to address the church and the labor question and to have a ministerial delegate, Rev. Charles Stelzle, both to the Chicago Federation of Labor and to the American Federation of Labor.

Methodists and Baptists, in contrast, despite their fewer ties to employers and more prominent social activist traditions, were often less willing to join labor's cause. The Methodist *Northwestern Christian Advocate* was a grand champion of the temperance movement and therefore slow to advocate more leisure time for workers. Also, the work ethic was firmly ingrained within Methodist tradition, and this was manifested repeatedly in its press. Workers needed to work more, not less. While the Baptists were not far behind the Methodists in temperance zeal, Baptist leaders were more concerned with spiritual reform and revival than industrial reform. As a result, Baptists did not concern themselves directly with economic or political reform questions, beyond their specific interest in the elimination of Sunday work, until the 1890s.

In making sense of the complex relationships between Protestants and eight-hour reformers in Chicago, it is helpful to return to the structural context of religious life in industrial cities. Unlike churches in smaller communities, urban religious leaders maintained a distinct relationship with its economic and political surroundings. Multiple economic interests competed with each other in large urban centers. Chicago was not a single company town. Consequently, it was not possible for a narrow band of economic elites to exercise the same kind of cultural control over the city's religious establishment as was possible in other settings. In the case of the textile town Gastonia, North Carolina, Pope (1942) reports that mill owners dominated Protestant churches both in terms of their numbers in congregations but also in terms of their ability to control the salaries and bonuses paid to clergy, which could be revoked if clergy expressed views contrary to those of the town's economic elites. Protestant congregations were also dominated by the wealthy, and this is likely to have dampened the enthusiasm of individual ministers for using their pulpit to support labor reform. This is certainly what many Chicago workers believed (Perry 1899).

The diversity of social relationships in an urban context requires a broadening of simple "dependence models" of religion to explain why religious leaders did or did not act to support labor reforms such as the eight-hour day. The social relationships between church leaders, employers, and workers were mediated through other institutional channels and value systems distinct from the structure of denominational finances. Newspapers, ministerial associations, denominational committees, and religious reform movements all represented spaces for clergy to engage industrial conflicts and development within a uniquely religious context. Through these channels, church leaders evaluated what was perceived to be the growing gap between religious ideals and industrial practice against their own understanding of legitimate Christian behavior for both employers and workers but also for themselves as the moral conscience of a new kind of society. Denominational newspapers in particular gave clergy and other interested voices from the religious community opportunities and some degree of autonomy to criticize the actions of employers in industrial conflicts and to offer their moral support for eight-hour reform without directly thundering prophetically from specific pulpits or from street corners. Reports and discussions of workers striking against Sunday labor, child labor, and long hours for women especially in 1893 and 1909 in the press moved church leaders to denominational action rather than at the parish level, without the fears of direct reprisals from particular business leaders sitting in the pews on any given Sunday morning.

Ongoing Challenges to Clergy-Labor Alliances

Since the late 1980s, studies of social movements have focused on the degree to which discourse shapes experience and how beliefs influence predispositions to social action (Snow et al. 1986; Baron 1991; Snow and Benford 1992; Wuthnow 1989). Religion finds a home among these studies because social movement analyses situate religion in institutional relationships of economics and politics while taking seriously the importance of religious beliefs and values for giving meaning to people's lives and moving them to actions.

Religious framing allows social movement participants to utilize religion's ideas about justice, its symbols and imagery, and its narratives to construct a moral rhetoric to aid movement mobilization and challenge. However, religious rhetoric as a source of values and as a means to interpret events and experiences does not by itself guarantee political success for those social movements who adopt it. Nor does it guarantee that others who also speak the language of religion will share the interpretation of religious meaning a movement seeks to impose on their reform efforts. What religious discourse must do for a movement, however, is to be perceived to get the movement closer to its goals, either in building intramovement solidarity or in achieving desired reforms. To the degree that religious rhetoric does so, it is likely to remain an active way movements understand themselves and their goals. To the degree that they do not achieve these ends, religious frames will be replaced by other forms of rhetoric that may better achieve them.

This admittedly instrumentalist approach to understanding religious rhetoric may be challenged for not taking the lived experience and religious commitment of workers or clergy seriously, since it may seem to make religious rhetoric a reflection of economic interests. But I do not see this as an either-or situation for social movements where either frames are instrumental reflections of other interests or else they are real and can be understood only as distinct from other interests. It is clearly both/and. Chicago's workers in craft unions, the Knights of Labor, and among socialist and anarchist labor organizations all expressed over and over again a deep commitment to Jesus Christ in his prophetic mission to create a more just human community. When they expressed it publicly, their faith was something real, and workers lived out their faith commitments instrumentally through concrete struggles for shorter hours. But for many reasons that they expressed to clergy and social reformers trying to attract workingmen and -women back to church, workers also made a distinction between their beliefs in the teachings of Christ and the practical and political actions of religious leaders facing concrete industrial problems in their own communities. Workers understood their faith in both subjective (as a means for giving meaning to one's life and actions) and instrumental (as a means to achieve practical outcomes for a movement) ways. As individuals, workers could be motivated to continue the struggle for an eight-hour day because it was God's will or as an authentic expression of the Golden Rule. As part of the labor movement, workers could disparage religion as an institution and reject framing strategies that did not help workers achieve their practical goals.

If the wide range of religious resources, including religious rhetoric, identified by Christian Smith (1996a) provides only a language but no pragmatic results to a movement, then religious resources risk being discarded for more practical resources. This is what happened to religious rhetorical strategies within the eight-hour movement and to the labor movement more broadly. David Burns (2010, 84) in *Life and Death of the Radical Historical Jesus* observes that a unique religious-political coalition was possible between Protestants and the labor movement. Churches engaged in open dialogue with trade unionists, socialists, and anarchists regarding the future of industrial capitalism. Burns notes that even labor radicals were inspired by the radical historical Jesus. Yet no matter how much labor reformers used biblical injunctions, narratives, theological traditions, or even the Sabbath as rhetorical means to mobilize support for reform, clergy would not respond in ways that would contribute to reform success, that is, by supporting strikes and labor's legislative agenda. Nor did religious appeals for concessions ever move employers to grant worker demands. When alliances with clergy kept producing nothing substantive for labor, labor developed other rhetorical strategies for action to achieve shorter hours. This is not to say that workers did away with their individual beliefs or that the eight-hour movement never involved religious rhetoric again, but, increasingly, the movement relied on other forms of rhetoric that were economic and political in nature that were perceived to be more effective in generating their desired industrial and legislative outcomes.

The key theoretical point to be made here is that religious rhetoric, expressed in social movement frames, is not a given in social conflicts. Religious rhetoric, expressed in the use of religious values, symbols, imagery, and narratives, emerges and is transformed by the social settings within which it exists. Protestantism was an important channel for both clergy and workers to address issues such as the workday. Redeeming time by reducing the workday was a challenge to traditional Protestant beliefs about the necessity of hard work and for mechanisms to keep the morally inferior workers away from vice. As it became clear to clergy that employers in their drive for profit were ignoring the welfare of the working classes, religious values regarding justice for the poor and oppressed eclipsed those centered solely on the work ethic and took root in Protestantism, expressed in the emerging Social Gospel. What brought Protestant clergy into the eight-hour movement and kept them there was their own interest in the furtherance of temperance, public education, workers' church attendance, and industrial harmony. These elements were fixed in the Social Creed of the churches and the eight-hour day. For Chicago workers, religious belief was at the foundation of eight-hour discourse and spurred on activity to win a shorter workday. Workers used religious rhetoric to critique industrial relations and conditions but also to condemn inaction on the part of those who should know better: Protestant clergy. As the marginalization of radical reform within the eight-hour movement became a prerequisite for gaining public sympathy, labor reformers exchanged prophetic arguments in favor of eight hours for more pragmatic ones focusing on the relationship between shorter hours and higher productivity by the workforce.

Religious rhetoric played an important role in how workers and clergy understood the goal of redeeming time in late-nineteenth-century Chicago. Religion was a means to interpret the changes that seemed to be turning the world upside down. But interpreting these changes was accompanied by calls to action to oppose those changes that were understood to be threatening the peace and stability of Chicago as well as undermining the role of clergy as moral arbiters of the community. While religious rhetoric was one source for eight-hour movement solidarity and activism, its ability to redeem time pragmatically and politically was based on how much potential allies shared not only the religious values being employed but also the implications of those values for strategies and tactics.

In his classic book *The Protestant Era,* theologian Paul Tillich made the following observation about the history of the rather poor relations between Protestantism and the labor movement. "If Protestantism had a deeper insight into these aspects of human history, it would have found an approach to the proletarian situation, and it would have been possible for it to give a better interpretation of the proletarian struggle than the socialists, with their hopeless mixture of mechanistic calculation of historical necessities and petty tactics, have provided" (1948, 174). Tillich argues here that there is no inherent opposition in the ideological basis of Protestantism and labor reform, as has been implied in many sociological studies of religion and industrial conflicts. Instead, opposition emerged between the two because of specific historical conditions and relationships between church leaders, workers, and employers. The history of Protestant involvement with Chicago's eight-hour movement bears this out.

Tillich's observation also contains some hope for the role religion plays in the contemporary labor movement. In many ways, the end of the twentieth century and the opening decades of the twenty-first are not dissimilar to the 1890s and 1900s. New technology and the penetration of global capitalism have created some new jobs, eliminated many others, and transferred production across the developing world. In the late summer of 1994, the United Auto Workers Union in Flint, Michigan, successfully struck against General Motors to protest mandatory overtime and seventy-hour workweeks. Similar scenarios have appeared in other industries that seek to cut their workforce while maintaining productivity levels. But in the midst of the economic recession, demands to redeem time through shorter hours are few, as most workers appear anxious to hold on to their job regardless of the hours they work. The question of redeeming time through increasing leisure and its morality is not currently a part of large-scale public discussion of the future of work, nor do religious leaders of any tradition seem ready to raise the issue. The next cycle of debate and protest over the hours we labor still lies ahead.

The study of the nineteenth-century labor movement, especially its fight for the eight-hour day, remains significant for the thinking about the religious and moral dimensions of work and global capitalism in our own day. Labor reform movements were never simply about higher wages or even fewer hours of work. The eight-hour movement embodied *moral* beliefs about the nature of work and leisure, the rights of wage earners to enjoy what they produced, and the best means for employers to ensure the welfare of their employees. Baptist Social Gospel advocate Walter Rauschenbusch, in *Christianity and Social Crisis,* raised a challenge to the religious community of his day:

> The Church has a tremendous stake in the social crisis. It may try to maintain an attitude of neutrality, but neither side will permit it. . . . If it loses the loyalty of the working class, it loses the very class in which it originated, to which its founders belonged, and which lifted it to power. . . . Protestantism, from the outset, entered into an intimate relationship with the intelligence and wealth of the city population. It throve with the class that espoused it. It lifted its class and its class lifted it. If the present struggle of wage-workers is successful, and they become the dominant class of the future, any religious ideas and institutions which they now embrace in the heat of struggle will rise with them to power and any institution on which they turn their back is likely to find itself left in the cold. The parable of the Wise and Foolish Virgins holds for entire nations and institutions as well as individuals. (1912, 331)

Rauschenbusch's challenge was issued a century ago. Yet it remains a prophetic warning to clergy and other people of faith as they find themselves drawn into conflicts not only to redeem time but actively to address the social consequences of the global capitalist economy for the lives of workers and communities in the twenty-first century.

NOTES

Introduction

1. Roediger and Foner's *Our Own Time: A History of American Labor and the Workday* (1989) remains the classic recent work on the history of the shorter-hours movement. Other important works include Rosenzweig's *Eight Hours for What We Will: Workers and Leisure in an Industrial City* (1983), the Labor Research Association's *History of the Shorter Work Day* (1942), Benjamin Hunnicutt's *Work without End* (1988), and Marion Cahill's *Shorter Hours: A Study of the Movement since the Civil War* (1932).

2. Higgins and Bole note that when Catholic clergy and lay activists were involved in the union organizing campaign of farmworkers in the 1970s, they "did not enter the dispute to tell Cesar Chavez or the growers how they should write their contracts" (1993, 63). In the heat of struggle, workers assumed that the church was supporting their vision of what should be put into the contracts as "justice," not only taking a neutral position on their right to organize and bargain.

3. Salvatore (1998) argues that Gutman, in his article on working-class religious culture, betrays his ignorance of both the religious mind of rank-and-file workers as well as the diverse cultural streams of religious tradition from which those workers built their religious mind. Salvatore's point notwithstanding, Gutman's assertion of the importance of the religious beliefs of rank-and-file workers nevertheless remains foundational for most of the research on religion and the labor movement over the past fifty years.

4. In the 1980s and early 1990s, a flourish of monographs and research articles took up the investigation of religion in the Gilded Age. Works by Kenneth Fones-Wolf (1989), Craig (1992), Murphy (1992), Halker (1991), and many others remain the significant foundations of all subsequent work on religion and labor. Still other studies have built on these earlier works documenting the centrality of religion in working-class culture and labor history before and after the late nineteenth century (see Cohen 1991; Pehl, 2012; E. Fones-Wolf and K. Fones-Wolf 2010; Bruno 2008; Roll 2010; Callahan 2009).

5. For examples of studies that document the impact of religious faith on the thinking of workers in the twentieth century, see also Roll's (2010) study of southern black and white farmers, E. Fones-Wolf and K. Fones-Wolf's (2010) discussion of Protestants and the CIO, Cohen's (1991) study of the New Deal, and Pehl's (2012) article on religion and struggles within the United Automobile Workers.

6. See, for example, the classic works in this area from the 1960s including Abell's *The Urban Impact on American Protestantism* (1962), Hopkins's *The Rise of the Social Gospel in American Protestantism* (1940), May's *Protestant Churches and Industrial America* (1963), and White and Hopkins's *The Social Gospel: Religion and Reform in a Changing America* (1976). More contemporary analyses include Curtis's *A Consuming Faith: The Social Gospel and Modern American Culture* (1991), Handy's *A Christian America: Protestant Hopes and Historical Realities* (1991), Phillips's *A Kingdom on Earth: Anglo-American Social Christianity* (1996), G. Smith's *The Search for Social Salvation: Social Christianity and America, 1889–1925* (2000), and Rossinow's (2005) article on Harry Ward and the Social Gospel.

7. In many twentieth-century examples, clergy have also been drawn into industrial conflicts based on their perception that the actions of employers were disrupting the stability of their communities. See, for example, Fantasia's (1988) analysis of a Methodist minister supporting strikers in Clinton, Iowa; Fuechtmann's (1989) study of clergy alliances with steelworkers in Youngstown, Ohio; and Mirola's (2003b) work on clergy-labor alliances in Detroit.

8. Among those that do stand out are Pope's *Millhands and Preachers* (1942), P. Johnson's *A Shopkeeper's Millennium* (1978), Sutton's *Journeymen for Jesus* (1998), K. Fones-Wolf's *Trade Union Gospel* (1989), and Fuechtmann's *Steeples and Stacks* (1989).

Chapter 1. A City of Industrial and Religious Extremes

1. There is an obvious problem with discrepancies in the Bureau of Labor Statistics tables. By one calculation, there were 1,172 strikes over hours between 1881 and 1886, while the summary table provided in the report suggests that there were almost 200 fewer strikes related to hours (Illinois Bureau of Labor Statistics 1888, 223, 230–33). Although this does warrant some caution in reading these reports, these data are used here simply to suggest general levels of strike activity in the period.

REFERENCES

Newspapers and Periodicals

Advance (Congregational). 1867–1910. Chicago.
Alarm (Anarchist). 1884–88. Chicago.
Bakers' Journal. 1888–92.
Chicago Boycotter (Trade and Labor Assembly). 1886. Chicago.
Chicago Daily Socialist. 1907–12. Chicago.
Chicago Daily Tribune. 1866–1912. Chicago.
Chicago Labor. 1893–94. Chicago.
Chicago Record-Herald. 1904. Chicago.
Christian Socialist. 1904–7. Chicago.
Comrade (Socialist). 1902–4. Chicago.
Dawn (Christian Socialist). 1889–96. Boston.
Eight-Hour Herald. 1893–98. Chicago.
Equity (Social Gospel). 1874–75. Boston.
Furniture Workers' Journal. 1885. New York.
Interior (Presbyterian). 1869–1912. Chicago.
Journal of United Labor (Journal of the Knights of Labor). 1883–93. Philadelphia.
Knights of Labor. 1886–92. Chicago.
Labor Balance (Social Gospel). 1877–79. Boston.
Labor Enquirer. 1887–88. Chicago.
Labor Holiday (Typographical Union No. 16). 1886. Chicago.
Living Church (Episcopal). 1878–1912. Chicago.
Northwestern Christian Advocate (Methodist). 1866–1912. Chicago.
Railroad Conductors' Brotherhood Monthly Magazine. 1877–78. Chicago.
Record (Trade and Labor Assembly). 1886–89. Chicago.
Socialist (Socialist Labor Party). 1878–79. Chicago.
Standard (Baptist). 1866–1912. Chicago.
Workers' Call (Socialist Labor Party). 1899–1903. Chicago.
Workingman's Advocate. 1866–72. Chicago.

Primary Sources

Addams, Jane. 1960 [1910]. *Twenty Years at Hull House.* New York: Signet.
Altgeld, John P. 1890. *The Eight-Hour Movement: An Address Delivered before the*

Brotherhood of United Labor at the Chicago Armory, 22 February 1890. Pamphlet. Chicago Historical Society.

Andreas, Alfred T. 1975 [1885]. *History of Chicago: From the Earliest Period to the Present Time.* 3 vols. New York: Arno Press.

Ayer, N. W., and Son. 1870, 1880, 1888, 1997, 1910. *American Newspaper Annual.* Philadelphia: N. W. Ayer and Son.

Bancroft, Hubert H. 1894. *The Book of the Fair.* New York: Bounty Books.

Bierbower, Austin. 1890. *The Socialism of Christ.* Chicago: Charles H. Sergel.

Bliss, William D. P., ed. 1897. "Shorter Hours Movement." In *The Encyclopedia of Social Reforms,* 1226–38. New York: Funk and Wagnall.

Bonney, Charles Carroll. 1886. *The Present Conflict of Capital and Labor: A Discourse.* Chicago: Chicago Sabbath Association.

Burrell, David J. N.d. *A Plea for Sunday Rest at the Columbian Fair.* Pamphlet. Chicago: Chicago Historical Society.

Carnegie, Andrew. 1962 [1889]. *The Gospel of Wealth, and Other Timely Essays.* Cambridge, Mass.: Harvard University Press.

Carwardine, William H. 1973 [1894]. *The Pullman Strike.* Chicago: Charles H. Kerr.

Cherouny, Henry W. 1905. "On the Eight-Hour Movement." *Inland Printer* 35 (June): 539–43.

Chicago Baptist Association. 1870–1910. *Proceedings.* Elgin, Ill.: Advocate Press and Bindery.

Chicago Congregational Association. N.d. "Sunday Schools and Societies in the Chicago Association." *Directory of the Congregational Churches.* Chicago: Advance.

Chicago Federation of Labor. 1905. *Minutes.* Chicago: Chicago Historical Society.

Chicago Sabbath Association. 1880–89. *Records.* Chicago: Chicago Historical Society.

Churches of Chicago. 1878. Chicago: Lakeside Press.

Citizens Association of Chicago Scrapbooks. 1886 and 1891. Chicago Historical Society.

Crafts, Wilbur F. 1885. *The Sabbath of Man: A Study of the Origin, Obligation, History, Advantages, and Present State of Sabbath Observance with Special Reference to the Rights of Workingmen.* New York: Funk and Wagnall.

Danyrid, Lemuel. 1889. *History and Philosophy of the Eight Hour Movement.* American Federation of Labor Eight-Hour Series, Pamphlet no. 3. Chicago: Newberry Library.

DeNormandie, James. 1892. *Sunday and the Columbian Fair.* Pamphlet. Chicago: Newberry Library.

Diocese of Chicago (Protestant Episcopal). 1866–1912. *Journal of the Proceedings of the Annual Convention.* Chicago: Gunthrop Warren.

Dovai, A. 1877. *Better Times!* Chicago: Social Democratic Printing Association.

"The Eight-Hour Law and Farm Labor." *Prairie Farmer* 19 (April 6, 1867): 217.

Ely, Richard T. 1896. *The Social Law of Service.* New York: Eaton and Mains.

———. 1902. "The Religious Press and the Labor Movement." *Central Christian Advocate* 3 (September): 6.

Fackel. September 14, 1884. "Sunday Observations." Reprinted in *German Workers in Chicago: A Documentary History of Working-Class Culture from 1850 to World*

War I, edited by Harmut Keil and John B. Jentz, 357–60. Urbana: University of Illinois Press.

General Assembly of the Presbyterian Church, USA. 1870–1910. *Minutes.* Philadelphia: Office of the General Assembly.

General Congregational Association of Illinois. 1870, 1880, 1890, 1900, 1910. *Minutes of the Annual Meeting.* Alton, Ill.: Perrin and Smith.

Gladden, Washington. "The Working People and the Churches." *Independent* (July 23, 1885): 944.

Gompers, Samuel. 1925. *Seventy Years of Life and Labor: An Autobiography.* New York: E. P. Dutton.

Gunton, George. 1889. *The Economic and Social Importance of the Eight-Hour Movement.* Eight Hour Series, no. 2. Washington, D.C.: American Federation of Labor.

International Typographical Union. N.d. *Eight-Hour Committee of the International Typographical Union and United Typothetae Association.* Miscellaneous pamphlets. Chicago: Chicago Historical Society.

Jones, S. 1871. *The Sunday Question and Self-Contradictions of the Bible.* Chicago: Religio-Philosophical Publishing House.

Kinney, H. 1892. *Why the Columbian Exposition Should Be Opened on Sunday.* Pamphlet. Chicago: Chicago Historical Society.

Lloyd, Henry Demarest. 1909. *Men, the Workers.* New York: Doubleday, Page.

Lum, Dyer D. 1970. *The Accused and the Accusers: The Famous Speeches of the Eight Chicago Anarchists in Court.* New York: Arno Press.

McNeill, George E. 1889. *The Eight Hour Primer: The Fact, the Theory, and the Argument. Eight Hours Series, No. 1.* Washington, D.C.: American Federation of Labor.

Methodist Episcopal Church. 1870–1912. *Register of the Rock River Annual Conference of the Methodist Episcopal Church.* Chicago: Methodist Book Depository.

Pentecost, Hugh. 1894. *Twentieth Century* (January 11): 6–8.

Perry, H. Frances. 1899. "The Workingman's Alienation from the Church." *American Journal of Sociology* 4 (March): 621–29.

Pomeroy, William C. 1894. *Stacks and Steeples: A Reply to an Address by Rev. William A. Burch, Pastor of Hamlin Avenue Methodist Episcopal Church, Brick Layer's Hall.* Chicago: Newberry Library.

Powderly, Terrance V. 1967 [1890]. *Thirty Years of Labor, 1859–1889.* New York: August M. Kelley.

Presbytery of Chicago. N.d. *Handbook of the Presbytery of Chicago.* Miscellaneous pamphlets, handbooks, and directories. Chicago: Chicago Historical Society.

Prescott, William B. 1905. "The Eight-Hour Movement." *Inland Printer* 35 (June): 345–50.

Protestant Episcopal Church. 1871–1910. *Journal of the General Convention.* Printed for the convention. Chicago: Seabury-Western Theological Seminary Library.

Rae, John. 1894. *Eight Hours for Work.* New York: Macmillan.

Rauschenbusch, Walter. 1912. *Christianity and Social Crisis.* New York: Association Press.

Retail Clerks' National Protective Association of America. 1891. *Declaration of Principles.* Madison: State Historical Society of Wisconsin.

Robertson. 1893. *The Eight-Hour Question*. Chicago: Newberry Library.
Robins, Raymond. 1908. *An Address to the National Protest Meeting of Labor*. Chicago: Chicago Historical Society.
Rogers, Edward H. 1872. *Eight Hours a Day's Work: A Lecture*. Boston: Weekly American Workman.
Sinclair, Upton. 1905. *The Jungle*. New York: Penguin Books.
———. 1952. *A Personal Jesus: Portrait and Interpretation*. New York: Evans.
Stead, William T. 1894. *If Christ Came to Chicago*. Chicago: Chicago Historical Bookworks.
Stevenson, Andrew. 1907. *Chicago: Preeminently a Presbyterian City*. Chicago: Winona.
Steward, Ira. 1873. *Poverty*. Pamphlet. Boston: Boston Eight-Hour League.
Stone, James M. 1852. *The Hours of Labor: Address to the Ten Hours State Convention and Report to the Legislature of Massachusetts*. Pamphlet. Lowell, Mass.: Ten Hours State Committee.
Strong, Josiah. 1885. *Our Country: Its Possible Future and Its Present Crisis*. New York: American Home Missionary Society.
Wilson, J. Stitt. N.d. *Christ's Solution of the Labor Problem*. Pamphlet. Chicago: Northwestern University Settlement.
Women's Trade Union League. 1909. *The Eight Hour Fight in Illinois by the Girls Who Did the Work*. Leaflet No. 4. Chicago: Women's Trade Union League of Chicago.
———. 1910. *Official Report of the Strike Committee*. Chicago: Women's Trade Union League of Chicago.
A Workingman. 1866. *Reason for Believing That the People Will Use Leisure Wisely with a Statement of the Character of the Eight-Hour Movement*. Pamphlet. Boston: Voice Printing and Publishing.

Government Documents

Burgess, Ernest, and Charles Newcomb, eds. 1931. *Census Data of the City of Chicago, 1920*. Chicago: University of Chicago Press.
City of Chicago. 1970. *The People of Chicago: Who We Are and Who We Have Been; Census Data on Foreign-Born, Foreign Stock, and Race, 1837–1970*. Chicago: Department of Development and Planning.
Illinois Bureau of Labor Statistics. 1888–1908. *Biennial Reports*. Springfield: H. W. Roker.
U.S. Bureau of Labor Statistics. 2013. *Economic News Release—Union Membership, 2012*. Washington, D.C.: Bureau of Labor Statistics Press Office.
U.S. Census Bureau. 1870. "Population." In *Ninth Census*. Washington, D.C.: Government Printing Office.
———. 1880. "Population." In *Tenth Census*. Washington, D.C.: Government Printing Office.
———. 1890. "Population." In *Eleventh Census*. Washington, D.C.: Government Printing Office.

———. 1900. "Population." In *Twelfth Census.* Washington, D.C.: Government Printing Office.
———. 1910. "Population." In *Thirteenth Census.* Washington, D.C.: Government Printing Office.
U.S. Senate. 1916. "Industrial Conditions and Relations in Chicago." In vol. 4 of *Industrial Relations: Final Report and Testimony.* Washington, D.C.: Government Printing Office.

Secondary Sources

Abell, Aaron. 1943. *The Urban Impact on American Protestantism, 1865–1900.* London: Anchon.
Adelman, William J. 1976. *Haymarket Revisited.* Chicago: Illinois Labor History Society.
Aiken, John R., and James R. McDonnell. 1970. "Walter Rauschenbusch and Labor Reform: A Social Gospeller's Approach." *Labor History* 11 (Spring): 131–50.
Aronowitz, Stanley. 1973. *False Promises: The Shaping of American Working Class Consciousness.* New York: McGraw-Hill.
Ashbaugh, Carolyn. 1976. *Lucy Parsons: American Revolutionary.* Chicago: Charles H. Kerr.
Atack, Jeremy, and Fred Bateman. 1991. "Whom Did Protective Legislation Protect? Evidence from 1880." No. 33 in National Bureau of Economic Research Working Paper Series on Historical Factors in Long-Run Growth. Cambridge, Mass.
Avrich, Paul. 1984. *The Haymarket Tragedy.* Princeton, N.J.: Princeton University Press.
Babb, Sarah. 1996. "'A True American System of Finance': Frame Resonance in the U.S. Labor Movement, 1866 to 1886." *American Sociological Review* 61: 1033–52.
Badger, R. 1979. *The Great American Fair: The World's Columbian Exposition and American Culture.* Chicago: Nelson-Hall.
Baltzell, E. Digby. 1964. *The Protestant Establishment: Aristocracy and Caste in America.* New York: Vintage Books.
Baron, Ava. 1991. *Work Engendered: Toward a New History of American Labor.* Ithaca, N.Y.: Cornell University Press.
Barrett, James R. 1987. *Work and Community in the Jungle: Chicago Packinghouse Workers, 1894–1992.* Urbana: University of Illinois Press.
Beckford, James A. 1989. *Religion and Advanced Industrial Society.* Boston: Unwin Hyman.
Beckner, Earl R. 1929. *A History of Labor Legislation in Illinois.* Chicago: University of Chicago Press.
Becnel, Thomas. 1980. *Labor, Church, and the Sugar Establishment: Louisiana, 1877–1976.* Baton Rouge: Louisiana State University Press.
Berlanstein, Lenard R. 1993. *Rethinking Labor History.* Urbana: University of Illinois Press.
Billings, Dwight B. 1990. "Religion as Opposition: A Gramscian Analysis." *American Journal of Sociology* 96, no. 1: 1–31.

Bonnett, Clarence E. 1956. *History of Employers' Associations in the United States.* New York: Vantage Press.

Bowman, Matthew. 2007. "Sin, Spirituality, and Primitivism: The Theologies of the American Social Gospel, 1885–1918." *Religion and American Culture* 17, no. 1: 95–126.

Brandeis, Elizabeth. 1966. "Hour Laws for Men." In *History of Labor in the United States, 1896–1932,* edited by John R. Commons et al., 3:540–63. New York: Macmillan.

Browne, Henry J. 1949. *The Catholic Church and the Knights of Labor.* Washington, D.C.: Catholic University Press.

Bruno, Robert A. 2008. *Justified by Work: Identity and the Meaning of Faith in Chicago's Working Class Churches.* Columbus: Ohio State University Press.

Burns, David. 2008. "The Soul of Socialism: Christianity, Civilization, and Citizenship in the Thought of Eugene Debs." *Labor* 5, no. 2: 83–116.

———. 2013. *The Life and Death of the Radical Historical Jesus.* New York: Oxford University Press.

Cahill, Marion Cotter. 1932. *Shorter Hours: A Study of the Movement since the Civil War.* New York: Columbia University Press.

Calhoun, Craig. 1982. *The Question of Class Struggle: Social Foundations of Popular Radicalism during the Industrial Revolution.* Chicago: University of Chicago Press.

Callahan, Richard J. 2009. *Work and Faith in the Kentucky Coal Fields: Subject to Dust.* Urbana: University of Illinois Press.

Cantwell, Christopher D. 2012. "The Bible Teacher: Piety and Politics in the Age of Fundamentalism." Ph.D. diss., Cornell University.

Carter, Heath W. 2010. "Scab Ministers, Striking Saints: Christianity and Class Conflict in 1894 Chicago." *American Nineteenth Century History* 11, no. 3: 321–49.

Cohen, Lizabeth. 1991. *Making a New Deal: Industrial Workers in Chicago, 1919–1939.* New York: Cambridge University Press.

Cort, John C. 1988. *Christian Socialism: An Informal History.* Maryknoll, N.Y.: Orbis Books.

Craig, Robert H. 1992. *Religion and Radical Politics: An Alternative Christian Tradition in the United States.* Philadelphia: Temple University Press.

Curtis, Susan. 1991. *A Consuming Faith: The Social Gospel and Modern American Culture.* Baltimore: Johns Hopkins University Press.

David, Henry. 1958 [1936]. *The History of the Haymarket Affair: A Study in the American Social-Revolutionary and Labor Movements.* New York: Russell and Russell.

Davis, Mike. 1986. *Prisoners of the American Dream.* New York: Verso.

Duis, Perry R. 1998. *Challenging Chicago: Coping with Everyday Life, 1837–1920.* Urbana: University of Illinois Press.

Ellingson, Stephen. 1995. "Understanding the Dialectic of Discourse and Collective Action: Public Debate and Rioting in Antebellum Cincinnati." *American Journal of Sociology* 101: 100–144.

Evans, Sara M., and Harry C. Boyte. 1986. *Free Spaces: The Sources of Democratic Change in America.* New York: Harper and Row.

Fantasia, Rick. 1988. *Cultures of Solidarity: Consciousness, Action, and Contemporary American Workers.* Berkeley: University of California Press.

Fetner, Tina. 2008. *How the Religious Right Shaped Lesbian and Gay Activism.* Minneapolis: University of Minnesota Press.
Fine, Sidney. 1953. "The Eight-Hour Day Movement in the U.S., 1888–1891." *Mississippi Valley Historical Review* 40 (December): 441–62.
Fink, Leon. 1985. *Workingmen's Democracy: The Knights of Labor and American Politics.* Urbana: University of Illinois Press.
Foner, Philip S. 1972. "Songs of the Eight Hour Movement." *Labor History* 13 (Fall): 571–88.
———. 1982. *The History of the Labor Movement in the United States.* Vols. 1 and 3. New York: International.
Fones-Wolf, Elizabeth, and Ken Fones-Wolf. 2010. "No Common Creed: White Working Class Protestants and the CIO's Operation Dixie." In *Rethinking U.S. Labor History,* edited by Donna T. Haverty-Stacke and Daniel J. Walkowitz, 111–36. New York: Bloomsbury Academic Press.
Fones-Wolf, Kenneth. 1989. *Trade Union Gospel: Christianity and Labor in Industrial Philadelphia, 1865–1915.* Philadelphia: Temple University Press.
Forbath, William E. 1991. *Law and the Shaping of the American Labor Movement.* Cambridge, Mass.: Harvard University Press.
Form, William H., and Delbert C. Miller. 1960. *Industry, Labor, and Community.* New York: Harper.
Foster, Gaines M. 2002. "Conservative Social Christianity, the Law, and Personal Morality: Wilbur F. Crafts in Washington." *Church History* 7, no. 4: 799–819.
Fowke, Edith, and Joe Glazer, eds. 1960. *Songs of Work and Freedom.* Chicago: Roosevelt University, Labor Education Division.
Fuechtmann, Thomas G. 1989. *Steeples and Stacks: Religion and the Steel Crisis in Youngstown.* New York: Cambridge University Press.
Gaventa, John. 1980. *Power and Powerlessness: Quiescence and Rebellion in an Appalachian Valley.* Urbana: University of Illinois Press.
Gerstle, Gary. 1989. *Working-Class Americanism: The Politics of Labor in a Textile City, 1914–1960.* New York: Cambridge University Press.
Ginger, Ray. 1958. *Altgeld's America: The Lincoln Ideal versus Changing Realities.* New York: Funk and Wagnall.
Glickman, Lawerence B. 1997. *A Living Wage: American Workers and the Making of Consumer Society.* Ithaca, N.Y.: Cornell University Press.
Goffman, Erving. 1972. *Frame Analysis.* New York: Harper and Row.
———. 1981. *Forms of Talk.* Philadelphia: University of Pennsylvania Press.
Gordon, David M., Richard Edwards, and Michael Reich. 1982. *Segmented Work, Divided Workers.* New York: Cambridge University Press.
Gramsci, Antonio. 1971. *Selections from the Prison Notebooks.* New York: International.
Green, James. 2006. *Death in the Haymarket.* New York: Pantheon Books.
Greenberg, Michael. 1980. "Revival, Reform, Revolution: Samuel Davies and the Great Awakening in Virginia." *Marxist Perspectives* 3, no. 2: 102–19.
Grob, Gerald. 1961. *Workers and Utopia: A Study of Ideological Conflict in the American Labor Movement, 1865–1900.* Evanston, Ill.: Northwestern University Press.
Gutman, Herbert G. 1966. "Protestantism and the American Labor Movement: The

Christian Spirit in the Gilded Age." *American Historical Review* 72 (October): 74–101.
Hackett, David G. 1991. *The Rude Hand of Innovation: Religion and Social Order in Albany, New York, 1652–1836.* New York: Oxford University Press.
Haines, Herbert. 1984. "Black Radicalization and the Funding of Civil Rights, 1957–1970." *Social Problems* 32: 31–43.
Halker, Clark D. 1991. *For Democracy, Workers, and God: Labor Song-Poems and Labor Protests, 1865–1895.* Urbana: University of Illinois Press.
Handy, Robert T. 1984. *A Christian America: Protestant Hopes and Historical Realities.* New York: Oxford University Press.
Haydu, Jeffrey. 1999. "Counter Action Frames: Employer Repertories and the Union Menace in the Late Nineteenth Century." *Social Problems* 46: 313–31.
Heidebrecht, Paul Henry. 1989. *Faith and Business Practice: Protestant Businessmen in Chicago, 1900–1920.* New York: Garland.
Higgins, George G., and William Bole. 1993. *Organized Labor and the Church: Reflections of a "Labor Priest."* New York: Paulist Press.
Hill, Christopher. 1984. *The World Turned Upside Down: Radical Ideas during the English Revolution.* New York: Penguin Books.
Hirsch, Eric L. 1990. *Urban Revolt: Ethnic Politics in Nineteenth Century Chicago Labor Movement.* Berkeley: University of California Press.
Hirsch, Susan E., and Robert I. Goler. 1990. *A City Comes of Age: Chicago in the 1890s.* Chicago: Chicago Historical Society.
Hobgood, Mary E. 1991. *Catholic Social Teaching and Economic Theory.* Philadelphia: Temple University Press.
Hobsbawm, Eric. J. 1983. *Industry and Empire.* New York: Penguin Books.
Hood, Robert E. 1990. *Social Teachings in the Episcopal Church: A Source Book.* Harrisburg, Pa.: Morehouse.
Hopkins, Charles Howard. 1940. *The Rise of the Social Gospel in American Protestantism, 1865–1915.* New Haven, Conn.: Yale University Press.
Howe, Irving. 1985. *Socialism in America.* New York: Harcourt, Brace, and Jovanovich.
Hudson, Winthrop S., ed. 1984. *Walter Rauschenbusch: Selected Writings.* New York: Paulist Press.
Hunnicutt, Benjamin K. 1988a. "The New Deal: The Salvation of Work and the End of the Shorter-Hours Movement." In *Worktime and Industrialization: An International History,* edited by G. Cross. Philadelphia: Temple University Press.
———. 1988b. *Work without End.* Philadelphia: Temple University Press.
Isaac, Larry. 2008. "Counterframes and Allegories of Evil: Characterizations of Labor by Gilded Age Elites." *Work and Occupations* 35, no. 4: 388–421.
Jaher, Frederic Cople. 1982. *The Urban Establishment: Upper Strata in Boston, New York, Charleston, Chicago, and Los Angeles.* Urbana: University of Illinois Press.
Jentz, John B. 1991. "Class and Politics in an Emerging Industrial City: Chicago in the 1860s and 1870s." *Journal of Urban History* 17 (May): 227–63.
Jentz, John B., and Richard Schneirov. 2012. *Chicago in the Age of Capital.* Urbana: University of Illinois Press.

Johns, W. 1967. *Dateline Sunday, U.S.A.: The Story of the Three and a Half Centuries of Sunday Law Battles in America.* Omaha, Neb.: Pacific Press.

Johnson, Curtis D. 1989. *Islands of Holiness: Rural Religion in Upstate New York, 1790–1860.* Ithaca, N.Y.: Cornell University Press.

Johnson, Paul E. 1978. *A Shopkeeper's Millennium: Society and Revivals in Rochester, NY, 1815–1837.* New York: Hill and Wang.

Johnston, Hank. 2005. "Comparative Frame Analysis." In *Frames of Protest: Social Movements and the Framing Perspective,* edited by Hank Johnston and John A. Noakes, 237–55. Lanham, Md.: Rowman and Littlefield.

Johnston, Hank, and John A. Noakes. 2005. *Frames of Protest: Social Movements and the Framing Perspective.* Lanham, Md.: Rowman and Littlefield.

Kahn, Shamus R. 2011. *Privilege: The Making of an Adolescent Elite at St. Paul's School.* Princeton, N.J.: Princeton University Press.

Karsner, Daniel. 1919. *Debs: His Authorized Life and Letters.* New York: Boni and Liveright.

Karson, Marc. 1958. *American Labor Unions and Politics, 1900–1918.* Carbondale: Southern Illinois University Press.

Kaufman, Stuart B. 1973. *Samuel Gompers and the Origins of the American Federation of Labor, 1848–1896.* Westport, Conn.: Greenwood Press.

Keil, Hartmut. 1983. "The German Immigrant Working Class of Chicago, 1875–90: Workers, Labor Leaders, and the Labor Movement." In *American Labor and Immigration History, 1877–1920: Recent European Research,* edited by Dirk Hoerder, 156–76. Urbana: University of Illinois Press.

Kelly, Alfred. 1938. "A History of the Illinois Manufacturers' Association." Ph.D. diss., University of Chicago.

Kinsley, Philip. 1946. *The "Chicago Tribune": Its First Hundred Years.* 3 vols. Chicago: Tribune.

Kornbluh, Joyce L. 1988. *Rebel Voices: An I.W.W. Anthology.* Chicago: Charles H. Kerr.

Labor Research Association. 1942. *The History of the Shorter Workday.* Pamphlet. New York: International.

Laurie, Bruce. 1980. *Working People of Philadelphia, 1800–1850.* Philadelphia: Temple University Press.

Lazerow, Jama. 1986. "Religion and Labor Reform in Antebellum America: The World of William Field Young." *American Quarterly* 38, no. 2: 265–86.

———. 1987. "Religion and the New England Mill Girl: A New Perspective on an Old Theme." *New England Quarterly* 60 (September): 429–53.

Lenhart, Thomas E. 1981. "Methodist Piety in an Industrializing Society, 1865–1914." Ph.D. diss., Northwestern University.

Lescohier, Don D. 1966. "The Hours They Work." In *History of Labor in the United States, 1896–1932,* 3:97–113. New York: Macmillan.

Levitan, Sar A., and Richard S. Belous. 1977. *Shorter Hours, Shorter Weeks: Spreading the Work to Reduce Unemployment.* Baltimore: Johns Hopkins University Press.

Magnuson, Norris. 1977. *Salvation in the Slums: Evangelical Social Work, 1865–1920.* Metuchen, N.J.: Scarecrow Press.

Marsden, George. 1992. "The Gospel of Wealth, the Social Gospel, and the Salvation of Souls in Nineteenth Century America." In *Protestantism and Social Christianity*, edited by Martin Marty, 3–14. New York: K. G. Saur.

Marx, Karl. 1972 [1843]. "Contribution to the Critique of Hegel's *Philosophy of Right*." In *The Marx-Engels Reader*, edited by Robert C. Tucker, 53–65. 2nd ed. New York: W. W. Norton.

———. 1986 [1846]. *The German Ideology*. New York: International.

May, Henry F. 1963. *Protestant Churches and Industrial America*. New York: Octagon Books.

McCartin, James P., and Joseph A. McCartin. 2007. "Working Class Catholicism: A Call for New Investigation, Dialogue, and Reappraisal." *Labor* 4, no. 1: 99–110.

McDonough, Peter. 1992. *Men Astutely Trained: A History of the Jesuits in the American Century*. New York: Free Press.

McGreevy, John T. 2003. *Catholicism and American Freedom: A History*. New York: W. W. Norton.

McLellan, David. 1987. *Marxism and Religion*. London: Palgrave Macmillan.

McTighe, M. J. 1994. *A Measure of Success: Protestants and Public Culture in Antebellum Cleveland*. Albany: State University of New York Press.

McVey, Frank L. 1903. "The Social Effects of the Eight-Hour Day." *American Journal of Sociology* 8 (January): 521–30.

Messer-Kruse, Timothy. 2011. *The Trial of the Haymarket Anarchists: Terrorism and Justice in the Gilded Age*. New York: Palgrave Macmillan.

Miller, Donald L. 1996. *City of the Century: The Epic of Chicago and the Making of America*. New York: Simon and Schuster.

Miller, Jon. 1993. "Missions, Social Change, and Resistance to Authority: Notes toward an Understanding of the Relative Autonomy of Religion." *Journal for the Scientific Study of Religion* 32, no. 1: 29–50.

Mirola, William A. 1999. "Shorter Hours and the Protestant Sabbath: Religious Framing and Movement Alliances in Late Nineteenth Century Chicago." *Social Science History* 23, no. 3: 395–433.

———. 2003a. "Asking for Bread, Receiving a Stone: The Rise and Fall of Religious Ideologies in Chicago's Eight-Hour Movement." *Social Problems* 50, no. 2: 273–93.

———. 2003b. "Religious Resources and Economic Protest: Possibilities and Constraints on Religious Coalition-Building in the Detroit Newspaper Strike." *Sociology of Religion* 64, no. 2: 443–62.

Montgomery, David. 1979. *Worker Control in America*. New York: Cambridge University Press.

———. 1981 [1967]. *Beyond Equality: Labor and the Radical Republicans, 1862–1872*. Urbana: University of Illinois Press.

———. 1987. *The Fall of the House of Labor*. New York: Cambridge University Press

Moore, Barrington. 1978. *Injustice: The Social Bases of Obedience and Revolt*. White Plains, N.Y.: M. E. Sharpe.

Murphy, Teresa Anne. 1992. *Ten Hours Labor: Religion, Reform, and Gender in Early New England*. Ithaca, N.Y.: Cornell University Press.

Nash, George H. 1970. "Charles Stelzle: Apostle to Labor." *Labor History* 11 (Spring): 151–74.

Nelson, Bruce C. 1988. *Beyond the Martyrs: A Social History of Chicago's Anarchists, 1870–1900*. New Brunswick, N.J.: Rutgers University Press.

———. 1991. "Revival and Upheaval: Religion, Irreligion, and Chicago's Working Class in 1886." *Journal of Social History* 25, no. 2: 233–53.

Nelson, Timothy J. 2009. "At Ease with Our Own Kind: Worship Practices and Class Segregation in American Religion." In *Religion and Class in America: Culture, History, and Politics*, edited by Sean McCloud and William A. Mirola, 45–68. Boston: Brill.

Oliver, Pamela E., and Hank Johnston. 2005. "'What a Good Idea!': Ideologies and Frames in Social Movement Research." In *Frames of Protest: Social Movements and the Framing Perspective*, edited by Hank Johnston and John A. Noakes, 185–203. Lanham, Md.: Rowman and Littlefield.

Olson, Laura R. 2000. *Filled with Spirit and Power: Protestant Clergy in Politics*. Albany: State University of New York Press.

Orsi, Robert A. 2003. "Is the Study of Lived Religion Irrelevant to the World We Live In? Special Presidential Plenary Address." *Journal for the Scientific Study of Religion* 42, no. 2: 169–74.

Oshatz, Molly. 2010. "No Ordinary Sin: Antislavery Protestants and the Discovery of the Social Nature of Morality." *Church History* 79, no. 2: 334–58.

Pacyga, Dominic A. 2009. *Chicago: A Biography*. Chicago: University of Chicago Press.

Payne, Elizabeth Anne. 1988. *Reform, Labor, and Feminism: Margaret Dreier Robins and the WTUL*. Urbana: University of Illinois Press.

Pehl, Matthew. 2012. "'Apostles of Fascism,' 'Communist Clergy,' and the UAW: Political Ideology and Working Class Religion in Detroit." *Journal of American History* 99 (September): 440–65.

Phillips, Paul T. 1996. *A Kingdom on Earth: Anglo-American Social Christianity*. University Park: Pennsylvania State University Press.

Pierce, Bessie Louise. 1940. *A History of Chicago*. 3 vols. New York: Alfred A. Knopf.

Piven, Frances Fox, and Richard A. Cloward. 1979. *Poor People's Movements: Why They Succeed, How They Fail*. New York: Vintage.

Pollard, Annie. 2009. "Working for the Sabbath: Sabbath in Jewish Immigrant Neighborhoods of New York." *Labor* 6, no. 1: 333–56.

Pope, Liston. 1942. *Millhands and Preachers*. New Haven, Conn.: Yale University Press.

Pride, Louis. 1987. *Chicago Pride: The Stockyards, Packingtown, and the Environs in the Nineteenth Century*. Urbana: University of Illinois Press.

Raboteau, Albert J. 1978. *Slave Religion: The "Invisible Institution" in the Antebellum South*. New York: Oxford University Press.

Rader, Benjamin G. 1966. "Richard T. Ely: Lay Spokesman for the Social Gospel." *Journal of American History* 53: 61–74.

Robertson, Darrel M. 1989. *The Chicago Revival, 1876: Society and Revivalism in a Nineteenth Century City*. Metuchen, N.J.: Scarecrow Press.

Rodgers, Daniel T. 1978. *The Work Ethic and Industrial America, 1850–1920*. Chicago: University of Chicago Press.

Roediger, David R., and Philip S. Foner. 1989. *Our Own Time: A History of American Labor and the Working Day*. New York: Verso.

Roediger, David R., and Franklin Rosemont. 1986. *The Haymarket Scrapbook*. Chicago: Charles H. Kerr.

Roll, Jarod. 2010. *Spirit of Rebellion: Labor and Religion in the New Cotton South*. Urbana: University of Illinois Press.

Rosenzweig, Roy. 1983. *Eight Hours for What We Will: Workers and Leisure in an Industrial City, 1870–1920*. New York: Cambridge University Press.

Rossinow, Doug. 2005. "The Radicalization of the Social Gospel: Harry F. Ward and the Search for a New Social Order, 1898–1936." *Religion and American Culture* 15, no. 1: 63–106.

Salvatore, Nick. 1998. "Herbert Gutman's Narrative of the American Working Class: A Reappraisal." *International Journal of Politics, Culture, and Society* 12, no. 1: 43–80.

Schneirov, Richard. 1997. *Labor and Urban Politics: Class Conflict and the Origins of Modern Liberalism in Chicago, 1864–97*. Urbana: University of Illinois Press.

Schneirov, Richard, and Thomas J. Suhrbur. 1988. *Union Brotherhood, Union Town: The History of the Carpenter' Union of Chicago, 1863–1987*. Carbondale: Southern Illinois University Press.

Schultz, Rima Lunin. 1986. *The Church and the City: A Social History of 150 Years at Saint James, Chicago*. Chicago: R. R. Donnelley and Sons.

Sizer, Sandra. 1992. "Politics and Apolitical Religion: The Great Urban Revivals of the Late Nineteenth Century." In *Protestantism and Social Christianity*, edited by Martin Marty, 15–32. New York: K. G. Saur.

Smith, Christian. 1996a. *Disruptive Religion: The Force of Faith in Social Movement Activism*. New York: Routledge.

———. 1996b. *Resisting Reagan: The U.S. Central America Peace Movement*. Chicago: University of Chicago Press.

Smith, Gary S. 2000. *The Search for Social Salvation: Social Christianity and America, 1880–1925*. New York: Lexington Books.

Smith, Lisa Ann, and Lori G. Beaman. 2010. "Displacing Religion, Disarming Law: Situating Quaker Spirituality in the 'Trident Three' Case." *Social Compass* 57, no. 4: 503–20.

Snow, David A., and Robert D. Benford. 1992. "Master Frames and Cycles of Protest." In *Frontiers in Social Movement Theory*, edited by Aldon Morris and Carol McClurg Mueller, 133–55. New Haven, Conn.: Yale University Press.

———. 2005. "Clarifying the Relationship between Framing and Ideology." In *Frames of Protest: Social Movements and the Framing Perspective*, edited by Hank Johnston and John A. Noakes, 205–11. Lanham, Md.: Rowman and Littlefield.

Snow, David A., E. Burke Rochford Jr., Steven K. Worden, and Robert D. Benford. 1986. "Frame Alignment Processes, Micromobilization, and Movement Participation." *American Sociological Review* 51 (August): 464–81.

Stackhouse, Perry. 1933. *Chicago and the Baptists: A Century of Progress*. Urbana : University of Illinois Press.

Stein, Leon, and Philip Taft, eds. 1969a. *Religion, Reform, and Revolution: Labor Panaceas in the Nineteenth Century.* New York: Arno Press and the New York Times.

———. 1969b. *Wages, Hours, and Strikes: Labor Panaceas in the Twentieth Century.* New York: Arno Press.

Steinberg, Marc W. 1999. "The Talk and Back Talk of Collective Action: A Dialogic Analysis of Repertoires of Discourse among Nineteenth Century English Cotton Spinners." *American Journal of Sociology* 105: 736–80.

Suggs, George G., Jr. 1970. "Religion and Labor in the Rocky Mountain West: Bishop Nicholas C. Matz and the Western Federation of Miners." *Labor History* 11 (Spring): 190–206.

Sutton, William R. 1998. *Journeymen for Jesus: Evangelical Artisans Confront Capitalism in Jacksonian Baltimore.* University Park: Pennsylvania State University Press.

Swartz, Heidi J. 2008. *Organizing Urban America: Secular and Faith-Based Progressive Movements.* Minneapolis: University of Minnesota Press.

Swift, David E. 1989. *Black Prophets of Justice: Activist Clergy before the Civil War.* Baton Rouge: Louisiana State University Press.

Szucs, Loretto Dennis. 1986. *Chicago and Cook County Sources: A Genealogical and Historical Guide.* Salt Lake City: Ancestry.

Tax, Meredith. 1980. *The Rising of the Women: Feminist Solidarity and Class Conflict, 1880–1917.* New York: Monthly Review Press.

Thompson, E. P. 1966. *The Making of the English Working Class.* New York: Vintage.

———. 1967. "Time, Work-Discipline, and Industrial Capitalism." *Past and Present* 38 (December): 56–97.

Tillich, Paul. 1948. *The Protestant Era.* Chicago: University of Chicago Press.

Tilly, Charles. 1978. *From Mobilization to Revolution.* Reading, Mass.: Addison-Wesley.

Valocchi, Steve. 1996. "The Emergence of the Integrationist Ideology in the Civil Rights Movement." *Social Problems* 43: 116–30.

Wade, Louise C. 1964. *Graham Taylor: Pioneer for Social Justice, 1851–1931.* Chicago: University of Chicago Press.

Weber, Max. 1958. *The Protestant Ethic and the Spirit of Capitalism.* New York: Scribner's Sons.

Weir, Robert E. 1996. *Beyond Labor's Veil: The Culture of the Knights of Labor.* University Park: Pennsylvania State University Press.

Westby, David L. 2005. "Strategic Imperative, Ideology, and Frames." In *Frames of Protest: Social Movements and the Framing Perspective,* edited by Hank Johnston and John A. Noakes, 217–35. Lanham, Md.: Rowman and Littlefield.

Whaples, Robert. 1990. "Winning the Eight-Hour Day, 1909–1919." *Journal of Economic History* 50 (June): 393–406.

Wheelock, Lewis F. 1956. "Urban Protestant Reactions to the Chicago Haymarket Affair." Ph.D. diss., Iowa State University.

White, Ronald C., and C. Howard Hopkins. 1976. *The Social Gospel: Religion and Reform in a Changing America.* Philadelphia: Temple University Press.

Williams, Rhys H., and Jeffrey Blackburn. 1996. "Many Are Called but Few Obey: Ideological Commitment and Activism in Operation Rescue." In *Disruptive*

Religion: The Force of Faith in Social Movement Activism, edited by Christian Smith, 167–85. New York: Routledge.

Winters, Donald E. 1985. *The Soul of the Wobblies: The I.W.W., Religion, and American Culture in the Progressive Era, 1905–1917.* Westport, Conn.: Greenwood Press.

Woodbridge, Mark E., ed. 1977. *American Federation of Labor and Congress of Industrial Organizations Pamphlets, 1889–1955.* Westport, Conn.: Greenwood Press.

Wuthnow, Robert. 1988. *The Restructuring of American Religion.* Princeton, N.J.: Princeton University Press.

———. 1989. *Communities of Discourse: Ideology and Social Structure in the Reformation, the Enlightenment, and European Socialism.* Cambridge, Mass.: Harvard University Press.

Zald, Mayer N. 1996. "Culture, Ideology, and Strategic Framing." In *Comparative Perspectives on Social Movements,* edited by Doug McAdam, John D. McCarthy, and Mayer N. Zald, 261–74. New York: Cambridge University Press.

INDEX

WILLIAM A. MIROLA is a professor of sociology at Marian University in Indianapolis. He is the coauthor of *Religion Matters: What Sociology Teaches Us about Religion in Our World.*

THE WORKING CLASS IN AMERICAN HISTORY

Worker City, Company Town: Iron and Cotton-Worker Protest in Troy and Cohoes, New York, 1855–84 *Daniel J. Walkowitz*
Life, Work, and Rebellion in the Coal Fields: The Southern West Virginia Miners, 1880–1922 *David Alan Corbin*
Women and American Socialism, 1870–1920 *Mari Jo Buhle*
Lives of Their Own: Blacks, Italians, and Poles in Pittsburgh, 1900–1960 *John Bodnar, Roger Simon, and Michael P. Weber*
Working-Class America: Essays on Labor, Community, and American Society *Edited by Michael H. Frisch and Daniel J. Walkowitz*
Eugene V. Debs: Citizen and Socialist *Nick Salvatore*
American Labor and Immigration History, 1877–1920s: Recent European Research *Edited by Dirk Hoerder*
Workingmen's Democracy: The Knights of Labor and American Politics *Leon Fink*
The Electrical Workers: A History of Labor at General Electric and Westinghouse, 1923–60 *Ronald W. Schatz*
The Mechanics of Baltimore: Workers and Politics in the Age of Revolution, 1763–1812 *Charles G. Steffen*
The Practice of Solidarity: American Hat Finishers in the Nineteenth Century *David Bensman*
The Labor History Reader *Edited by Daniel J. Leab*
Solidarity and Fragmentation: Working People and Class Consciousness in Detroit, 1875–1900 *Richard Oestreicher*
Counter Cultures: Saleswomen, Managers, and Customers in American Department Stores, 1890–1940 *Susan Porter Benson*
The New England Working Class and the New Labor History *Edited by Herbert G. Gutman and Donald H. Bell*
Labor Leaders in America *Edited by Melvyn Dubofsky and Warren Van Tine*
Barons of Labor: The San Francisco Building Trades and Union Power in the Progressive Era *Michael Kazin*
Gender at Work: The Dynamics of Job Segregation by Sex during World War II *Ruth Milkman*
Once a Cigar Maker: Men, Women, and Work Culture in American Cigar Factories, 1900–1919 *Patricia A. Cooper*
A Generation of Boomers: The Pattern of Railroad Labor Conflict in Nineteenth-Century America *Shelton Stromquist*
Work and Community in the Jungle: Chicago's Packinghouse Workers, 1894–1922 *James R. Barrett*
Workers, Managers, and Welfare Capitalism: The Shoeworkers and Tanners of Endicott Johnson, 1890–1950 *Gerald Zahavi*
Men, Women, and Work: Class, Gender, and Protest in the New England Shoe Industry, 1780–1910 *Mary Blewett*

Workers on the Waterfront: Seamen, Longshoremen, and Unionism in the 1930s *Bruce Nelson*

German Workers in Chicago: A Documentary History of Working-Class Culture from 1850 to World War I *Edited by Hartmut Keil and John B. Jentz*

On the Line: Essays in the History of Auto Work *Edited by Nelson Lichtenstein and Stephen Meyer III*

Labor's Flaming Youth: Telephone Operators and Worker Militancy, 1878–1923 *Stephen H. Norwood*

Another Civil War: Labor, Capital, and the State in the Anthracite Regions of Pennsylvania, 1840–68 *Grace Palladino*

Coal, Class, and Color: Blacks in Southern West Virginia, 1915–32 *Joe William Trotter Jr.*

For Democracy, Workers, and God: Labor Song-Poems and Labor Protest, 1865–95 *Clark D. Halker*

Dishing It Out: Waitresses and Their Unions in the Twentieth Century *Dorothy Sue Cobble*

The Spirit of 1848: German Immigrants, Labor Conflict, and the Coming of the Civil War *Bruce Levine*

Working Women of Collar City: Gender, Class, and Community in Troy, New York, 1864–86 *Carole Turbin*

Southern Labor and Black Civil Rights: Organizing Memphis Workers *Michael K. Honey*

Radicals of the Worst Sort: Laboring Women in Lawrence, Massachusetts, 1860–1912 *Ardis Cameron*

Producers, Proletarians, and Politicians: Workers and Party Politics in Evansville and New Albany, Indiana, 1850–87 *Lawrence M. Lipin*

The New Left and Labor in the 1960s *Peter B. Levy*

The Making of Western Labor Radicalism: Denver's Organized Workers, 1878–1905 *David Brundage*

In Search of the Working Class: Essays in American Labor History and Political Culture *Leon Fink*

Lawyers against Labor: From Individual Rights to Corporate Liberalism *Daniel R. Ernst*

"We Are All Leaders": The Alternative Unionism of the Early 1930s *Edited by Staughton Lynd*

The Female Economy: The Millinery and Dressmaking Trades, 1860–1930 *Wendy Gamber*

"Negro and White, Unite and Fight!": A Social History of Industrial Unionism in Meatpacking, 1930–90 *Roger Horowitz*

Power at Odds: The 1922 National Railroad Shopmen's Strike *Colin J. Davis*

The Common Ground of Womanhood: Class, Gender, and Working Girls' Clubs, 1884–1928 *Priscilla Murolo*

Marching Together: Women of the Brotherhood of Sleeping Car Porters *Melinda Chateauvert*

Down on the Killing Floor: Black and White Workers in Chicago's Packinghouses, 1904–54 *Rick Halpern*
Labor and Urban Politics: Class Conflict and the Origins of Modern Liberalism in Chicago, 1864–97 *Richard Schneirov*
All That Glitters: Class, Conflict, and Community in Cripple Creek *Elizabeth Jameson*
Waterfront Workers: New Perspectives on Race and Class *Edited by Calvin Winslow*
Labor Histories: Class, Politics, and the Working-Class Experience *Edited by Eric Arnesen, Julie Greene, and Bruce Laurie*
The Pullman Strike and the Crisis of the 1890s: Essays on Labor and Politics *Edited by Richard Schneirov, Shelton Stromquist, and Nick Salvatore*
AlabamaNorth: African-American Migrants, Community, and Working-Class Activism in Cleveland, 1914–45 *Kimberley L. Phillips*
Imagining Internationalism in American and British Labor, 1939–49 *Victor Silverman*
William Z. Foster and the Tragedy of American Radicalism *James R. Barrett*
Colliers across the Sea: A Comparative Study of Class Formation in Scotland and the American Midwest, 1830–1924 *John H. M. Laslett*
"Rights, Not Roses": Unions and the Rise of Working-Class Feminism, 1945–80 *Dennis A. Deslippe*
Testing the New Deal: The General Textile Strike of 1934 in the American South *Janet Irons*
Hard Work: The Making of Labor History *Melvyn Dubofsky*
Southern Workers and the Search for Community: Spartanburg County, South Carolina *G. C. Waldrep III*
We Shall Be All: A History of the Industrial Workers of the World (abridged edition) *Melvyn Dubofsky, ed. Joseph A. McCartin*
Race, Class, and Power in the Alabama Coalfields, 1908–21 *Brian Kelly*
Duquesne and the Rise of Steel Unionism *James D. Rose*
Anaconda: Labor, Community, and Culture in Montana's Smelter City *Laurie Mercier*
Bridgeport's Socialist New Deal, 1915–36 *Cecelia Bucki*
Indispensable Outcasts: Hobo Workers and Community in the American Midwest, 1880–1930 *Frank Tobias Higbie*
After the Strike: A Century of Labor Struggle at Pullman *Susan Eleanor Hirsch*
Corruption and Reform in the Teamsters Union *David Witwer*
Waterfront Revolts: New York and London Dockworkers, 1946–61 *Colin J. Davis*
Black Workers' Struggle for Equality in Birmingham *Horace Huntley and David Montgomery*
The Tribe of Black Ulysses: African American Men in the Industrial South *William P. Jones*

City of Clerks: Office and Sales Workers in Philadelphia, 1870–1920 *Jerome P. Bjelopera*

Reinventing "The People": The Progressive Movement, the Class Problem, and the Origins of Modern Liberalism *Shelton Stromquist*

Radical Unionism in the Midwest, 1900–1950 *Rosemary Feurer*

Gendering Labor History *Alice Kessler-Harris*

James P. Cannon and the Origins of the American Revolutionary Left, 1890–1928 *Bryan D. Palmer*

Glass Towns: Industry, Labor, and Political Economy in Appalachia, 1890–1930s *Ken Fones-Wolf*

Workers and the Wild: Conservation, Consumerism, and Labor in Oregon, 1910–30 *Lawrence M. Lipin*

Wobblies on the Waterfront: Interracial Unionism in Progressive-Era Philadelphia *Peter Cole*

Red Chicago: American Communism at Its Grassroots, 1928–35 *Randi Storch*

Labor's Cold War: Local Politics in a Global Context *Edited by Shelton Stromquist*

Bessie Abramowitz Hillman and the Making of the Amalgamated Clothing Workers of America *Karen Pastorello*

The Great Strikes of 1877 *Edited by David O. Stowell*

Union-Free America: Workers and Antiunion Culture *Lawrence Richards*

Race against Liberalism: Black Workers and the UAW in Detroit *David M. Lewis-Colman*

Teachers and Reform: Chicago Public Education, 1929–70 *John F. Lyons*

Upheaval in the Quiet Zone: 1199/SEIU and the Politics of Healthcare Unionism *Leon Fink and Brian Greenberg*

Shadow of the Racketeer: Scandal in Organized Labor *David Witwer*

Sweet Tyranny: Migrant Labor, Industrial Agriculture, and Imperial Politics *Kathleen Mapes*

Staley: The Fight for a New American Labor Movement *Steven K. Ashby and C. J. Hawking*

On the Ground: Labor Struggles in the American Airline Industry *Liesl Miller Orenic*

NAFTA and Labor in North America *Norman Caulfield*

Making Capitalism Safe: Work Safety and Health Regulation in America, 1880–1940 *Donald W. Rogers*

Good, Reliable, White Men: Railroad Brotherhoods, 1877–1917 *Paul Michel Taillon*

Spirit of Rebellion: Labor and Religion in the New Cotton South *Jarod Roll*

The Labor Question in America: Economic Democracy in the Gilded Age *Rosanne Currarino*

Banded Together: Economic Democratization in the Brass Valley *Jeremy Brecher*

The Gospel of the Working Class: Labor's Southern Prophets in New Deal America *Erik Gellman and Jarod Roll*

Guest Workers and Resistance to U.S. Corporate Despotism *Immanuel Ness*

Gleanings of Freedom: Free and Slave Labor along the Mason-Dixon Line, 1790–1860 *Max Grivno*

Chicago in the Age of Capital: Class, Politics, and Democracy during the Civil War and Reconstruction *John B. Jentz and Richard Schneirov*

Child Care in Black and White: Working Parents and the History of Orphanages *Jessie B. Ramey*

The Haymarket Conspiracy: Transatlantic Anarchist Networks *Timothy Messer-Kruse*

Detroit's Cold War: The Origins of Postwar Conservatism *Colleen Doody*

A Renegade Union: Interracial Organizing and Labor Radicalism *Lisa Phillips*

Palomino: Clinton Jencks and Mexican-American Unionism in the American Southwest *James J. Lorence*

Latin American Migrations to the U.S. Heartland: Changing Cultural Landscapes in Middle America *Edited by Linda Allegro and Andrew Grant Wood*

Man of Fire: Selected Writings *Ernesto Galarza, ed. Armando Ibarra and Rodolfo D. Torres*

A Contest of Ideas: Capital, Politics, and Labor *Nelson Lichtenstein*

Making the World Safe for Workers: Labor, the Left, and Wilsonian Internationalism *Elizabeth McKillen*

The Rise of the Chicago Police Department: Class and Conflict, 1850–1894 *Sam Mitrani*

Workers in Hard Times: A Long View of Economic Crises *Edited by Leon Fink, Joseph A. McCartin, and Joan Sangster*

Redeeming Time: Protestantism and Chicago's Eight-Hour Movement, 1866–1912 *William A. Mirola*

The University of Illinois Press
is a founding member of the
Association of American University Presses.

Composed in 10.5/13 Minion Pro
by Lisa Connery
at the University of Illinois Press
Manufactured by Sheridan Books, Inc.

University of Illinois Press
1325 South Oak Street
Champaign, IL 61820-6903
www.press.uillinois.edu